108481

DATE DUE			

Studies in Comparative Politics

Peter H. Merkl, editor

Studies in Comparative Politics is designed to make available to students and teachers comparative studies of substantive interest and innovative approach. Written for classroom use, they range over a broad spectrum of topical subjects and lend themselves in particular to supplementing course content in a comparative direction.

POLITICAL CULTURE &
GROUP CONFLICT IN
COMMUNIST
CHINA

ALAN P.L. LIU

CLIO BOOKS
CALIFORNIA   ENGLAND

The author and publisher are pleased to note the following sources of quoted material which appear in the text of this book:
RED GUARD, copyright © 1971 by Gordon A. Bennett and Ronald N. Montaperto. Reprinted by permission of Doubleday & Company, Inc., and George Allen & Unwin Ltd.
THE REVENGE OF HEAVEN by Ken Ling. Copyright © 1972 by Dr. Ivan London and Miriam London. Reprinted by permission of G. P. Putnam's Sons and the Sterling Lord Agency, Inc.

Library of Congress Cataloging in Publication Data
Liu, Alan P   L   1937–
    Political culture and group conflict in Communist China.
    (Studies in comparative politics; 4)
    Bibliography: p.
    Includes index.
    1. China—Politics and government—1949–
2. Political participation—China. 3. Elite (Social sciences)—China. I. Title. II. Series.
JQ1516. L56   301. 6'3'0951   74-14195
ISBN 0-87436-196-6
ISBN 0-87436-197-4 pbk.

Second paperback printing, May 1977

American Bibliographical Center—Clio Press
2040 Alameda Padre Serra
Santa Barbara, California 93103

European Bibliographical Center—Clio Press
Woodside House, Hinksey Hill
Oxford OX1 5BE, England

Manufactured in the United States of America

The Text for *Political Culture and Group Conflict in Communist China* was designed by Liz Maynard using Trump Medieval for the body and Carolus for display. Scott Campbell designed the cover. Composition was by Computer Typesetting Services, Inc., Glendale, Calif. Offsetting and bindery were by the Crawfordsville, Ind. division of R. R. Donnelley and Sons Co.

To My Wife
LILLIAN

CONTENTS

viii *Contents*

PART THREE: CONFLICT & ORDER

PREFACE

The following study is about the intensive and widespread group conflicts in China in the so-called Cultural Revolution from 1966 to 1969. My reasons for writing this book are two. In terms of substance it is my long-standing interest to understand and analyze the prospect of national integration in China. For that purpose a study of group interaction is essential. In terms of the method of study, it is also my long-standing goal to link Chinese studies with general social science concepts. But I have no interest in grand theorizing, neither am I satisfied with mere chronicling of events. Some kind of ordering of raw data is essential if one is to derive meaning from facts.

Part I of the book gives a panoramic view of the conflicts between 1966 and 1968. It is a sort of a map in which only the most outstanding and crucial features of the terrain are presented. It analyzes the conditions that brought forth the conflicts such as elite legitimation, loosening of social control, nationwide emulation of the events in few focal points and the causes for the eventual outbreak of violence.

Part II deals with the constitutive parts of the conflicts. It discusses the motivation and behavior of each conflicting group, i.e., students, workers, peasants and veterans.

Part III describes how the leaders brought the conflicts to an end, and the reactions of the conflicting groups to the reimposition of control.

The sources on which this study is based are ordinarily used by all serious students of Communist Chinese affairs. Three types of sources may need clarification for those unfamiliar with research problems in studying a "closed" system like China. First, I have used broadcasting reports from China and from Western news agencies. I did not monitor those broadcasts; but rather analyzed the systematic recording of Chinese broadcasts and news reports from Western correspondents in China prepared by U.S. government agencies. Almost all serious scholars in Chinese studies have found such reports useful and reliable. The broadcasts are more informative than the bland reports of the official press on the local situation in China during the Cultural Revolution. Second, I used information from Red Guard publications. Persons who do not have specific evidence to discredit this source often object to the use of these documents in research; their objections are often based on vague suspicion. These critics, however, do not object to the use of official media which, in reality, may be more misleading than the uncensored Red Guard papers. In any case, the value of the Red Guard papers is well stated by Sidney Greenblatt:

> Cultural Revolution Red Guard publications, though by no means free of partisanship, were freed of official censorship. Furthermore, the authors and editors of Red Guard publications were committed to revealing the disparity between revolutionary pronouncements, policies, social values and practices, and the actual revisionism they disguised. To serve this commitment fresh information was drawn from internal organizational files "captured" or "released" for Red Guard use. These factors alone helped to produce a new version of social reality in Communist China. . . . These passionately partisan documents yielded new insights into the sources of social conflict, the methods of social control, and the dynamics of social organization [*Chinese Sociology and Anthropology*, Spring-Summer 1970].

For anyone who wants to study the motivation and behavior of conflicting groups in China between 1966 and 1968, the Red Guard documents are the voice of these groups and should be the primary source. There is no apparent objection to the use of Mao's works to study his motivation and behavior. Third, I relied on five eyewitness accounts to enliven and affirm information from documentary sources: (1) *Haifeng Wen-hua Ke-ming Kai-shu* [A General Account of the Cultural Revolution in Haifeng County] by Hai Feng; (2) *Kuang-chou Ti-ch'u Wen-ke Lieh-chen Shu-lueh* [An Account of the Cultural Revolution in the Canton Area] by Hai Feng; (3) *Shanghai Journal* by Neale

Hunter; (4) *Red Guard* by Gordon Bennett and Ronald Montaperto;
and (5) *The Revenge of Heaven* by Ken Ling. Naturally these sources
are subject to some bias but I was impressed by the close correspondence
among them on the process and nature of the mass movement in the
Cultural Revolution. Furthermore, using other scholars' methods of
reducing personal bias in interview data, I have drawn personal experiences from these eyewitness accounts, not political value judgments.
The high degree of uniformity in the experience data convinced me
of their authenticity. Moreover, since I lacked research support for
interviewing in America and abroad, I used these eyewitness accounts
as a "next best" alternative. Undoubtedly some critics will charge that
some of these accounts are biased, and the burden of proof is on them—I
hope they will be specific in their reviews. I have criticized some of
these sources myself in the footnotes. After all, I use the sources selectively.

This book was first presented as a conference paper in 1973 and
it received two criticisms. One purely partisan young scholar commented
that he agreed with the content of the paper, but that I could have
written "something more positive about China." This criticism revealed
his misunderstanding of the role of conflict in society ("conflict is
bad") and the partisan attitude shared by a few well-established "China
scholars." My belief is that China should be studied as it "is," not as
it "ought to be." A scholar free of censorship has the right to choose
any topic for his research and writing; objective and scholarly criticism should thus be directed to the way a particular topic is handled,
not the selection of the topic.

The second criticism was more academic. I was asked, "Is your study
in perspective?" The critic suggested that a minority of the Chinese
population was involved in the conflicts and that disturbances did not
occur in all the cities. To this well-intentioned criticism, I direct the
following statement by Lewis Coser in reply:

> It would be a major analytical error to argue that groups threat-
> ening violence or actually engaged in violence can be disregarded,
> because they are typically small in numbers. If we are concerned
> with historical change we must attend to articulate minorities at
> least as much as to habitually inert and mute majorities. Given
> the psychic costs that are always involved in the uses of violence,
> it is to be expected that only relatively small numbers of men
> will at any given time be ready to engage in a politics of violence.
> For only a few will the psychic rewards of violence outweigh the
> cost. But the very fact that they are able to break with the habitual
> wont and use of the political game gives them a specific weight
> that is out of proportion to their sheer numbers [*Continuities
> in the Study of Social Conflict* (New York, 1967), p. 107].

I want to express my gratitude to my colleague Peter Merkl, who encouraged me to expand the earlier paper to book length and gave me valuable suggestions on the revision of the manuscript. I am equally grateful to Allen S. Whiting for his comprehensive criticism of the earlier paper. I also appreciate Professor Donald Treadgold's passing on to me a critique of my paper by a graduate student at the University of Washington, which alerted me to the type of negative comments that this book might receive from certain quarters. I owe a debt to Mr. Chih-ping Chen of the Reading Room of the Center for Chinese Studies, University of California at Berkeley, for his cooperative and generous assistance in my research there in the summer of 1973, and finally, I appreciate the interest shown by the Editor, Clio Books, Lloyd Garrison.

I want to thank the Regents of the University of California for granting me summer fellowships in 1972 and 1973 to enable me to do research in Santa Barbara and Berkeley. The views expressed in the book are, naturally, mine.

SANTA BARBARA, CALIFORNIA

December 1975.

CHRONOLOGY

Elite Mobilization for Conflict (May–August 1966)

May 24   Announcement of reorganization of Peking Municipal Party Committee.

May 25   First wall poster appeared at Peking University, attacking the university president. Student movement led by Nieh Yuan-t'ze, teaching assistant at the Department of Philosophy.

June 1   Nationwide broadcasting and publicity of Nieh's poster.
           Beginning of student attack of individual teachers all across the nation.

June–July Dispatching and controversy over the "work teams" at various colleges.

July 1   Public purge of the officials of the Party Propaganda Department.

July 18   Mao ordered the withdrawal of the "work teams" from campuses.

August 1–12	The 11th Plenum of the Eighth Party Central Committee. Student observers attended the plenum, first time in the history of the Communist Party. Mao published his own wall poster—"Bombard the Headquarters!"
August 18	Mao and Lin Piao reviewed Red Guard parade in Peking. Formation of Red Guards all over the nation. Start of Red Guards' "Destroy the Four Olds" movement and violence against persons of "Seven Black Elements" category. Beginning of "link-up" movement of students; Peking students set up liaison stations in various cities in the provinces.

Group Violence Caused by Local Elites' Self-Defense (September 1966–February 1967)

September	Beginning of Red Guard attack on local Party authorities. Physical clashes between workers and students allied with local Party authorities and Peking Red Guards, together with their local supporters (radicals).
October	Red Guard papers in Peking attacked openly Liu Shao-ch'i, revealing the depth of elite division. More clashes between Red Guards and local authorities over background materials.
November	Rebel and Red Guard organizations formed in factories and mines. First workers' group formed in Shanghai on the 9th. The next day, Shanghai workers started the "Anting Incident."
December	Attack on local authorities and formation of Red Guards spread to the countryside. Mass rallies in Peking, subjecting Peng Chen, Lu Ting-i and Lo Jui-ch'ing to public humiliation. Directive from State Council on the 31st ordering military training of students.

January 3	Shanghai newspaper *Wen-hui Pao* taken over by a rebel group. Wave of rebels' taking over of Party newspapers in China.
January 9	Mao in Peking called on the Red Guards to seize power from local Party authorities.
January 11	Directive from State Council to put banks and radio stations under army control. Party Central Committee called on workers to resist "economism." First seizure of power in Shansi province. Takeover of governmental agencies in Peking by various Red Guard groups. Wave of "power seizure" in provincial capitals.
January 23	Army ordered by Mao to "support the left" and suppression of the veterans' group in Harbin. Start of radical Red Guards' raids into army bases across the nation.
February 3	Party Central Committee and State Council ordered the cessation of "link-up" movement by Red Guards.
February 12	Party Central Committee and State Council ordered to dissolve "cross-trade" organizations among workers, students and veterans.
February 23	Bloody clash between radical Red Guards and the army in Ts'inghai province.

Suppression of the Radicals by the Army (March–April 1967)

March 7	Mao ordered the army to discipline the students.
March 18	The army was ordered to supervise factories. Start of the movement by the army to suppress the radical Red Guard groups across the nation.
April 6	Directive from the Central Military Affairs Commission censuring the army's suppression of the radical students. Rise of incidents of violent clashes between

radical and conservative organizations among students and workers in China.

Withdrawal of Army Authority and Escalation of Group Violence (May–December 1967)

May 6	Bloody clashes between radical students and conservative workers in Chengtu, Szechwan province, and Chengchow, Honan province.
June–July	Start of "struggle with modern weapons" among Red Guard and workers' groups.
July 20	"Wuhan Incident" in which two emissaries from the Central Cultural Revolution Group of Peking were detained by a mass organization of workers, supported by local army commander and garrison units.
August–September	Start of purge of "ultra-leftist" leaders in Peking. Increase in violent conflicts among Red Guard and workers' groups all over China.
September 24	Mao Tse-tung concluded an inspection trip.
October 11	The *Shen-wu-lien* group in Hunan publicized its critique of China under the rule of the Communist Party.
October 15	Government initiated the "grand alliance" movement to merge Red Guard and rebel groups within each organization, so to break up the "cross-trade" associations.
December	Party organizations at regional level revived.

Resistance to Reimposition of State Authority (1968)

January	Movement started to accelerate the establishment of revolutionary committees in the provinces.
February	More purges of "ultra-leftists" in Peking.
March 24	Purge of Chief of Staff Yang Cheng-wu and Peking Garrison Commander Fu Chung-pi. Violent conflict among Red Guard groups reported in Shansi, Kweichow, Ts'inghai and Szechwan.

April	Violent conflict reported in Shensi and Liaoning.
May–August	Violent conflicts reported in Kwangtung, Kiangsu, Hunan, Yunnan, Fukien and Kwangsi.
June 10	Special "Central Support-the-Left Force" formed and dispatched to provinces to suppress group conflict.
September	Last revolutionary committees set up in Tibet and Sinkiang.

PART
ONE
CONFLICT
PROCESS

1

GROUP CONFLICT

In 1969, a young Chinese in Hong Kong recalled the intense group conflict during the so-called Great Proletarian Cultural Revolution in which he was a participant and stated:

> In a society rent with class struggle like ours, nobody could remain aloof from the movement. After going through the Cultural Revolution, some people were inevitably promoted because they stood staunchly on the side of the revolutionary faction. . . . Others were capped with political hats and subjected to struggle or thought reform. Thus, everyone naturally took the view that one's political standpoint was a matter of life and death. People hotly contested the issues arising in the course of the movement, fervently hoping that they themselves would end up in the group considered to be the genuine revolutionary left. Such intense competition inevitably produced factions which, never successfully controlled, finally indulged in the extreme of physically attacking each other. . . .[1]

At about the same time, a young Chinese in Taiwan who was also a former Red Guard in mainland China between 1966 and 1968 perceptively pointed out another underlying force to the group conflict in

China at that time. "As the Cultural Revolution progressed," says Ken Ling, "people generally seemed unwilling to keep their places; they tried to move out of bad areas to better ones, from lower positions in society to higher ones."[2]

This study is about the various socioeconomic-political forces that brought forth the intense and violent group conflict in the Cultural Revolution in China. Since there is already an abundance of historical narratives on this subject, we shall take a more analytical and conceptual approach. That requires us to be explicit about the underlying frame of reference against which we interpret the Chinese data. What follows is a brief discussion on the four components of group conflicts: source, mobilization, conflict process and termination (or resolution). We will be mainly summing up the systematic studies on social conflict by Anthony Oberschall, Raymond Mack, Richard Snyder, Neil Smelser, Ralf Dahrendorf and Lewis Coser.[3]

Sources of Conflict

The sources of group conflict are generally either sociological or cultural.

Sociological sources of group conflict, in turn, are of two kinds: those having to do with the existing mode of conflict regulation in any society and those resulting from social and economic changes.

In this study, the existing mode of conflict regulation distinguishes between those societies in which conflict has been institutionalized and those in which institutionalization of conflict has been of a very low degree. The former type of conflict relations is characterized by "explicit rules, predictable behavior, and continuity, as in the case of collective bargaining."[4] The latter type is characterized by "an absence of agreed procedures for review of relations, and by discontinuity of interaction or drastic shifts in the mode of resolution."[5] In addition, institutionalization of conflict is either centralized or decentralized. Centralized institutionalization of conflict means regulation by legal norms enforced from outside the conflict system. In decentralized institutionalization, "the conflict relation may be autonomous in the sense that the parties voluntarily establish an informal social control of their interactions."[6] In reality all societies combine both methods; it is the relative weight assigned to each mode of regulation by any particular society or government that differentiates one society from another.[7]

On the whole, societies that decentralize institutionalization of conflict tend to keep future conflict relations within their present mode of explicit rules of interaction, continuity of interaction, interdependence of parties and the creation of new norms. Societies that centralize institutionalization of conflict relations tend to perpetuate the conditions that initially brought centralization into being, i.e., chronic recurrence of unsettled issues, an absence of voluntarily agreed-upon procedures for regulation of relations and significant probability of sudden and, possibly, violent conflicts.[8]

The Communist political system typically centralizes institutionalization of group conflict. Outwardly Communist systems project an image of order and tranquillity. Inwardly, Communist systems are characterized by uninstitutionalized conflict. Consequently there is an increased probability that sudden and violent conflicts will take place in Communist nations, particularly in those undergoing rapid social and economic changes. There are several possible reasons.

First, the integration of state and society in Communist nations is heavily dependent on the unitary organization of Communist parties. As a result, elite dissension is more disruptive in Communist nations than in nations which have a pluralistic base of national integration.

Second, it is well known that the conditions which are conducive to organizations are lacking in Communist societies. Communist governments preempt and expropriate the formation of voluntary groups and their functions of interest articulation. Since these organizations are the primary units of group conflict, their suppression means "a permanent, and often growing, quantity of unreleased pressure in totalitarian states which imbues their latent political conflicts with an intensity unknown in free societies, where pressure is released almost as soon as it is created."[9]

Third, political institutions dominate Communist governments at the expense of other institutions and so all manner of conflicts are politicized. Such politicization heightens the awareness of the elite and the masses of authority relationships. In other words, there is a heightened consciousness of authority-subject relations in Communist societies. According to Dahrendorf, authoritative relations in society are a fundamental source of group conflict.[10] The tactics of total politicization thus constantly provoke conflict. Another result of politicization is the difficulty of separating conflict over norms and conflict over values. Thus a strike for higher wages must appear as a political challenge, not simply as a means of gaining economic improvement.[11] Conflicts in Communist systems have a high probability of escalation. Furthermore, total politicization tends to severely restrict (if not eliminate) the role of *impartial* mediators in a conflict situation and without them conflict resolution and institutionalization are difficult to achieve.[12] Dahrendorf asserts that in totalitarian societies, "whatever conflicts do occur involve both rulers and ruled with their whole personalities; and if these conflicts become open and violent, the cost of defeat is too high for both parties to allow graceful retreat."[13]

So far we have discussed a sociological source of conflict relating to existing modes of conflict regulation in society. The second sociological source of group conflict is social and economic change. This source of conflict is well understood so the following discussion is brief. Social change, according to Mack and Snyder, shifts "the bases of potentially antagonistic interests and the relative power positions of individuals and groups."[14] Changes like population growth, invention, urbanization and mobility affect the sources of conflict, the nature and number of parties in conflict, the instrumentalities of conflict, the issues of conflict, modes of settlement, and so on. Economic growth, according to Mancur Olson, Jr., "can significantly increase the number of losers," since it tends to increase the inequality of incomes and sharpen a decline in consumption due to governmental policies of capital formation and resulting short-term downswings.[15]

In developing nations, Communist or not, social and economic changes are inseparably part of the wholesale change known as "modernization" or "nation building". Hence, conflicts generated by social and economic changes are compounded by those generated by political changes. The latter often result in expanding governmental power. Conflicts are created by clashes between central governments and hitherto autonomous regions and between ethnic groups who lived in separate areas before nation-building began. The governments of developing nations are often inefficient and they lack sufficient authority. These factors further generate conflicts because of governmental failures to meet the demands of the people. Even governments having power initially based on populistic mass movements, e.g., the Chinese Communist Party, eventually lose popularity. Smelser notes four reasons why ideological mass movements are quite likely to occur in new revolutionary regimes. First, newly legitimized governments tend to define protest movements in ideological ("value-oriented") terms. Second, the social disorganization created by revolutionary upheavals keeps the level of strain in society high. Third, there is great pressure on the government to mobilize the population because of revolutionary involvement in foreign and civil wars. Fourth, the machinery of social order under a new revolutionary government is not institutionalized so it is often applied with a heavy hand to compensate for a lack of established legitimacy.[16]

So much for the sociological sources of group conflict. The other major source of group conflict, as we stated at the outset, is cultural. Almost all students of social conflict recognize that aside from the social and economic factors, there are attitudinal, psychological and cultural sources of group conflict. Thus Oberschall states: "Discontents and conflicts are found in all social systems, yet some conflicts are more likely to arise in and be chronic to societies with particular social and institutional structures and, once they occur, are less likely to be resolved in a peaceable manner in some institutional settings than in others."[17] Mack and Snyder mention that cultural and social values may either neutralize or dominate conflicting values.[18]

Specifically, a culture affects group conflicts in at least three ways: (1) by defining and activating conflict situations; (2) by legitimizing aggressive acts against certain persons or groups; and (3) by regarding conflict as a general norm of interpersonal relationship. For example, according to Smelser, one of the necessary conditions to a collective movement is a strain in the social system but, then, strain is "also defined by cultural standards and personal expectations."[19] Oberschall states that "even violence is subject to norms embedded in the culture."[20] According to Berkowitz, "Attitudes governing the moral propriety of hostile behavior also govern the likelihood that a person will act aggressively."[21] As to the acceptance of conflict as a norm, Mack and Snyder state: "In general, it might be expected that the more central conflict is to the operations of a group or organization, the more highly developed will be the techniques of conflict waging."[22] It might be argued that it is impossible for large groupings (e.g., nations) to accept conflict as a central norm, but it is quite possible for a group of leaders to have that orientation. Moreover, elite group values necessarily affect the people at large, particularly the young generation in developing nations.

The most important element in the cultural source of conflict is the role of the elite. Di Palma asserts that

> . . . social and economic cleavages, mass attitudes, and demands usually become relevant and enter the political system when structured and directed by elites and institutions. Moreover, mass beliefs and demands are to some extent affected by communications from the system's elites. Mass cleavages and demands can become critical under certain conditions, but these conditions are very largely shaped by elite responses and inducements. . . . It can be more useful and creative to entertain the opposite notion that it is mass behavior that reflects elite and institutional inducements, or at least operates within the conditions created by the latter.[23]

We have stated earlier that cultural legitimization of aggression toward certain groups or individuals is itself a source of conflict. It is clear that elites, the cultural guardians, carry out this legitimization. Berkowitz states that

the people about us may lessen or eliminate . . . aggression anxiety
if they define hostile behavior as being socially proper in a given
situation. Adult permissiveness toward aggression may result in
such a social definition of aggression for children, the children
transferring their "superego functions" to the watching adult.[24]

"Authorities," says Berkowitz, "have sometimes fomented aggression
against particular groups because they believed such hostility would
help them achieve other, nonaggressive goals."[25]

Elites have the potential for inciting "strategic aggression," but it is
equally likely that elites can "defuse" and terminate a conflict situation.
Elites (e.g., the elite led by Gandhi) can also promote a culture of civility
among their followers.[26] Furthermore, leaders are often granted a degree
of freedom of action by their followers which enables them to employ
peaceful means even if their followers are "jingoistic." Thus elites
influence the attitudes and values of their followers in conflict situations
but no particular type of influence can be ascribed to elite behavior.

The interaction between elites and masses with respect to values and
attitudes in general, and group conflict in particular, is a major element
of the "political culture" of a particular nation. Political culture is
defined by Lucian Pye as

the set of attitudes, beliefs, and sentiments which give order and
meaning to a political process and which provide the underlying
assumptions and rules that govern behavior in the political system.
It encompasses both the political ideals and the operating norms
of a polity. Political culture is thus manifestation in aggregate form
of the psychological and subjective dimension of politics.[27]

Elsewhere Pye states that political culture includes "explicit citizenship
training and conscious learning about the workings of the political
system."[28] In other words, the role of elites in creating and maintaining
a particular political culture is crucial. Moreover, in their discussions
of the general substance of political culture, Pye, Sidney Verba and
Myron Weiner have all, directly or indirectly, touched upon the handling of conflict situations. Pye has commented extensively on the
attitude of trust versus distrust in the elites of developing nations.[29]
Verba regards the identification with one's fellow citizens as one of
the four dimensions of political culture.[30] Weiner, in particular, has
commented on the "conflict resolution" in Indian political culture.[31]

Two broad sources of conflict, the sociological and the cultural, have
been discussed. But, students of social conflict note that sociological
and cultural sources of conflict do not themselves activate conflict
actions. Other conditions must be present to induce groups to engage
in conflict.

Mobilization for Conflict

Group conflict takes place when five conditions are present: divisions among the elite, loosening of social control, a precipitating event or events, availability of focal points, and communication.[32]

The integration of any nation is dependent on the unity and integrity of its top leaders; consequently, when a prolonged and serious dissension exists among the leaders, the people become disoriented. An elite division signals an opportunity for the assertion of the grievances of the hitherto discontented groups and the probability of group conflict is raised accordingly. This is particularly true in Communist nations where integration is critically dependent on the Communist Party and its professed ideological validity.

When elite dissension is accompanied by a loosening of social control, the probability of group conflict is further increased. There are two types of social control. One is almost synonymous with the normative order of society. The other employs specific agencies of government, namely, the police, troops, militia, National Guard, yeomanry, court officials, and the like.[33] In Communist China, the second type is simply known as "the instruments of proletarian dictatorship." The loosening of both types of social control clearly tends to activate group conflict. Oberschall notes that in the case of the broad type of control,

> a period of liberalization after a long period of oppression allows the surfacing of long-dormant grievances and demands going far beyond those initially voiced and anticipated by the authorities, the mobilization of discontented groups and the anticipation of reforms that cannot be realistically instituted in a short time. The subsequent ineffective attempts to crack down upon the activities of freshly mobilized groups increase and unite opposition and precipitate social disturbances on a wider scale.[34]

The loosening of the second type of social control tends to lower the quotient of the "risk/reward ratio" of discontented groups so their willingness to participate in conflict is enhanced.[35]

When the aforementioned conditions are present, the tendency for various groups to engage in conflict is further heightened when certain events are interpreted by the groups concerned as a legitimization of their desire for conflict, i.e., when "precipitating events" or "precipitating factors" occur. In other words, the subjective interpretation of events is important. Rumors frequently become such "precipitating events."

Oberschall notes that conflicts spread from "focal points," i.e., the locus of the political center of gravity. "Successes of insurgents at the focal point signal the loosening and weakening of social control at its center of greatest strength, and therefore provide the hope of success for protesters and a clear-cut precipitating occasion on which all attention is centered."[36] It is noted that the existence of "focal points" indicates that a degree of integration or "nationalization" of communication and public opinion has already taken place within the political system.

It is self-evident that there must be communication between groups and localities before widespread group conflict can occur. Before any *national* conflict movement can take place, it is also noted that a degree of prior nationalization of public communications must also exist.

A review of these five conditions for conflict mobilization reveals an interesting and somewhat ironic fact. Highly monistic political systems (e.g., the Communist nations) are conducive to mass group conflict, since they depend upon an "exemplary center" and the effectiveness of a separate and distinct structure of social control (e.g., the K.G.B. in the Soviet Union and the Public Security Ministry in China) for national integration. Yet the rationale for monistic power structures is their supposed ability to maintain unity and reduce conflict.

The five conditions for conflict mobilization deal mainly with the initiation and subsequent spread of group conflicts. Once a movement of group conflicts is generated, however, its further development depends partly on another set of factors.

Conflict Process & Termination

The additional factors that determine the form, intensity, duration, limits and resolution of conflict include: the substance (i.e., the type) of conflict, the number and internal structure of parties in conflict, the means used in conflict, the reaction of the rest of society in general and authorities in particular, and the availability of impartial mediators.

Mack and Snyder classified thirteen types of conflict, and their classification is related to the resolution of conflict through "trade."[37] Generally speaking, all conflicts can be classified as to whether they are amenable to compromise or "trade" types of settlement. Thus ideological and cultural conflicts are not as amenable to settlement through compromise as conflicts over bread-and-butter issues. Lewis Coser distinguishes realistic and unrealistic types of conflict. He asserts that realistic conflicts "arise from frustration of specific demands within the relationship and from estimates of gains of the participants and which are directed at the presumed frustrating object"; nonrealistic conflicts "are not occasioned by the rival ends of the antagonists, but by the need for tension release of at least one of them."[38] Common sense indicates that the realistic type of conflict is more amenable to a trade kind of settlement than unrealistic conflicts. Clark Kerr notes the distinction between real and induced conflicts, "the latter being cases where representatives of conflicting groups have ends to be gained (e.g., their own prestige) apart from the ends in dispute between groups."[39] The induced type of group conflict is obviously difficult to resolve through trade.

The duration and intensity of group conflicts are affected by the number of groups and the degree of their internal organization. On the number of participants, Mack and Snyder suggest the following hypotheses which, as we shall see later, seem to have been borne out by the group conflicts in China's Cultural Revolution:

> 1. The larger the number of parties, the more difficult it will be to discover a common solution, in which all parties can achieve at least some gain over previous power positions;
> 2. The larger the number of parties, the less intense will be the nonrealistic components of the conflict relationship;
> 3. There is a persistent tendency to reduce multiple-party conflict to two-party conflict via coalitions and blocs.[40]

However, the degree of internal discipline and organization in each conflicting group has ambiguous results in the analysis of conflict processes. Groups with high levels of internal discipline and cohesion may permit their representatives to conduct negotiations flexibly and thus bring conflict to an early end, but they may also enable the leaders to prolong conflicts, since in these groups the probability of the presence of unrealistic or induced conflict is increased. The fanatical internal discipline of small sect-like combat groups often accounts for their tendency to engage in prolonged and violent conflicts.[41]

Oberschall notes that the role of authorities such as police is a crucial factor in group conflict either because they initiate violence or because they show partiality.[42] In this connection, it is relevant to mention the argument of some psychologists that aggressive or hostile acts do not necessarily result in "catharsis"; on the contrary such acts lead to further hostile actions on the part of the initiator.[43] Nonviolent means are "not likely to be successful unless there exist third parties or an independent public opinion whose support can be mobilized and who in turn will bring pressures to bear on the agents of social control and the government."[44]

The reaction of governmental authorities influences the conflict process. Note that authorities either use repressive ("riot-control") or accommodative ("interest-aggregation") measures to control conflict. The effectiveness of the riot-control approach depends primarily on the degree of isolation—social or physical—of the conflict movement. Repression by authorities can be highly effective when the groups in conflict lack public support or when they are confined in areas that can be sealed off. Accommodative measures demand that the groups be legally and publicly "recognized."

> As soon as conflict groups have been permitted and been able to organize themselves, the most uncontrollably violent form of conflict, that of guerrilla warfare, is excluded. Moreover, the very act of organization presupposes some degree of recognition which in turn makes the most violent forms of conflict unnecessary and, therefore, unlikely.[45]

But, the possibility that an authority may use one of the two measures initially and switch to the other as conflict continues cannot be precluded.

To bring group conflict to an early, less costly and mutually satisfying end, the availability of an impartial (depending on the recognition of the parties to conflict) mediator is vitally important. As Mack and Snyder point out: "The pressure for liquidation or control of social conflict from disinterested but affected bystanders is one of the primary limits on its duration, extension, and intensity."[46] It is important to note that in conflict situations where no challenge to the authorities is involved, the authorities often act as mediators. In this circumstance, an indication of partiality on the part of the mediating authority will cause a violent and radical turn in the conflict process.

The above sketch of the major concepts of group conflict in recent scholarly works validates the crucial importance of the role of elites in structuring conflict situations. The top leaders decide the type of social and economic change that a nation will undergo and those changes in turn create various patterns of strain in different social groups. The national elites, particularly in developing nations, promote distinct types of political culture which have important influences on interpersonal and intergroup relationships. The mobilization of group conflict and the subsequent course of a conflict movement are partly determined by elite actions as well, although once a conflict situation is widespread other factors, possibly outside of elite control, contribute to the movement. Ultimately, conflict resolution is significantly determined by the actions of authorities.

Consequently the organization of the following chapters emphasizes the role of Chinese political leaders in the creation, development and termination of group conflict in China from 1966 to 1969. The new political culture and its effects on the youth of China are dealt with first. The other major sociological sources of group conflict, e.g., the way of handling existing conflicts and the effects of social and economic changes, are discussed along with each social group, i.e., youth, workers, peasants and veterans. The impact of social and economic changes differs from group to group and the nature of each group's discontent varies accordingly.

Notes

1. Gordon A. Bennett and Ronald N. Montaperto, *Red Guard: The Political Biography of Dai Hsiao-ai* (Garden City, N.Y., 1972), p. 181.

2. Ken Ling, *The Revenge of Heaven: Journal of a Young Chinese* (New York, 1972), p. 147.

3. The conceptual elaboration in this chapter is based mainly on the following works: Lewis Coser, *The Functions of Social Conflict* (New York, 1956); Ralf Dahrendorf, *Class and Class Conflict in Industrial Society* (Stanford, Calif., 1959); Raymond W. Mack and Richard C. Snyder, "The Analysis of Social Conflict—Toward an Overview and Synthesis," *Journal of Conflict Resolution*, Vol. 1, No. 2 (June 1957); Anthony Oberschall, *Social Conflict and Social Movements* (Englewood Cliffs, N.J., 1973); and Neil J. Smelser, *Theory of Collective Behavior* (New York, 1963).

4. Mack and Snyder, "Analysis of Social Conflict," p. 220.

5. Ibid., p. 243.

6. Ibid., p. 244.

7. Since one major function of all forms of social structure is to regulate conflict, a more comprehensive discussion of the relationship between social order and conflict is needed for any "theory" of group conflicts. For that purpose, see Oberschall, *Social Conflict*, pp. 120–123.

   Mack and Snyder have discussed mainly how institutionalized conflicts tend to give rise to a decentralized approach and uninstitutionalized conflicts to a centralized approach ("Analysis of Social Conflict," pp. 243–244). I have extended their thesis by noting that future conflicts tend to follow existing modes of conflict regulation and that the centralized approach has a higher probability of sudden and explosive eruptions of disorganized conflicts.

9. Dahrendorf, *Class and Class Conflict*, p. 315.

10. Ibid., p. 176.

11. Oberschall, *Social Conflict*, p. 70.

12. Mack and Snyder, "Analysis of Social Conflict," p. 226; Oberschall, *Social Conflict*, pp. 266–267.

13. Dahrendorf, *Class and Class Conflict*, p. 317.

14. Mack and Snyder, "Analysis of Social Conflict," p. 225.

15. Mancur Olson, Jr., "Rapid Economic Growth as a Destabilizing Force," *Journal of Economic History*, Vol. 23, pp. 539–552, as quoted in Oberschall, *Social Conflict*, p. 38.

16. Smelser, *Theory of Collective Behavior*, pp. 332–333.

17. Oberschall, *Social Conflict*, p. 64.

18. Mack and Snyder, "Analysis of Social Conflict," p. 247.

19. Smelser, *Theory of Collective Behavior*, p. 51.

20. Oberschall, *Social Conflict*, p. 333.

21. Leonard Berkowitz, *Aggression: A Social Psychological Analysis* (New York, 1962), p. 103.

22. Mack and Snyder, "Analysis of Social Conflict," p. 235.

23. Giuseppe Di Palma, *The Study of Conflict in Western Society: A Critique of the End of Ideology* (Morristown, N.J., 1973), pp. 8–9.

24. Berkowitz, *Aggression*, p. 103.

25. Ibid., p. 194.

26. For more discussion on this, see Irving L. Janis and Daniel Katz, "The Reduction of Intergroup Hostility: Research Problems and Hypotheses," *Journal of Conflict Resolution*, Vol. 3, No. 1 (March 1959).

27. Lucian W. Pye, "Culture and Political Science: Problems in the Evaluation of the Concept of Political Culture," *Social Science Quarterly*, Vol. 53, No. 2 (September 1972).

28. Lucian W. Pye, "Introduction: Political Culture and Political Development," in Lucian W. Pye and Sidney Verba, eds., *Political Culture and Political Development* (Princeton, N.J., 1969), p. 9.

29. Lucian W. Pye, *Politics, Personality, and Nation Building: Burma's Search for Identity* (New Haven, 1962).

30. Sidney Verba, "Conclusion: Comparative Political Culture," in Pye and Verba, *Political Culture*, pp. 535–537.

31. Myron Weiner, "India: Two Political Cultures," in Pye and Verba, *Political Culture*, pp. 213–218.

32. Since these concepts are largely self-explanatory and they are from the works of Smelser and Oberschall, our discussion will be brief.

33. Smelser, *Theory of Collective Behavior*, p. 17; Oberschall, *Social Conflict*, p. 32.

34. Oberschall, *Social Conflict*, p. 77.

35. Ibid., pp. 157–172.

36. Ibid., p. 140. Oberschall's "focal points" correspond to what Karl Deutsch calls a "nuclear area or ecumene" (or "key cities" or "nodal areas") in *Nationalism and Social Communication* (Cambridge, Mass., 1953), pp. 37–63.

37. For more on conflict resolution by "trade" or "exchanges," see Sidney R. Waldman, *Foundations of Political Action. An Exchange Theory of Politics* (Boston, 1972). For descriptions of these 13 types of conflict, see Mack and Snyder, "Analysis of Social Conflict," pp. 219–221.

38. Coser, *Functions of Social Conflict*, p. 49.

39. C. Kerr, "Industrial Conflict and Its Mediation," *American Journal of Sociology*, Vol. 60 (1954), p. 230, as cited in Mack and Snyder, "Analysis of Social Conflict," p. 220.

40. Mack and Snyder, "Analysis of Social Conflict," p. 230.

41. See Coser's discussion of these sect-like groups in Coser, *Functions of Social Conflict*, pp. 95–104.

42. Anthony Oberschall, "Group Violence: Some Hypotheses and Empirical Uniformities," *Law & Society Review*, Vol. 5, No. 1 (August 1970), p. 77.

43. Berkowitz, *Aggression*, p. 227; Janis and Katz, "Reduction of Intergroup Hostility," pp. 92–93.

44. Oberschall, *Social Conflict*, p. 321.

45. Dahrendorf, *Class and Class Conflict*, p. 213.

46. Mack and Snyder, "Analysis of Social Conflict," p. 226.

2

POLITICAL CULTURE

In late August 1966, after Mao's first public review of the "Red Guards" in Peking, those young rebels launched the "Destroy the Four Olds" campaign ("old ideas, old culture, old customs, and old habits") throughout China. They went on a rampage; they changed street and store names, forcibly cut people's hair (long hair was regarded as bourgeois), destroyed art wares and monuments, and broke into the houses of "revisionist" teachers and "black elements" (i.e., former landlords and rich peasants, "counter-revolutionaries," "bad people," and "rightists"). Ken Ling recalled his activities during this period in mainland China in these words:

> . . . I seldom stayed at home. When I did go home, I would first go to school, take a bath, put [on] everyday clothes and return, pretending that nothing unusual had happened. I realized that what I was doing contradicted what I had been taught at home. . . . Like an actor playing two roles, I was a notorious Red Guard outside but a compliant son at home. When I was asked to do household chores, I never scorned them because I was now a Red Guard leader. But when mother asked me not to overdo collecting evidence on teachers, I no longer obeyed her.[1]

Ken Ling perceptively notes the clash of two cultures in China today, the parochial culture of the old and the "subject-participant" culture of the new.

The Chinese Communists are among the most determined leaders of the developing nations to create a new political culture. If Myron Weiner's statement, "the changing character of political attitudes and the political process is increasingly the consequence of the introduction of new governmental institutions and of governmental activities,"[2] is true of India, it is even more true with respect to the political culture of China. According to Weiner, changes in the Indian political culture are brought about by the "expanding net of the government," "the dispersion of power" and "the democratization of power." In China, mass political mobilization, rather than "democratization of power," has increased tremendously since 1949.[3] The changes in political culture can be expected to be more pronounced in China than in India.

The Cultural Revolution is an ideal opportunity to study changes in Chinese political culture. During that period the bias which prevented reliable analysis of the public's attitude toward the government, i.e., the controlled communications system, was temporarily removed. Travel restrictions were lifted. More important, the Party regulations and guidance which had played a central role in the life of the Chinese were absent. Consequently, the Cultural Revolution also presents the opportunity to study the psychology and personality of Chinese youth. In that situationally ambiguous period the distinction between the unique personality traits of each subgroup and individual and the universal cultural traits of a whole people or nation was greatly sharpened. The common mode of behavior and thought of Chinese youth in that period of situational flux provides a means of analyzing the impact of a state inculcation of a new political culture.[4]

The following discussion of the political culture in China observes Mack and Snyder's prescription that psychological (or cultural) propositions require the nature of the analytical units to be clearly denoted; and that motivations, values and attitudes as group characteristics be related to specific situations and in the context of a particular conflict interaction.[5] The analytic unit in this study consists of Chinese youths generally in the 15- to 22-year-old age group. The conflict situation encompasses the actions of those youths in the Cultural Revolution between 1966 and 1969, specifically their relationships to political authority and themselves. The following discussion of the Chinese political culture pertains mainly to this group.

There are two relevant aspects of political culture: the Chinese accentuation of politics, and the habitual teaching of dual standards of political civility to the young generation. Both of these factors have an important bearing on group conflict in the Cultural Revolution. The statement by the former Red Guard quoted at the beginning of Chapter 1 clearly shows how "politicization" gave rise to factionalism and violent struggle. The young people of China were taught a dual standard of political civility—aggression against "the enemy" and comradeship with "the people"—that accounts for the factionalism and group violence characteristic of the Cultural Revolution. The results of an accentuation of politics for the young generation of China, e.g., the heightening of political sensitivity, a degree of precocity, a "hair-splitting" mentality, class consciousness, a "statist" tendency, and acceptance of socialist values such as puritanism, egalitarianism and populism, will be treated first. Then the systematic inculcation of a dual standard of political civility will be analyzed. It will be shown that this duality was manifested in linguistic reforms under the Communist rule after 1949, particularly in the polarization of new terms. The dual standard was taught in specific mass campaigns and in the regular school curricula. Finally, this analysis will show how the emulation of the army by young mainland Chinese served to inculcate the new ethos of duality in political civility.

Accentuation of Politics

The first thing that almost all Chinese, adult or children, quickly learned after 1949 is that politics is now a central part of their life. In China even a minimal involvement requires a working knowledge of the official ideology (at least an ability to use a few necessary terms). Even minimal political activity means regular exposure to political propaganda or agitation, attendance at endless meetings, participation in public demonstrations and the regular articulation of support for the government's policy. The active participants must do more—i.e., "read between the lines" of official pronouncements and newspaper editorials to adapt to policy changes.

The primacy of politics resulted in a heightened political sensitivity among the youth of mainland China. Ken Ling recalled his experience in the initial period of the Cultural Revolution in 1966:

> We all had had premonitions of the forthcoming movement. In the newspapers during the month of May there had been violent criticism of the literature, plays and movies called "poisonous weeds." As the outside disturbances had penetrated our classrooms, our teachers had lost their usual lively manner and appeared uneasy. Many of them were worshipers of the poisonous weeds. They had become very cautious and no longer told us little personal

anecdotes. *Mainland youth of my generation, living in an unpre-*
dictably changing society, had cultivated a sensitivity on political
matters. Looking at our teachers, we guessed that they must be
recalling the terrible lessons of the cruel "anti-rightist"* struggle
of nine years before [emphasis added].[6]

According to another former high school student named Dai Hsiao-ai,
"Everyone naturally took the view that one's political standpoint was
a matter of life and death."[7]

The accentuation on politics seemingly developed a degree of precocity in Chinese youth, e.g., a certain impatient desire to participate in
adult activities. Dai Hsiao-ai, who was then in a high school in Canton,
testified, "Just before the Cultural Revolution I felt that there was nothing
we could not accomplish if we tried. We all felt this way. We were
ready for anything."[8] Once having participated in the terror against
the so-called black elements (families of former landlords, rich peasants, "bad persons," "counterrevolutionaries," and "rightists," i.e., outcast groups in China), Dai relished this experience of destruction: "We
felt like adults, really for the first time."[9] Ken Ling states that after
he participated in terrorizing and mistreating teachers in the first stage
of the Cultural Revolution (June to August 1966), "I was surprised
at the great change in myself during such a short period. My carefree
student days and adolescence were over. Although I was only sixteen,
I felt I was a man, with a man's share of responsibility."[10] It is significant
that Dai and Ken expressed similar feelings after participating in violent
acts against outcast groups which were fully sanctioned by the authorities. Violence enables a person or a group to claim "full manhood
hitherto denied to them by the powers that be."[11] In the case of Chinese
youths, years of political instruction which made no distinction between
adults and children, created a certain "activated state" in their minds.
The officially sanctioned aggression against some out-groups brought
this state to maturation. In this respect, it is relevant to mention that
researchers studying the effect of the mass media on the youth of
America and England found that early exposure to a mass medium
(e.g., television) tends to create precocious anxieties about growing up
among 13- to 14-year-olds.[12] The massive and pervasive political education in mainland China after 1949 probably produced a similar effect
by precipitating youthful sensitivity and anticipation concerning adult
political roles.

The emphasis on the primacy of politics is also a reflection of the
"operating norm" of Chinese Communist leaders which tended to
inculcate a "hair-splitting" mentality among youth in mainland China

---

*"Anti-rightist" struggle refers to the Communist Party's counterattack on
the intellectual critics in the "Hundred Flowers" campaign of 1957.

and which is the dominant trait of elite political cultures as well. A discerning former English teacher in Shanghai reports that during the Cultural Revolution the views of his students did not differ much so that "they had to keep their eyes peeled for the characteristics they *thought* they should find in their opponents" [emphasis original]. The same teacher found a rebel group's "hair-splitting" attack on a Shanghai newspaper "comic" but then stated that the rebels "had to be very sharp to find discrepancies, for a general attack might cast aspersions on the men in power in the capital—the Rebels' own mentors."[13] Dai Hsiao-ai stated that "conducting unmerciful struggles against people who committed the 'one-character mistake' *(i tzu chih ts'o)* was actually quite common."[14] The Red Guards, according to Chou En-lai, tried to find "cracks between the Party Center and the Central Cultural Revolution Group with a magnifying glass."[15] Again and again during the Cultural Revolution there were instances when members of the Central Cultural Revolution Group who had wielded the weapon of "one-character mistake" to condemn fallen leaders (e.g., Liu Shao-ch'i or Peng Chen) found the youthful rebels turning the tables on them. In one instance Chen Po-ta, chief editor of *Hungchi*, was hard pressed by a group of Red Guards objecting to an editorial. He pleaded with them in desperation:

> Some say that they have found "conspiracy" in the editorial. I do not think there is. You can not condemn others to death on account of one essay. In that case no one can write essays anymore. I never thought so much resistance could arise because of this. This proves that your political sensitivity is sharper than mine.[16]

The record of this episode shows that Chen's listeners were not satisfied. The "hair-splitting" style of politics was the result of the conduct of top leaders and their adoption of an esoteric and controlled communications system. The search for facts behind thick layers of official propaganda requires mainland Chinese to read between the lines.[17]

The sharpening of general political sensitivity is accompanied by a greatly heightened class consciousness among youths in mainland China. The two former high school students, Dai Hsiao-ai and Ken Ling, testify to the intense class consciousness among students. Dai recalled that in the beginning of the Cultural Revolution (June 1966) student attitudes varied according to class backgrounds. Students of the "worker-peasant" class felt a strong sense of legitimacy in their actions. Those of bourgeois backgrounds experienced vague fears and anxiety. Students whose parents were high civil and military officials—the "new class"—eventually became "royalists" who defended the "establishment." Class discrimination sometimes became violent. Dai described how students, said to be "Seven Kinds of Black," were detained, cursed, beaten up and turned back at the Peking Railway Station in the first wave of the "link-up" movement during the fall of 1966. Such encounters created fear among those in Dai's group who came from middle-peasant backgrounds.[18] The student composition of each school was also class-bound. Ken Ling reports that "the overwhelming majority of students . . . were of five black classes; this was one of its exceptional characteristics" in the Amoy Eighth Middle School, which he attended.[19] The vocational school Dai attended in Kwangtung, however, was composed mainly of students from "correct" class backgrounds. This youthful class consciousness was undoubtedly the result of state inculcation. Dai reports that the young people in a village he visited responded to the appeal of class struggle, while the adults freely communicated with "black elements" without evidence of mutual antagonism.[20] Ma Sitson, former director of the Central Music Academy in Peking, recalled that "the children were fiercest of all"[21] in the violence and terror visited by Red Guards against teachers and other "black elements" in June 1966.

Years of political exhortations, coupled with a monistic power structure and many paternalistic policies of the Communist government, have decidedly created a statist or centralist political orientation among the young generation in mainland China. At the beginning of the Cultural Revolution students all over China almost unthinkingly followed the direction of Party representatives and launched merciless struggles against some of their most respected teachers. For example, the "slightest suggestion that anyone was working against the common good or the teachings of Chairman Mao would provoke a flurry of indignant posters" among students in Shanghai.[22] In many cases young people were only too glad and, indeed, impatient to serve the state.[23] Some Chinese students did rebel against the government; there were many such rebellions and very violent ones at that. But in rebelling against authority, Chinese students managed to "have their cake and eat it too" by directing their antipathy toward nearby, regional officials while voicing allegiance to the remote, central authority. Psychologically this behavior is rational because the regional officials often frustrated the students. Prior to the Cultural Revolution, aggression or hostile acts against local officials were inhibited by fear of punishment. During the Cultural Revolution such aggression was sanctioned by the highest authority of the land, hence the dialectical synthesis of a simultaneous rebellion and expression of allegiance to authority.

In the absence of the usual controls, Chinese students during the period between 1966 and 1969 returned to seemingly archaic patterns of traditional behavior and thought, thus signifying that the government's policy of "primacy of politics" was less than a total success.

But by rebelling against local authorities while swearing allegiance to the national authority, the students unexpectedly carried out the official policy of "using the ancient to benefit the present." Students all over China sent delegations to Peking "to file a complaint to the capital" (*pei-shang kao-chuan*) during the autumn of 1966. As Ken Ling explained, the phrase "to file a complaint to the capital" was from a traditional opera "in which the hero set out for the capital to file a complaint, accompanied by servants bearing his coffin to show his determination to fight to the death."[24] Thus the traditional practice of commoners (as children) telling grievances to higher authorities (as parents) for the wrongs done by lesser officials unexpectedly bolstered the authority of Mao, who was actually calling for "destruction of the old."[25] The statist orientation of Chinese youth occasionally enabled the central leaders to emasculate the young rebels. For example, a group of rebels from a film studio asked Chiang Ch'ing for instructions, and she replied: "Don't ask me for instructions. We are all comrades."[26] Even at the height of the youthful anarchy, directives from the Central Cultural Revolution Group in Peking often could make or break a local rebel group.[27] The basic allegiance of Chinese youth to the central authority most strongly distinguished them from the youth in Hungary in 1956.[28] In the Hungarian revolution, the behavior of youths (some very young) in the streets of Budapest showed no trace of any subject orientation.

The Chinese Communist inculcation of a strong statist orientation among many youths of China was accompanied by the widespread acceptance of some of the broad principles of the Communist government. A study of the political orientation of Soviet citizens during the early 1950s by Bauer and Inkeles distinguishes between the acceptance of a system as opposed to acceptance of a regime. Soviet citizens generally accepted the system of socialism but many rejected a particular regime, e.g., that of Stalin. Studies of the orientation of students in Poland and Yugoslavia in the 1960s also show that there was a general acceptance of the broad values of the socialist regime.[29] The attitudes of Chinese students in the "Hundred Flowers" campaign of 1957 and in the Cultural Revolution seem to conform to this general pattern.[30] The former Cantonese Red Guard, Dai Hsiao-ai, reportedly "reject[ed] not the values expressed by the Chinese political system, but the institutions and personalities which constituted the system."[31] When Shanghai students attacked and seized a Party-run newspaper in 1966, it was observed that "not once during the whole affair was there the slightest whisper of dissatisfaction with the press in general or with the strict Party control of news and information. . . . No one challenged the right of a paper to run a line; the argument was whether the line was 'progressive' or 'reactionary' "[32] "Maoist" puritanism and its attack on the "moral degeneration" of fallen leaders and their families seemed to have genuine popular support among Chinese youth.[33] Puritanism, egalitarianism and populism seem to have been widely accepted values.

The political culture of Chinese youth discussed so far was highly conducive to group conflict. The sharpened political sensitivity in China accentuated the authoritative relations in society which themselves are a fundamental source of group conflict. These factors and the tendency toward "hair-splitting" by the youth of China combined with the pervasive class consciousness also directly contributed to group conflict. Furthermore, they accentuated the proclivity of Chinese leaders to use strategic aggression against certain out-groups in order to accomplish their political purposes. The statist and allegiant attitudes of Chinese youths made them especially responsive to the direction of their leaders. These factors engendered widespread group conflict in the Cultural Revolution but the teaching of a dual standard of political activity was also part of the Communist Party's mobilization for group conflict from 1966 to 1969.

A Dual Standard of Political Civility

One astounding phenomenon of the Cultural Revolution was the prevalence of incivil words and deeds on the part of both the elite groups and the masses. Political civility refers to "the degree to which more or less formal norms of courtesy tend to dampen the harshness of political disagreement."[34] Incivility means either a low degree or the complete absence of norms of courtesy in political interactions. In China, even while the rebelling youths were not engaging in the widespread violence, they fantasized incivil and aggressive acts toward real or imaginary opponents. These fantasies were expressed in the language of the Red Guards. Ken Ling recalled the roadside slogans he observed while travelling back to Amoy in October 1966, "most of which began with the words 'down with,' 'burn,' 'bombard,' 'fry in oil,' or 'hang' and ended with the name of some leading member of the Amoy Municipal Party Committee."[35] Hunter vividly describes the scene in Shanghai in November 1966:

> Characters 3 feet high, painted in bold black strokes, shouted "Bombard the Municipal Committee!" and "Burn Mayor Ts'ao Ti-ch'iu!" And soon it became quite common to see breathtaking threats like "Any Rat that Dares to Try and Shift the Revolutionary Pacemakers Half a Hair's Breadth off Course Will Be Smashed to a Pulp!" I asked some of my students (who had taken a moderate

position) what they thought of this language. They laughed un-
comfortably and mumbled that the slogans, though "admirably
strong," were "of course not to be taken literally."[36]

The rationalization of Hunter's "moderate students" cannot be taken
literally, for violent acts committed by the Red Guards closely fitted
their violent words. Both the fantasy and the reality of political incivility
among Chinese youth were the result of a long-standing state policy
to teach the young dual standards of political civility; aggression against
certain out-groups was explicitly legitimized by that new political ethos.
The foundation of this new ethos was the language.

Language & Incivility

If a political culture "is the product of both the collective history
of a political system and the life histories of the individuals who cur-
rently make up the system,"[37] then one can hardly play down the role
of language in transmitting and transforming a political culture. Language is an important medium in socializing the young and transmitting
the collective history of a political system. So far as group conflict is
concerned, Berkowitz states that "people may develop hostile attitudes
toward particular groups merely because their parents, friends, and
associates have repeatedly coupled unpleasant words with the sight of
these groups or even the utterance of their names." And, "many words
have aggressive connotations and thus carry with them associated ideas
and feelings that can facilitate aggressive behavior."[38]

The Chinese Communists are probably the most conscious and serious
of all the world leaders in attempting to change the attitudes and
behaviors of their people by creating a new language. After 1949, a
wholesale language reform began in China. Li Chi attributed the language
revolution to three forces: (1) the need to meet the demands of a new
social, political and economic order; (2) the use of language as a weapon
of psychological warfare in the interests of the Communist Party; and
(3) the assertion of hitherto inarticulate social groups.[39] The first two
conditions have given rise to many "hair-splitting terms of classification"
which "were a matter of life and death with many people."[40] Terms
of dual nature abound in China. One set of terms is designed to arouse
class hatred and instigate action, composed mainly of "words savoring
of astringency or bitterness or suggesting threat or passionately cruel
impulse." Another set of terms is "couched in words of soothing cheer,
promise and warmth in order to produce the picture of a splendid
prospect and induce action of another type."[41] Naturally the astringent
terms are intended for the out-groups, former landlords and the "black
elements." The soothing words apply to individuals, Communist leaders,

model workers or peasants, the army, and martyrs. Extremely aggressive and hostile acts are permitted in dealing with out-groups and the most sentimental type of attachment is shown to the others.

Chinese political linguists also injected a large dose of military vocabulary into their language and this is undoubtedly related to the experience of the Chinese Communist elites. However, the origin of this language policy is of less interest than its possible effects. Li Chi points out:

> It is a conventional practice in wars of all kinds for the two opposing camps to draw clear lines of demarcation and glare at one another over an unbridgeable gap. It is considered necessary if feelings of hostility are to be kept ablazing. Slogans, praises of one's own side and abuses of the enemy, in order to reduce human relationships and values into two simple groups, have traditionally been part of the wartime uses of a language to maintain hostility. Mao Tse-tung says, "If you are a proletariat literary man, you will not sing the praises of the bourgeois class but sing the praises of the proletariat class and the working people. You must be one of the two. . . ."[42]

In disseminating a language of dualities, the Chinese leaders actually polarized the population. The young were thus prepared by the state to engage in hostile and incivil acts against individuals or groups that ran afoul of the authorities.

This language policy bore rich fruit during the Cultural Revolution. The polarity of language reached a state where there was a sole guiding light on one side—the all-powerful Olympian image of Chairman Mao— and on the other side denigrative images of Mao's opponents that employed "fantasies stemming from the backward countryside and city corners."[43] The victims, especially independent intellectuals, were "vilified as beasts, insects, or reptiles of the most vicious or meanest kind. . . . They have been, depending upon the context, variously nicknamed *ch'ai-lang* (voracious wolves) . . . *tu-she* (poisonous snakes) . . . *chi-sheng ch'ung* (parasitic worms) and *hai-jen ch'ung* (injurious vermin)." All this "indicates that, at least on the semantic level, the Chinese Communists refuse to accept their enemies as human beings."[44]

There is every reason to take the incivility and double standard in the language of the Red Guards and even the elite press seriously, since "nation-wide turmoils have attended them, and . . . violent words have been followed up with violent action."[45]

The Red Guards and their mentors did not hesitate to resurrect terms from old myths of bygone days and bizarre images from folk religions even while calling for "destruction of the old."[46] It was noted earlier that the statist orientation of Chinese youth in the Cultural Revolution was bolstered by the traditional subject mentality among the Chinese and that the authorities in Peking probably encouraged such a union. Those authorities obviously resorted to the same tactics in legitimizing hostile acts against out-groups.

By disseminating a language of militancy, encouraging the ethos of an unambiguous attitude toward friend and foe and legitimizing aggression toward the enemy, the Chinese Communists impart to their people their own operative norms, their formula of success. The authorities in Peking, proud of their achievement and committed to a populistic ideology, seek to transform their people after their self-image. To accomplish such a serious task, Chinese leaders emphasize the self-conscious codification of their experiences and resort to mass mobilization to teach people an elite code of conduct.

Transmission of Incivility

By codifying their experiences of political conflict, Communist leaders emphasize the dialectical or dual nature of political conflict and civility. Before his downfall in the Cultural Revolution, Liu Shao-ch'i's essay, "On Intra-Party Struggle," was regarded as an authoritative codification of political conflict and civility within the Communist Party. The most important aspect of this document is Liu's set of *procedural* rules which define legitimate intra-Party struggle to deal with political disagreements and mistakes made by Party cadres.[47] The procedural rules presumably maintain a degree of political civility within the Party.

The duality of Liu's rule of civility lies in his emphasis on *intra*-Party struggle. He condemned the use of "dissension and cunning schemes" and "administrative procedures—investigation, imprisonment and trial . . ." as methods of intra-Party struggle. Nowhere in Liu's essay is there a statement that such methods are wrong in dealing with any political disagreement, within or without the Communist Party.

This conditional nature of political civility was given ultimate legitimacy by Mao Tse-tung in June 1949 in his essay "On People's Democratic Dictatorship." Mao made a distinction between "people" and "reactionary," and between democracy and dictatorship. "Democracy," wrote Mao, "is practiced within the ranks of the people, who enjoy the rights of freedom of speech, assembly, association, and so on. The right to vote belongs only to the people, not to the reactionaries. The combination of these two aspects, democracy for the people and dictatorship over the reactionaries, is the people's democratic dictatorship." The often repeated statement that "to be kind to the enemy is to commit a crime against the people" is derived from Mao's dualistic standard. Unlike Liu, however, Mao did not establish a set of procedural rules or specific criteria distinguishing "people" from "reactionary." In 1957, Mao reiterated these dual standards albeit with different names, e.g., "contradictions among the people" (nonantagonistic) and "contradiction between the people and the enemy" (antagonistic). As Lowell Dittmer states it, the two contradictions are based on "a *subjective* distinction ultimately dependent on the definition of an authority standing above the conflict."[48]

In essence, the political code of conduct promoted by the Chinese Communists requires the Chinese people to develop a dual personality. They must learn to display "boundless love" for the people and "boundless hate" for the enemy. Toward the enemy, no-holds-barred struggle and aggression are permitted and even encouraged. Initially the people, young and old, learned how the incivil aspect of the new code of conduct worked by observing the parade of mass campaigns from 1950 to 1952. The major campaigns were Land Reform, Suppression of Counterrevolutionaries, Three-anti, Five-anti, and Thought Reform of Intellectuals. The targets of struggle included groups supposedly part of "the people," the petty bourgeoisie in the Three-anti and Five-anti campaign and university professors in the Thought Reform campaign. Nonetheless, a no-holds-barred struggle was begun against these groups in the campaigns. The campaign "Purge of Counterrevolutionaries" (*Sufan*) in 1955 employed the type of "unprincipled methods of struggle" condemned by Liu Shao-ch'i in "On Intra-Party Struggle" against a group of dissenters *within* the Party. The line between "people" and "enemy" and between intra- or extra-Party struggle was thin indeed, and the demand for incivility toward "the enemy" never abated.

Since 1962, mass campaigns on mainland China have accentuated the theme of class hatred. This is partly due to the declining prestige of the Communist Party which resulted from the failure of the Great Leap Forward. The emphasis on class hatred was intended to remind people of the basic link between the Party and the interest of the masses (to renew the primordial attachment to the Party). This emphasis also reflected the conflict between Peking and Moscow, because Mao and other Chinese leaders considered one of the most important sources of "Soviet revisionism" to be a blurring of the line between socialism (represented by the proletariat, China and other "fraternal" nations) and capitalism (the bourgeoisie and the U.S.). But the overall effect of the emphasis on class hatred was the exacerbation of differences in society and the undermining of any prospect for political civility. Hu Yao-pang, director of the Young Communist League until January 1967, said in the Ninth Congress of the League in 1964:

> Modern revisionists advocated the absurd view of "nation of all
> the people" and "party of all the people," denying class struggle.
> They use hypocritical "love for mankind" to blur youth's distinc-

tion between us and the enemy. They talk about: "all men are friends, comrades and brothers," and so on. Chairman Mao says it well: "There is no love without cause in the world. Neither is there hate without cause. As for the so-called 'love for mankind,' this kind of love had long disappeared as soon as mankind had been split into classes. . . . We cannot love our enemy or the ugly things in society. Our aim is to destroy these things." Just think, how can there be love between the murderous and greedy imperialists and the oppressed people, between exploiter and exploited? How can the workers and peasants in a socialist nation be "friends, comrades and brothers" to opportunists and those who steal state property?[49]

To prevent young mainland Chinese from blurring the line between "us" and the "enemy," the Communist Party conducted numerous campaigns "recalling past miseries" *(Yi-k'u)* in schools and for the public at large. In these campaigns old peasants and workers were invited to tell students about their sufferings under the Kuomintang, the landlords, the Japanese and imperialists, and contrast that with their present conditions. These campaigns seemed to achieve the intended effect by arousing class hatred among impressionable youngsters and evoking gratitude to the Communist Party. As Dai Hsiao-ai testified: "Sometimes these accounts were very moving; I almost always came away with a feeling that I owed a great deal to the party and to Chairman Mao for making things so much better for me."[50] The campaign "recalling bitterness" on mainland China was similar to psychotherapy, in which the patients are told to recall earlier frustrations to reduce inner tension. The only difference is that the campaigns in China were used not to reduce pent-up stress, but to provoke listeners to anger. In this respect, the Chinese approach is more valid than that of Western therapists. Berkowitz, for example, argues strongly that

> . . . free expression of aggression may have other, unfortunate outcomes. Because of the associations they have, these thoughts could cause people to remember the particular aversive events that had provoked them, and perhaps other unpleasant experiences as well. They also think of the people they want to hurt, their frustraters, and these images also elicit aggressive reactions. Recalling and reliving their anger, these people have stirred themselves up still more.[51]

The "unfortunate outcomes" are exactly what the Chinese leaders wanted from the campaigns "recalling past miseries." "Hatred," said Chou En-lai, "is a mighty lever in society."[52] The leaders of China were gratified when the students almost unthinkingly terrorized their teachers and the families of "black elements" in response to the campaigns.[53]

The inculcation of "righteous hatred and aggression" is, of course, not a post-1962 phenomenon, though the campaigns after that time accentuated that ethos. Furthermore, this theme was not merely incorporated in mass campaigns directed toward adults or near-adults. It has been a part of the school curriculum from the primary level to the upper grades since 1949. The most authoritative study of this technique is a content analysis of a set of elementary school grammar readers (*yü-wen*) used in mainland China to conduct instruction in Mandarin (or "common speech," *pu-tun-hua*) by Ridley, Godwin and Doolin. Their analysis of the readers noted that a major theme, prosocial aggression, appears regularly in textbooks and increases in frequency as the grade level rises. "It frequently accompanies war stories." The three authors speculated about the conflicting themes of "altruism, kindness, and consideration for others" in the readers and of " 'prosocial aggression' allowing unlimited aggression against those deemed to be enemies of society." They conclude that this type of socialization might "lead to a general emotional shallowness on the part of the individual, who would respond as he knows he should, but at heart knows he is only playing a game that he must play and that everyone else is playing too."[54] The speculation about the possibly playful effect of teaching prosocial aggression is contrary to the experience in China. In the Cultural Revolution, there was a close fit between the violent words and the violent deeds of the Red Guards. It has already been shown that the very young were particularly class conscious and violent, and Berkowitz's thesis that language instigates aggressive acts is more plausible than the speculation about playfulness.

The teaching of prosocial aggression is not confined to classrooms and school grounds in China; the language reform after 1949 has already been mentioned. Moreover, young people in China were socialized by the mass media as soon as they left their families and school. For example, the Chinese Communists have endeavored to reform classical Chinese drama and turn it into a medium of political socialization since 1949. Classical dramas in China are like folk songs in that they contain social protests against the oppressive norms of traditional society. They also contain substantial violence and are extremely popular among the Chinese people and are thus an effective *mass* medium. The Communists intended to stress and promote the parts of classical drama that emphasized rebellion against the old (i.e., the feudal system) and the spirit of conflict while suppressing the parts lacking that type of appeal.[55] According to one Red Guard publication, Chou En-lai attributed some Red Guard violence to the effect of drama. Chou, while talking to a group of Red Guards from Manchuria on September 28, 1967, chided them for torturing their victims and asked: "Did you not learn this from stage? Don't we want to destroy the old and promote the new? Why, then, do you still learn from that?"[56]

The discussion has so far concerned the general transmission and teaching of a new political ethos, i.e., the dual approach to civility, in mainland China. To make this process meaningful to young people, the Chinese authorities have repeatedly launched "hero worship" campaigns. The most noteworthy of these campaigns emulate groups or individual martyrs associated with the army.

Army as the Model

The army is the only social group in China that has been used as the model for nationwide emulation. There are other models from the ranks of workers and peasants selected for public emulation but no campaign has urged people to learn from peasants *qua* peasants or workers *qua* workers. The whole nation, however, was engaged in the "Learn from the People's Liberation Army" campaign in 1964. Mao Tse-tung's statement that "soldiers are just workers and peasants in uniform" does not contradict this analysis; on the contrary, it accentuates the importance and prestige of the army.[57]

From 1963 until the Cultural Revolution was initiated, one campaign after another used the army as a model and dominated the mass media on mainland China. Throughout these campaigns the ethos of "boundless hatred" for class enemies and "boundless love" for the people supposedly emulated true (onetime living) examples. The first and most spectacular campaign of this type was "Learn from Lei Feng." The Party propagandists altered the story of Lei Feng's martyred childhood a few times and all versions stressed Lei's capacity for class hatred.[58] Lei's English biography begins with a chapter entitled "Bitter Hatred" and the text starts with a passage from Lei Feng's diary:

> Although I was only a child at the time I was filled with hatred for imperialism and the dark society I lived in, for I knew they were murderous and inhuman. I yearned for some of my own people to come and save me, for then I would get hold of a gun and shoot down those dirty brutes and avenge my parents.[59]

Lei Feng had an exemplary childhood in terms of "boundless hatred for the enemy." His father's death was indirectly caused by Japanese troops; his elder brother died of tuberculosis due to capitalist exploitation in his factory; and his younger brother died of undernourishment, while his mother hanged herself after being raped by a landlord. A substantial number of Chinese youth had less exemplary backgrounds.

Consequently, the Party leaders needed to bridge the gap. Wang Chieh served as just such a bridge.

Wang "belonged to a new generation of Chinese youth who have matured . . . quickly under the brilliance of Mao Tse-tung's thought . . ." and was a middle school student "from an ordinary peasant family" when he joined the army.[60] Thus his background did not predispose Wang to the new ethos; he learned from others through campaigns of "recalling past bitterness and miseries." Wang's biographer records his "political socialization":

> From the stories told by the men at the "recall bitterness" meetings, it emerged that out of ninety-odd men in the company, sixty-six had fathers or brothers who had worked as farmhands for landlords, and fifty-six had had their homes broken up and relatives killed by the imperialists, Kuomintang reactionaries or landlords. For instance, while the father of one of the men, Tsao Chien-yueh, was being taken away by Japanese invaders, his grandmother was bayoneted to death. Chu Yu-pei also had a bitter story to tell. He could still vividly remember the time when he had to go begging as a little boy. His parents were so poor that they didn't even have a rice bowl, so he had to collect scraps of food with a broken tile. From these and many other painful tales of the old society, young Wang Chieh learned about the bitter past of his comrades-in-arms. He began to see the real meaning of classes, oppression and exploitation, the reason for revolution. No longer able to control his anger and hatred, he jumped on the platform and declared: "Comrades, I haven't been through the bitterness you've suffered, but I feel as if all your sufferings have happened to me as well. I'm determined to avenge my class brothers!"[61]

The public campaigns were reinforced by incorporating the military spirit in formal pedagogy, in the reading and extracurricular activities of students. Ridley, Godwin and Doolin reported that

> War stories, containing descriptions of violence and death, were the fourth most frequent contextual unit. These stories appear to perform two functions. On the one hand, they permit the use of heroes and heroines exemplifying the highest possible sacrifice for one's country, and on the other hand they enable the regime to elaborate on the nature of righteous struggle.[62]

Dai Hsiao-ai reports that active military training was carried out in high schools under the direction of army officers. Teachers and students were part of the militia and learned how to handle weapons and practiced live firing. Students genuinely enjoyed the experience and truly admired the army. Dai and Ken Ling testify that the initial enthusiasm of high school students for joining the Red Guards in 1966 was based on the belief that they were becoming "the reserve force for the army."[63] The official report about the first Red Guard group, the "Peking Militant School of Red Guards" on the campus of Ts'inghua University, corroborates that report. Members of the Peking group went to the drilling ground

> for an hour's military training every morning, doing bayonet charging, target aiming and shooting, hand-grenade throwing and other basic drills. . . . They also hold discussions with the People's Liberation Army men . . . and study their high political consciousness, strict organization and discipline and skillful military technique. They are serious about preparing themselves to be good reserves for the People's Liberation Army.[64]

The success of the "Learn from the Army" campaigns obviously can be attributed to numerous sources, including a reliance on adolescent psychology and the rising nationalism in China. In this analysis, the army worship campaigns are significant because they reinforced a double standard of civility. The ethic of the army legitimized and institutionalized aggression toward the enemy and extolled comradeship in its own ranks.

Any observations regarding the transmission of the elite political culture to the youth of mainland China lead inevitably to the conclusion that the Communist authorities have attempted to institutionalize aggression in Chinese society, i.e., the authorities define aggression against certain groups as legitimate and proper and actually encourage the public to commit such aggressive acts. The behavior of the Red Guards and other groups in the Cultural Revolution indicates that Chinese authorities have achieved some success. Janis and Katz have systematically explored the implications of institutionalized aggression regarding group conflict. According to these psychologists, institutionalized aggression produces three psychological dangers: the release of latent hostilities under conditions of social sanction of violence; the apathetic condoning of any institutionally approved practice; and the perpetuation and intensification of institutionalized violence.

Under ordinary circumstances, latent personal hostility and aggression are kept in check by social norms and institutions. But then the norms legitimize and even instigate aggression, latent hostility is released and the response tends to go beyond the bounds of sanctioned behavior. Institutionalized aggression inflicts wounds upon its victims that are deeper than those inflicted by personalized aggression. Personalized aggression leads to personalized resentment and institutionalized aggression "induces in its victims more displacement and more generalized hostility." The victims of institutionalized aggression have no recourse to any form of counteraggression, since the punishment awarded them is legal and proper. "The result is often intense generalized hatred." In extreme cases, it may result in identification with an aggressor.[66]

When hostile and violent actions against certain out-groups are sanctioned by authorities, the general public tends to view the aggression as an objective event and accept the actions passively. Passive acceptance results from the development of a double standard; one standard of morality for the kin group and another for all other groups. Such dual ethics are sometimes justified on the basis of social myths, e.g., racial superiority or correction of historical wrongs. The authorities in China actively prepared the people, and youth in particular, for a double morality.

Institutionalized aggression tends to perpetuate and intensify group violence. Violence against certain groups becomes an "ongoing concern" and special institutions are set up, staffed by professionals, to perpetuate it. Because there is a need to adapt to such roles, individuals intimately associated with such institutions develop vested interests and values which maintain the institution and its practice. There is a tendency in such organizations to match unusual institutional roles and basic personality types, e.g., brutal roles undergo a process of self-selection. The Chinese setting is unique in that the government seeks to institutionalize aggression without too much professionalization. Mao emphasizes mass participation in violence and in production; some individuals, however, are more involved and "good at it" than others. Nevertheless, the Public Security Ministry remains a powerful institution. In this respect, the remarks by a former resident of mainland China are significant:

> In every group on mainland China, be it an office, a school, a factory or a village, you encounter this phenomenon. That is, you always find one group that punishes (call it the activists or the ruling faction) and another group that is punished. The latter has acquired this status either because of their background, history, past mistakes or just stubborn character; they are subject to criticism and struggle always as if that was their fate.[67]

Subsequent chapters will discuss the dangers of institutionalized aggression at work in group conflicts in China during the Cultural Revolution.

Before we leave this lengthy discussion of the new political culture in mainland China, it is necessary to anticipate critical comments of this analysis and description. It may be argued that the discussion has not sufficiently noted the emphasis given in the official Chinese Communist ideology of Mao's "cure the disease and save the patient." His seeming civility toward those who erred, however, has a narrow and specific application; it means the sparing use of capital punishment against political dissenters. Ironically, this lowest denominator of civility (by and large observed by Mao in cases of onetime high level Party officials) is responsible for the development of other forms of political struggle and institutionalized aggression in China including public humiliations, denunciation by close friends and relatives, labor reforms, and discrimination against children. These forms of aggression are not capital punishment, nor are they common expressions of civility. The evidence of discrimination and aggression against the innocent offspring of the "black elements" is simply too much and too obvious to cite.

The new political culture on mainland China actively prepares Chinese youth for conflict. The heightened political sensitivity and the teaching of double standards of political civility among mainland Chinese youth constitute the subjective precipitating factor in the mass conflict from 1966 to 1968, which was later accompanied by a set of objective factors producing conflict. The objective factors consist of a series of events, e.g., elite division and communications and the collapse of social controls. The fusion of subjective and objective factors led to large-scale group conflict in the Cultural Revolution.

Notes

1. Ken Ling, *The Revenge of Heaven: Journal of a Young Chinese* (New York, 1972), p. 46.

2. Myron Weiner, "India: Two Political Cultures," in Lucian W. Pye and Sidney Verba, eds., *Political Culture and Political Development* (Princeton, N.J., 1969), p. 202.

3. See, for example, James R. Townsend, *Political Participation in Communist China* (Berkeley, Calif., 1969), and *Politics in China* (Boston, 1974), pp. 179–285; also my *Communications and National Integration in Communist China* (Berkeley, Calif., 1971).

4. The discussion of an interplay between personality and the influence of environmental factors on a person follows Fred Greenstein's line of reasoning in *Personality and Politics* (Chicago, 1972). That approach also conforms to Oberschall's specification as to when psychological concepts should be introduced in accounting for group conflicts: "As social control in a group or collectivity becomes weaker, usually because of greater heterogeneity of group elements and a looser group structure, the scope of individual choice for both means and ends is greater. Thus the risk/reward ratios resulting from external social control and opportunities for material gain and social ascent will elicit a greater variability of responses by group or collectivity members. Hence, intervening variables will be

of help in reducing unexplained variance of behavior responses, including often psychological variables." Anthony Oberschall, *Social Conflict and Social Movements* (Englewood Cliffs, N.J., 1973), p. 176. Oberschall actually refers to the idiosyncratic behavior of individuals under conditions of situational ambiguity but this analysis adapts that concept to investigate common modes of behavior—*spontaneous* common behavior—under situational ambiguity to test the genuine impact of Chinese Communist politicization of the youth culture.

5. Raymond W. Mack and Richard C. Snyder, "The Analysis of Social Conflict—Toward an Overview and Synthesis," *Journal of Conflict Resolution*, Vol. 1, No. 2 (June 1957), pp. 232–233.

6. Ken Ling, *The Revenge of Heaven*, p. 13.

7. Gordon A. Bennett and Ronald N. Montaperto, *Red Guard: The Political Biography of Dai Hsiao-ai* (Garden City, N.Y., 1972), p. 181.

8. Ibid., p. 27.

9. Ibid., p. 78.

10. Ken Ling, *Revenge of Heaven*, p. 32.

11. Lewis A. Coser, *Continuities in the Study of Social Conflict* (New York, 1967), p. 80.

12. Joseph T. Klapper, *The Effects of Mass Communication* (Glencoe, Ill., 1961), pp. 219–221.

13. Neale Hunter, *Shanghai Journal: An Eyewitness Account of the Cultural Revolution* (Boston, 1969), pp. 118, 175.

14. Bennett and Montaperto, *Red Guard*, p. 117, explain the "one-character mistake." The authors note that "mistakenly omitting characters is a common problem among all writers in Chinese . . . during the Cultural Revolution the consequences of such an accidental mistake were obviously regarded as being more serious than might have been the case in ordinary times or in less intense political movements."

15. Ting Wang, ed., *Chung-kung Wen-hua Ta-ke-ming Tze-liao Hui-pien* [A Collection of Documents on the Great Proletarian Cultural Revolution], Vol. 6 (Hong Kong, 1972), p. 26 (hereafter cited as *Collection of Documents*). This is a collection of original documents dealing with the Cultural Revolution in Central-South China.

16. This document is contained in "Group VI-1" of the microfilm data entitled *Red Guard Publications* made available by the Association of Research Libraries—Center for Chinese Research Materials, Washington, D.C. Altogether, there are 12 reels of these data. Hereafter they will be referred to as RGP, together with the identification of each reel. In this case, Chen conducted the conversation with a group of Peking students at the office of *Jen-min Jih-pao* [People's Daily] on October 25, 1966.

17. For a general discussion on the effects of totalitarian communications systems, see Ithiel de Sola Pool, "Communications in Totalitarian Societies," in Wilbur Schramm and Ithiel de Sola Pool, eds., *Handbook of Communications* (New York, 1973); for specific examples of this pertaining to China, see Tung Chi-ping and Humphrey Evans, *The Thought Revolution* (New York, 1966), pp. 128–129, 145–146; Hunter, *Shanghai Journal*, p. 93.

18. Bennett and Montaperto, *Red Guard*, pp. 90, 4, 5, 43, 44, 65, 71, 72.

19. Ken Ling, *Revenge of Heaven*, p. 23.

20. Bennett and Montaperto, *Red Guard*, pp. 103–104.

21. Ma Sitson, "Cruelty and Insanity Made Me a Fugitive," *Life*, Vol. 62, No. 22 (June 2, 1967), p. 29.

22. Hunter, *Shanghai Journal*, p. 46.

23. Bennett and Montaperto, *Red Guard*, pp. 26, 37, 41.

24. Ken Ling, *Revenge of Heaven*, p. 64.

25. For manifestations of old traditional values and attitudes, see Ken Ling, *Revenge of Heaven*, pp. 19, 42, 225; Bennett and Montaperto, *Red Guard*, pp. 103, 214.

26. *Survey of China Mainland Press* (Hong Kong: U.S. Consulate General), No. 3902, p. 7 (hereafter referred to as SCMP).

27. See Hunter's description of the fate of the Red Revolutionaries in Shanghai, *Shanghai Journal*, pp. 237–243; Dai Hsiao-ai's descriptions of the suspension of the debate on the class composition of the Red Guards and the calling off of a hunger strike in Bennett and Montaperto, *Red Guard*, pp. 134, 177.

28. Paul Kecskemeti, *The Unexpected Revolution* (Stanford, Calif., 1961), p. 81.

29. Emilia Wilder, "Impact of Poland's 'Stabilization' on Its Youth," *Public Opinion Quarterly*, Fall 1964, pp. 447–452; Stanislaw Skrzypek, "The Political, Cultural, and Social View of Yugoslav Youth," *Public Opinion Quarterly*, Spring 1965, pp. 87–106.

30. For discussion of the attitudes of Chinese students during the "Hundred Flowers" campaign of 1957, see Roderick MacFarquhar, *The Hundred Flowers Campaign and the Chinese Intellectuals* (New York, 1960), pp. 130–173; Dennis J. Doolin, *Communist China: The Politics of Student Opposition* (Stanford, Calif., 1964).

31. Bennett and Montaperto, *Red Guard*, p. 227.

32. Hunter, *Shanghai Journal*, p. 176.

33. Ibid., p. 274.

34. Gabriel A. Almond and G. Bingham Powell, Jr., *Comparative Politics: A Developmental Approach* (Boston, 1966), p. 56.

35. Ken Ling, *Revenge of Heaven*, p. 101.

36. Hunter, *Shanghai Journal*, pp. 132–133. Even Mao Tse-tung was said to have been embarrassed by the use of violent words and the accompanying struggle by violence; he was said to have demanded a more "sophisticated" form of struggle against his "opponents" instead of always employing terms like "smashing so and so's head." Be that as it may. One can hardly, however, believe that Mao was not aware of the fact that this ethos of incivility is a result of years of political education, much of it modelled after his writings. See *Miscellany of Mao Tse-tung Thought* (1949–1968), Part II, Joint Publications Research Service (February 20, 1974), p. 454.

37. Lucian W. Pye, "Introduction: Political Culture and Political Development," in Pye and Verba, *Political Culture*, p. 8.

38. Leonard Berkowitz, "Words and Symbols as Stimuli to Aggressive Responses," in John F. Knutson, ed., *The Control of Aggression* (Chicago, 1974), pp. 116, 120.

39. Li Chi, *General Trends of Chinese Linguistic Changes under Communist Rule* (Berkeley, Calif., July 1956), pp. 12–14.

40. Ibid., p. 16.

41. Ibid., p. 21.

42. Ibid., pp. 26–27. For more on the use of military terms, see T. A. Hsia, *Metaphor, Myth, Ritual and the People's Commune* (Berkeley, Calif., June 1961).

43. H. C. Chuang, "Preface," *The Great Proletarian Cultural Revolution: A Terminological Study* (Berkeley, Calif., August 1967), pp. iii–iv.

44. Ibid., p. 24.

45. Ibid., p. ii. Only the most partisan observers ignored or even denied violence by the Red Guards; unfortunately Neale Hunter is one of them. His account is still highly valuable, but note that one major "theme" of Hunter's book takes issue with American newspapers on their reports about violence in China during the Cultural Revolution. Actually Hunter left China in April 1967, i.e., before the outbreak of mass violence. He obviously was not invited to witness the terror and violence against the "black elements" in August–October 1966. For these accounts, one has to rely on Ma Sitson, Dai Hsiao-ai (in Bennett and Montaperto, *Red Guard*) and Ken Ling.

46. Chuang, *Great Proletarian Cultural Revolution*, pp. 22–23.

47. Conrad Brandt, Benjamin Schwartz and John K. Fairbank, *A Documentary History of Chinese Communism* (New York, 1966), pp. 356–372.

48. Lowell Dittmer, "The Structural Evolution of 'Criticism and Self-Criticism'," *The China Quarterly*, October–December 1973, p. 714.

49. *Chung-kuo Ch'ing-nien*, No. 14 (1964), p. 12.

50. Bennett and Montaperto, *Red Guard*, pp. 22–23.

51. Berkowitz, "Words and Symbols as Stimuli to Aggressive Responses," p. 140.

52. Hans Granquist, *The Red Guard: A Report on Mao's Revolution*, trans. Erik J. Friis (New York, 1967), p. 33.

53. See, for example, the striking identity of thought and behavior of Ken Ling and Dai Hsiao-ai in their description of participation in terror and violence in Ken Ling, *Revenge of Heaven*, pp. 32–33, and Bennett and Montaperto, *Red Guard*, p. 39.

54. Charles Price Ridley, Paul H. B. Godwin and Dennis J. Doolin, *The Making of a Model Citizen in Communist China* (Stanford, Calif., 1971), pp. 144–145, 198–199. Their conclusion about the "playful" effects are undoubtedly influenced by the late T. A. Hsia's analysis of the war metaphors in the Chinese language; see T. A. Hsia, *Metaphor, Myth, Ritual*, p. 5.

55. For a general discussion of the reform of classical drama on mainland China, see Richard F. S. Yang, "The Reform of Peking Opera under the Communists," *The China Quarterly*, July–September 1972; also my *The Use of Traditional Media for Modernization in Communist China* (Cambridge, Mass., October 1965).

56. The whole document is reprinted in Chao Tsung (Chung), "An Account of the 'Great Proletarian Cultural Revolution,' " (Part 58), *Tsukuo* [China Monthly], No. 104 (November 1, 1972), p. 31 (Chinese text).

57. Mao reportedly made this statement in a speech to the Central Committee Cultural Revolution Group in August 1967. The speech was reprinted in the Red Guard publication, *Wu-ch'an-chieh-chi-chih-shen* (Wuchow, Kwangsi), No. 10 (January 1, 1968). It is reprinted in Chao Tsung, "An Account of the 'Great Proletarian Cultural Revolution,' " (Part 55), *Tsukuo*, No. 101 (August 1, 1972), and also in *Yi-chiu Liu-pa Chung-kung-nien-pao* [1968 Yearbook on Chinese Communism] (Taipei, 1969), pp. 773–774 (hereafter cited by English title).

58. Jacques Marcuse, "The Myth Who Speaks for Mao," *New York Times Magazine*, November 1, 1964; Vincent V. S. King, *Propaganda Campaigns in Communist China* (Cambridge, Mass., January 1966), pp. 16–41.

59. Chen Kuang-sheng, *Lei Feng, Chairman Mao's Good Fighter* (Peking, 1968), p. 1.

60. "A Song in Praise of Revolutionary Youth—The Story of Wang Chieh, Chairman Mao's Good Soldier," in *The Diary of Wang Chieh* (Peking, 1967), p. 2.

61. Ibid., p. 3.

62. Ridley, Godwin and Doolin, *Making of a Model Citizen*, pp. 163–164.

63. Bennett and Montaperto, *Red Guard*, pp. 23, 67; Ken Ling, *Revenge of Heaven*, p. 36.

64. NCNA, October 12, 1966, in SCMP, No. 3802, p. 14.

65. Irving L. Janis and Daniel Katz, "The Reduction of Intergroup Hostility: Research Problems and Hypotheses," *Journal of Conflict Resolution*, Vol. 3, No. 1 (March 1959), pp. 96–99. The remainder of the discussion is based on this article, so attributions to this work are not repeated.

66. There is evidence that the children of the so-called black elements on mainland China were victims and developed this kind of response; see David Raddock, "Innocents in Limbo: China's Youths Recall," *Current Scene*, Vol. 10, No. 6 (June 10, 1972), pp. 13–14.

67. Chin Chien-li, *Pei-kuo Chien-wen-lu* [Odyssey in North China] (Hong Kong, 1973), p. 564. On mainland China, as other witnesses testified, some Communist cadres were known as "veterans in struggle" *(tou-chen lao-shou)* and in the campaigns of the 1950s, "tiger beaters" were sent from the national center to all localities to conduct struggle campaigns. Hence, aside from the professionals of the Public Security Bureau, there are numerous "specialists in violence" at large.

3

MOBILIZATION
FOR CONFLICT

C hapter 2 discussed one of the
important conditions for large-scale group conflicts in China, its political
culture. The new political ethos brought by the Communist leaders
of China emphasizes conflict as the norm of interpersonal relationships
and institutionalizes aggression toward certain groups and individuals.
Chapter 3 discusses two other conditions for conflict: the way the
Communist government managed conflicts before the Cultural Revolution and the actual conditions for mobilization.

Conflict Management before 1966

The model used in this book to analyze group conflict distinguishes
two types of conflict relations, institutionalized and uninstitutionalized.
Furthermore, the institutionalization of conflict is either centralized
or decentralized. Centralized conflict relies mainly on outside control
to regulate conflict relations, whereas decentralized conflict is resolved
mostly through adjustments made between conflict groups. The centralized institutionalization of conflict tends to perpetuate the conditions

that initially brought centralization into being: chronic recurrence of unsettled issues, an absence of voluntarily agreed-upon procedures for regulation of relations and significant probability of sudden and, possibly, violent conflicts. Communist political systems tend to rely on centralized ways of handling conflict by means of monistic power structures and the expropriation of intermediate groups and politicization of conflict relations. The political system on mainland China has achieved all the conditions of centralized institutionalization of conflicts.

Since 1949 the Chinese Communists have simultaneously created large and complex organizations to politicize the population and concentrated effective power to a high degree. The most impressive development was the creation of about 164 mass organizations of various types (professional, political, social and religious). Among the outstanding organizations, each with several million members, were the Young Communist League, the All-China Federation of Trade Unions and Women's Associations. These are politicized organizations, with little or no "subsystem autonomy." Or, to borrow Lasswell and Kaplan's distinction between "ruling class" and "dependent class,"[1] these mass organizations on mainland China have been "dependent organizations" in that they are indulged by the ruling organization—the Communist Party—but do not share in the rule. In terms of communication, these organizations are all linked with the Communist Party but not with each other. They are like the spokes of a wheel connected to a hub (the Party), but without an outer rim or any direct connections between the spokes.[2] These national organizations "expropriate functions formerly reserved to intermediate groups and the family."[3] But in China the process of nationalization is partly expropriation and partly preemption, since the Communist Party created organizations in hitherto unorganized spheres or masses, especially in the countryside. Public communication on mainland China is similarly organized. Thus human communication is substantially nationalized by these organizations and the mass media. Spontaneous lateral communication is actively discouraged and suppressed. This kind of nationalization is likely to result in the atomization of social groups and the displacement of genuine conflicts among the people, since spontaneous human communication is kept at a minimum. The Communist Party uses nationalized organizations to control conflict and promote aggression against officially designated objects whether or not these conflicts or aggressions have any real basis in society. Consequently, genuine conflict in society, e.g., conflict between the Party and the masses, is displaced and that displacement creates "dammed-up tension in the individual, creating potentialities for disruptive explosion."[4]

The policies of the Chinese Communist Party have not been consistent with respect to the two gross strains in Chinese society, the rural-urban gap and the antagonism resulting from regional differences. Politically, in education and communications, the Chinese Communist government stresses unity by promoting a common national identity. Even in this aspect of the regime's policy the official tactic is integration through segregation, e.g., prevention of the free flow of communication and movement between urban and rural areas and among provinces. All communications must be mediated through the Communist authority.[5] Despite these policies, there have been significant resettlements of the population in China since 1949. Many southerners have been sent to frontier regions and northern parts of China. Large numbers of demobilized soldiers have been formed into "Production and Construction Corps" to develop new farms and even cities on China's northern frontiers. These movements, however, have been under strict governmental control. Settlers remain segregated in separate farms in new territories and, in any case, they usually inhabit thinly populated areas.[6] In southern and southwestern China, where regionalism has been strong, no such large-scale population movement took place until the start of the "youth to the countryside" campaign in the early 1960s. The initial and conflict-prone consequences of this forced "downward transfer" policy will be discussed later. Even those youths live in separate quarters in the countryside. The government's policy of divide and rule in these regions of strong localist sentiment (by appointing northerners to positions of real power) *initially* provokes, instead of minimizes, provincial antagonism.[7]

Spontaneous communications among the people, however, can not be suppressed entirely and, after all, the ultimate aim of the Communist Party is to achieve national integration. But for the moment the Chinese leaders are not ready to entrust national integration to the people themselves through mutual adjustments. Whenever and wherever the Communist Party finds it difficult to reduce or suppress spontaneous communications, e.g., during the traditional Chinese New Year (now renamed "Spring Festival"), it attempts to forestall undesirable consequences through political intervention. Before soldiers, workers, employees or students return to their families for the annual celebration (not all of them are allowed to return home every year), the news media in China usually report campaigns involving "political preparation for home visits." Undoubtedly, part of the political preparation instructs vacationers what to say to their kin and friends and what to expect at home. The purpose is to minimize the natural reaction to gaps between the expectations of the people and reality and the difference between statements and living experience. At the same time, the government sponsors "get-together" events between groups, e.g., between the army and peasants, army and students, workers and peasants, intellectuals and worker-peasants, and so on. These events are part of the government's policy to politicize spontaneous human relations, and they are designed to inculcate comradeship instead of friendship.[8] This process of integration through segregation involves the Communist Party as the sole mediator in group interactions.

The official policy until the disaster of 1959 actually sharpened urban-rural and regional economic differences.[9] As long as the Communist Party maintained effective power, however, these differences were controlled. As soon as Party control became ineffective, latent and suppressed antagonism exploded. The Chinese Communists have also been promoting class consciousness, hence class conflict, among peasants and workers in mainland China. Yet the Communists maintain strict control over conflicts and direct them to designated objects. The channelization of class conflict depends upon the effective operation of the Communist Party and mass organizations.

This kind of centralized institutionalization of conflict relations results in a superficial image of order and contentment which often impresses foreign visitors, the Chinese themselves and even Mao Tse-tung. For example, Dai Hsiao-ai, a former Red Guard of Kwangtung, described his classmates and the school in general as "happy and content" before the outbreak of group conflict in the Cultural Revolution. Yet, Dai's biographers report, "within months, this close knit and smoothly functioning unit was to be torn apart by the conflict of forces whose very existence would have been denied before the Cultural Revolution."[10] Dai was amazed by the deep resentment of those teachers who were not members of the Communist Party and suffered discrimination in promotion and other matters.[11] As the Cultural Revolution unfolded in Shanghai, Neale Hunter recalled, "I had to admit that my first impressions of the city had been superficial." The people were not as united as Hunter first thought. "There were deep undercurrents of discontent, wide rifts between factions of the Party, bitter personal feuds in the administration, and many doubts about the program for the future."[12] Most significantly, despite the political education absorbed by the Chinese people since 1949, Hunter states that "few were aware of the exact composition of their government" before the Cultural Revolution.[13] Since the Chinese government maintains the sole right to inform its people about politics and is responsible for public political education, the general public's lack of knowledge on the composition of government can be attributed partly to a deliberate obscuration by the government's propaganda and partly to the people's covert resentment against too much politicization of their lives.[14]

This type of centralized regulation of communications and conflict also results in an ever-widening distance between leaders and followers. Leaders actually become quite fearful of genuine contact between themselves and their subjects. Mao Tse-tung is the most eloquent spokesman of this aspect of Chinese politics (he is perhaps also the only one who can *afford* to be populistic from time to time). In July 1966, for example, Mao ordered the withdrawal of the so-called work teams from schools and thus gave a free hand to students revolting against school and Party authorities. He berated his colleagues at the highest level of the power structure in strong terms:

> The work teams have become counterrevolutionary since they obstructed [students'] revolution. The students at the University of Communications in Sian were prevented from telephoning [the Party Center]; they were not allowed to come to the [Party] Center. Why are you afraid of letting people come to the Center? Let them come and besiege the State Council. . . . In some places [students] were forbidden to besiege the newspaper office and they were not permitted to go to the provincial Party headquarters or the State Council. Why are you so afraid? When [the students] do get to the State Council, only minor officials are there to receive [the students] and these officials cannot explain things well. If you do not show yourselves in person, then I shall do so. You are always so afraid, afraid of counterrevolutionaries or war. How could there be so many counterrevolutionaries?[15]

Or, as Mao commented perceptively to a group of Party officials during his inspection tour in August–September 1967:

> Why were some cadres subject to mass criticism and struggle? One reason is that they have carried out a counterrevolutionary and bourgeois line so the people are angry. The other is that being high officials they put on airs and were haughty. They would not consult the masses and treat the people with equality. They did not practice democracy and were in the habit of instructing and berating the people. They had seriously alienated themselves from the people. So the people had reactions but could not express them. These reactions exploded during the Cultural Revolution. Once they erupted, the situation becomes serious and the officials were embarrassed. We must learn a lesson from this, solve this problem of upper-lower relationship and handle the cadre-mass relationship well. From now on, all cadres must go to the lower level to see for themselves and consult the masses more.[16]

Above all, Mao admitted that the force of conflict in the Cultural Revolution "developed so rapidly as to surprise" him.[17] However, Mao's instruction to cadres quoted here indicates that he sees no need (or is unaware of the need) to change the system of centralized regulation of conflict.

As the discontent of each major social group on mainland China is discussed in later chapters, it becomes apparent that the dissatisfaction of groups first expressed in the "Hundred Flowers" campaign of 1957 remained in force or even became more intense during the Cultural Revolution. The centralized institutionalization of conflict relations tends to perpetuate uninstitutionalized conflicts including the recurrence of chronically unsettled issues. At the individual level, such systems seem to create intrapersonal conflicts as well. The late Edgar Snow, certainly not an "anti-Mao" writer, testified to the high incidence of nervous illness in China:

> I have no statistics on neurasthenic diseases in China but the number of cases I have encountered in hospitals and sanatoria seems *very high*. The inner tensions caused by social pressures of the *kind of system* Communists are trying to create are obviously severe, outlets are few, and it is not surprising that the demand for consultations with Chinese therapists is great [emphasis added].[18]

The intense conflicts which occurred during the Cultural Revolution could also be due to China's heterogeneous society with many ethnic, religious, linguistic and cultural divisions. This type of society is more likely to be "the locus of all manner of discontents and conflicts and . . . these conflicts are more difficult to pursue in a non-violent and institutionalized manner than in societies that are homogeneous in these characteristics."[19] The main thesis here is that the centralization of institutionalized conflicts under the Communist regime tends to prolong and intensify preexisting conflicts and also creates new ones along the way.

Mobilization for Conflict

Spontaneous group conflict in Communist states takes place when there are serious divisions among the elite, a loosening of social control, and in the presence of precipitating events, with precise focal points and communications. These are all necessary conditions for group conflict and they must all be present in order to cause conflict, but they do not necessarily follow a particular sequence. Furthermore, some events may assume more than one role, particularly with respect to the last three, i.e., precipitating event, focal point or mode of communications.[20] All the necessary conditions for group conflict were present in the Cultural Revolution.

From May to December 1966, Peking was naturally a focal point for Party authorities and students in China. Every major event in Peking in connection with the Cultural Revolution in this period precipitated events for student movement in other cities of mainland China. The critical events in Peking started with the public airing of perhaps the severest elite division in the history of the Chinese Communist Party. On May 24, it was announced that a total changeover of the top leaders of the Municipal Party Committee had taken place. Most noteworthy was the dismissal of Peng Chen, then Mayor of Peking and a member of the Politburo. One day later, students challenged the school and Party authorities in Peking University for the first time; a group of philosophy students led by a young female teaching assistant named Nieh Yuan-t'ze put up posters accusing the university president of insincerity in carrying out the Cultural Revolution. The challenge to school authority by Nieh and her colleagues may have been prearranged by the "left wing" leaders in charge of the Cultural Revolution.[21] If so, the leaders followed the natural and empirical causation of mass movement because subsequent events in Peking unmistakably evidenced an elite division, loosening of social control, and the communication of events in Peking to other parts of China.

On the same day that Nieh's poster appeared, three Party media of major influence were being reorganized: the *Peking Daily* and the journal *Front* (both organs of the Municipal Party Committee) and, at about the same time, the most authoritative newspaper in China, the *People's Daily*, organ of the Central Committee of the Communist Party.[22] The Peking branch of the Young Communist League was also reorganized. These changes were indications of elite division. The factor of communication was clearly evident on June 1, 1966, when Mao ordered Nieh's poster to be broadcast by the Central People's Broadcasting Station to the whole nation. The poster was also published in the *People's Daily* the next day. Shortly thereafter another precipitating event occurred—the State Council decreed suspension of regular classes in high schools, colleges and universities. Students were encouraged to criticize all aspects of the educational system and the *People's Daily* published reports of the activities and views of this movement in Peking. It is particularly important to note that a group of high school girls in Peking addressed their letters to Mao Tse-tung, thus signifying Mao's support and legitimization of student movements.[23] The letters also symbolized the prominence of women in the Cultural Revolution, to be discussed in later chapters.

The elite division in Peking continued after June 1966, over the problem of social control. Students in Peking and elsewhere in China were aroused by the events of May and June and "work teams" were dispatched by Party authorities to schools ostensibly to maintain a degree of direction and control over the students. Mao's statement on the actions of the work teams already quoted accused the teams of becoming counterrevolutionary by preventing students from appealing to the Party Center. Liu Shao-ch'i was allegedly the culprit guilty of suppressing students.[24] In retrospect, the work teams were a precipitating factor in the enlargement of the student rebellion. They arrived when student expectations had already been aroused by the events of May and June and they introduced "a sharp new deprivation in the midst of generally difficult conditions."[25] Such events either aggravate existing strains or create new ones. In Peking, the work teams reportedly divided students and incited struggles among students. They classified students into right, left and middle groups and conducted ruthless struggles against "rightists." Students in Peking were generally fearful, since it was reported that personal dossiers were being compiled by the work teams.[26] Mao ordered control over students to be removed and on July 18 the work teams were withdrawn from schools.

In August, Mao further precipitated the student movement by granting personal approval and encouragement and by lifting all social controls. Mao transmitted his directions via the public media to the entire country. Mao took the following actions: he wrote a personal letter to the Red Guard group in the high school attached to Ts'inghua University in Peking (August 1); published his own "wall poster" attacking the "work teams" in the Eleventh Plenum of the Eighth Party Central Committee; completed his first public review of a Red Guard parade accompanied by other Party leaders on August 18 in Peking; and initiated the "Destroy the Four Olds" movement in Peking. The Red Guards in their "destruction of the old" conducted violent and terroristic attacks (even including killing) on selected groups and individuals in Peking and elsewhere, thus pointedly demonstrating that social control no longer applied to them.[27] Students finally, as Mao had hoped, conducted a spontaneous challenge of local Party authorities. To make the movement nationwide, Mao reversed the totalitarian method of suppressing spontaneous lateral communications among the people and ordered a "link-up" movement whereby students all over the nation were allowed to go to Peking to be reviewed by Mao and exchange revolutionary experiences with each other.[28] The result, as Mao himself stated it, was that "Red Guards in the whole country were mobilized and went on charging— charging with such force as to amaze you."[29]

The events in Peking constitute what is known as an initial or real phase of collective behavior. These initial events produce a "drawing in" effect and the "derived phase" of collective behavior then takes place.[30] The response of various localities in China to the events in Peking constitute the "derived phase" of the student movement in June–December 1966. The events in Peking were highly contrived in that the actions of students were probably guided step by step by Mao's colleagues until after August, while the events in the provinces were more spontaneous and complex. The legitimacy of local authorities in China is dependent on the approval of national leaders like Mao, so once central endorsement is withdrawn, local Party officials face challenges to their authority from all directions. Students and discontented individuals within and without local Party institutions often took independent and unpredictable actions. The first wall poster attacking the county Party authority in the county of Haifeng, Kwangtung province, was said to have preceded Nieh's poster by ten days.[31] If this is true, then it is symptomatic of later developments in Kwangtung and elsewhere. That is, it became increasingly clear that a total break had occurred among the top Party leaders so many local leaders decided to join the rebels' side for opportunistic or other reasons. This further split the provincial elites and aggravated group conflict.

The broadcast and publication of Nieh's poster in the national media on June 1, 1966, elicited an almost immediate response from students in various localities of China. In Canton, wall posters appeared in high schools and universities within a week.[32] At the Foreign Languages Institute of Shanghai, where Neale Hunter was employed as an English language teacher, the first wall poster appeared one day after the publication of Nieh's.[33] In the middle school where Ken Ling was a graduating senior, regular classes were suspended and a campaign of poster writing began.[34]

The authority of local Party leaders began to disintegrate. The more active and motivated students all over China initiated direct contact with the students in Peking and followed the national media closely to plan their next move. They no longer treated local Party leaders as the spokesmen of the Party Center. The reactions of local Party leaders further split their own ranks and undermined their authority. In some places, e.g., Dai Hsiao-ai and Ken Ling's high schools and Hunter's languages institute, Party leaders tried to divert the attack to individual teachers. When this proved to be inadequate, lower level Party officials were sacrificed. For example, at Dai Hsiao-ai's school, the work team sent by provincial Party leaders directed students to attack the principal who had directed students to attack teachers earlier.[35] Elsewhere in Canton, similar tactics were used by municipal Party leaders who sacrificed their subordinates—Party branch secretaries—so as to divert student attention.[36] At the languages institute in Shanghai, Hunter observed the same sequence of events. The Party secretary of the institute was at first content with students' criticism and humiliation of individual teachers. Then the Party secretary singled out one of the vice-presidents, a veteran Party member, for public attack and that enabled the Party Committee to maintain control over the institute for the moment.[37] In the end these local authorities merely exacerbated the split within their ranks, reduced their prestige and emboldened the students.

The students, particularly the most active and motivated ones, were increasingly defiant toward local leaders. They felt their strength growing as they discovered each other through more direct communication and as they observed the loosening of social control. For example, Dai Hsiao-ai was led to question the tactics of the school principal, i.e., his selection of an ever larger number of teachers to be attacked, because "students returning from weekly visits home reported evidence of widespread activity in other quarters of the city, particularly in other schools" where "the students themselves had played an active role."[38] From then on, Dai and a group of activists began to take independent actions. They caused the provincial Party authority to send a work team which resulted in the downfall of the school principal. Similarly, a group of students from the South China Technical Institute (College) in Canton established direct correspondence with Peking students after the broadcast of Nieh's poster. They circulated "news from Peking" and "letters from Peking" among the students. On June 24, the activists posted wall bulletins containing a highly inflammatory message from Peking: "Except for Chairman Mao and the Party Center, all other Party authorities are subject to question." The students at the institute were instantly aroused; "they passed the word and copied the bulletins." An alarmed provincial Party authority intimidated the students by keeping them under surveillance and also by resorting to wall posters to counterattack. On June 26, five students from the institute departed from Canton for Peking to "file a complaint" to the Center. Significantly, although the students were supposed to be under the constant surveillance of the Public Security Bureau, they were not arrested or obstructed in their trip to Peking.[39] In nearby Haifeng county, the writer of the first poster to precede Nieh's poster in Peking was not punished, though everyone in the county expected the authorities to arrest the writer.[40]

At the Foreign Languages Institute in Shanghai the tactics initiated by the institute's Party secretary, i.e., the sacrifice of lower cadres and teachers, were briefly effective in early June 1966, but on July 5 the situation "was radically changed by an open letter . . . sent by some graduates of our Institute who had gone to Peking No. 2 Foreign Languages Institute for further studies." The gist of the letter "was that the revolutionary masses of the Shanghai Institute should not waste their time on small fry but should strike at the heart of the trouble—the

Party Committee itself!"[41] The more independent-minded students at the institute responded almost instantly; on the same day, five students from the Spanish Department put up a long poster listing seven grievances against the Party hierarchy at the institute.[42] The subsequent formation of work teams by local Party authorities did not deter the students. Even threats by the Shanghai police chief were ignored because the radicals considered them idle and even hoped for a confrontation which would mobilize others and discredit the authorities.[43]

Shortly after the withdrawal of the work teams, Peking delivered a *coup de grâce* to local Party authorities when Mao's review of the Red Guards on August 18 was broadcast to the nation. In the next few days, students all over China demanded to form their own Red Guards. Many Red Guard groups were actually organized by local Party authorities to meet the demand of students, but the radical and independent-minded ones formed their own organizations without seeking an authoritative endorsement.[44] The students were basically divided between Red Guards endorsed by Party authorities (known as conservatives) and those without Party endorsement (the radicals or revolutionaries). Local Party leaders were on the defensive and the loss of authority of these onetime powerful people was often dramatic. In the case of Dai Hsiao-ai, the loss of power on the part of local and provincial Party leaders was exposed in a mass meeting on September 1, which was attended by five thousand Red Guard representatives. The meeting was disrupted by a group of Red Guards angered by their exclusion. As Dai vividly recalled:

> Then something happened which left me stunned. The Chairman grabbed the microphone and asked that, for their own safety, all Party leaders and other officials leave the room. I couldn't believe my eyes when they all complied without a word. They didn't even try to make peace but simply left. In ordinary times, we wouldn't have dared even to raise our voices to each other before them but now they obeyed what amounted to an order from a student. Now I also realized why they had said nothing in the meeting. They were actually frightened by the Red Guards and powerless before them. It was then that I first realized that school Party committees were not the only casualties of the Cultural Revolution. The movement had also affected the provincial and city Party organs. I was shocked.[45]

The loss of authority of local Party leaders and the control of students over their own movement that followed the formation of Red Guards can be further deduced by the appearance of focal points. In Canton, for example, students were saying: "For national situation, focus on Peking University; for Canton situation, focus on Chungshan University."[46] The most popular student leader in the area, Wu Ch'uan-p'in, came from Chungshan University in Canton. In Shanghai, though Neale Hunter has not stated it explicitly (obviously, for he had not actually been a part of the movement), it is clear that Futan University was a focal point for Shanghai students. Futan University was the first to contact Peking students before August 1966 and was the center of the radical movement. Even the mayor of Shanghai, Ts'ao Ti-ch'iu, went to Futan to appease the radicals. The students of Futan spearheaded the local "link-up" movement to break down the past barriers between students in the same city.[47]

Meanwhile, from September to November, a vast communication movement took place in China, the so-called "link-up" movement. Millions of students converged on Peking to be reviewed by Mao and other leaders. At the same time students from Peking and North China descended upon the cities and towns in central and southern China. The "link-up" movement gave added impetus to the collapse of local Party authority. In many areas, the Red Guards were still dominated by local Party authorities and the "link-up" movement loosened the last semblance of their control over students. The movement "radicalized" more students as those from other areas witnessed the radicalism of students in the capital. A sense of peer rivalry was aroused and students from other areas determined to match or exceed the radical efforts of the Peking Red Guards.[48]

During the "link-up" movement, local Party authorities and even the people in general were less concerned about the activities of the radicalized "local boys" than they were about the arrival of *agents provocateurs*, i.e., students from Peking and Northeast China. Those students established local liaison centers in the major cities of China.[49] Most of the students from Peking belonged to the so-called Third Headquarters known to be under the direction of Mao's wife and her colleagues so the local authorities could not afford to offend them. The Red Guards from Peking clarified the goals of the Cultural Revolution, particularly in directing local Red Guards toward local Party leaders as a target.[50] The Peking Red Guards also passed on the formula of organization to local students, spearheaded audacious attacks on Party headquarters and dared local groups to do the same.[51] Ken Ling described the first attack on local Party authorities in Amoy in August 1966:

> This was the first time that people dared to behave in such a reckless manner in front of the headquarters of the Municipal Party Committee. Partly it was because we had been emboldened during the past month or so by the violent struggles against the teachers and the raids on homes and libraries; partly it was due to the agitation of the Peking Red Guards, who had come along

with us. When we hesitated to barge into a formerly forbidden area, they goaded us, saying we had no guts and were like "women with bound feet."

"In Peking, we even dared rebel against the central leaders," they said. "Why should you be afraid here?"[52]

The "link-up" movement activated traditional provincialism and antagonism among people from different regions. Before the Cultural Revolution government control over travel and communications kept traditional enmity in bounds and the "link-up" movement released latent hostilities. Local Party authorities appealed to the traditional local sentiments to restrain and expel Peking Red Guards. The local authorities also recruited willing workers and peasants to attack local radicals allied with the Peking Red Guards. This tactic initiated the nationwide phenomenon of "struggle between students, workers and peasants" and the result was the enlargement of group conflict.

The "link-up" movement also loosened social control and produced a "drawing in" effect among the entire population. New groups began to join the movement, particularly workers in cities and peasants on the outskirts of large cities. According to Ken Ling, "As the Cultural Revolution progressed, people generally seemed unwilling to keep their places; they tried to move out of bad areas to better ones, from lower positions in society to higher ones."[53] "From November on," says Hunter, "the movement expanded to include the industrial workers. . . . Whether Peking wanted this to happen or not, it was inevitable."[54] The student rebellion, particularly the "link-up" movement, signalled a fissure in the social order and the situation was conducive to the expression of suppressed desires and grievances. In some areas, law and order were seriously eroded. Ken Ling described the situation in Amoy:

> In August fake Red Guards began to appear. Gangsters became "Red Guards" at night, practicing extortion on lovers in the parks and dark alleys and committing robbery. Some even organized into groups and raided the homes of richer families in broad daylight. It was the beginning of a descent into chaos with disturbances everywhere and thieves and prostitutes conspiring together. Stores would lock up their doors after dark, and people would be afraid to wear necklaces, wristwatches or ride bicycles on the streets.[55]

In the conceptual language of collective behavior, a "social contagion" was occurring in China toward late 1966.

The "contagion" and "descent into chaos" gathered momentum in January 1967, when a new movement and a new national focal point emerged. Shanghai became the new focal point and the "January revolution," consisting of two "power seizures," occurred during the first week of January—two Shanghai dailies with national influence were expropriated on January 3 and 5 and the leaders of the Municipal Party Committee were openly brought to trial on January 6. The "January revolution" was almost immediately endorsed by Mao, who stated that Shanghai would be "the prime mover" in the nationwide development of the Cultural Revolution.[56] Shanghai indeed became a focal point for the "power seizure" which quickly spread all over China. A dramatic radio broadcast from Lhasa, Tibet, illustrates the effect of events in Shanghai:

> The seizure of power by the revolutionary rebels of *Wen Hui Pao* and *Liberation Daily* in Shanghai greatly inspired the journalists in Lhasa. On 11 January the revolutionary rebels of the Lhasa Wired Broadcasting Station succeeded in taking over the station. In quick succession the rebels of NCNA's Tibet branch and the Tibet People's Broadcasting Station followed suit. . . .[57]

In other provinces the Red Guards, joined by workers, took over the press and the whole regional Party structure as well. In Shanghai, the Municipal Party Committee was seized by rebel groups on January 15. In Peking, Red Guard groups took over national governmental agencies.

The "January revolution" inspired by Shanghai subsequently spread to the entire country and finally brought "social contagion" to a peak. The fissure opened by the "link-up" movement became a chasm. The "power seizure" pushed the paralysis of local authorities, a loosening of social control, the free flow of communications, participation of new groups, violence and conflicts to the point of total normlessness. In Shanghai, "the disgrace of the Party leaders triggered an immediate, widespread, and organized reaction."[58] The city was temporarily paralyzed by mass walkouts of workers and the supply of water, electricity and coal was interrupted. Rail traffic, postal and telegraph services were suspended. The rebels in power found it necessary to threaten the workers with police measures. But "the police force was as divided as any other organization" and "the whole Police Department was turned upside down on January 11 by a group that raided the central offices of the Public Security Bureau and every single one of its district and county branches."[59] In many cities, the "power seizure" included raiding of Public Security Bureaus, once the most feared "instrument of proletarian dictatorship." In Canton, it was reported that a rebel group, a thousand strong, raided the city Public Security Bureau on the night of January 21. Significantly, the rebels in this case were helped by a rebel group within the Bureau who acted as a "fifth column."[60] Ken Ling states that he participated in the raid against the Amoy Public Security Bureau on January 25.[61] The regional and local authority structure was so badly fractured that "power seizure" extended to residential and neighborhood committees. An *Anhwei Daily* article (February 17) accused the rebels of using cruel methods to punish cadres of neighborhood committees and of breaking into police stations to acquire archives.[62] No semblance of local authority remained in late January 1967 as shown by the phenomenon of "economism," i.e., the practice of paying workers extra or advance wages and allowing peasants to divide all their produce as income by employers or cadres. The rebels and Cultural Revolution leaders in Peking charged that local authorities deliberately resorted to "economism" to induce workers and peasants to fight against Red Guards. At best that charge was partly true—local Party officials responded to those particularistic demands because they no longer had authority to impose rules and regulations.

The formal national media which precipitated the mass movement in the autumn of 1966 were overcome by rumors, Red Guard tabloids and wall posters which, by late January 1967, began to influence the behavior of groups in conflict. The rumors reflect the mentality of different groups. Some were unclear as to the goal of the Cultural Revolution and the rumors justified their fears and their reasons for engaging in conflict. For example, during January in Peking, it was rumored that "Danger of a Fascist Party is imminent," "The Chinese race is in danger" and "The two-line struggle at the Center is very intense; Chairman Mao is in the minority."[63] Some rumors justified what Ken Ling describes as people's unwillingness to "keep their places." Mass walkouts by workers were often accompanied by rumors of this kind. On January 16, a radio broadcast in Canton mentioned the rumor that the national leaders were coming to the south and that it had incited "workers of other places to leave their production posts, to wreck the production and construction of the Central-South Region."[64] Other rumors announced the entrance of new groups into the expanding conflict. Thus on January 19, 1967, the State Council issued a public notice denying there was an alleged new directive from the government concerning "temporary workers" (noncontract workers).[65] The particularistic interest of the noncontract workers will be discussed in later chapters.

Apparently, the Red Guards and the "power seizure" movement stimulated some people out of the normal apathy and passivity often found in highly authoritarian or totalitarian states. The public began to look for excitement. In January 1967, for example, people in Canton were particularly keen about the rumors concerning T'ao Chu, once the most powerful Party leader in Kwangtung (he was the director of the Central-South China Bureau of the Chinese Communist Party). T'ao was suddenly promoted to the national position of Acting Director, Department of Propaganda of Party Central Committee, in March 1966.

Just as suddenly he was dismissed and disgraced in early January 1967. A rumor alleging that T'ao had been escorted to Wuhan and was about to be sent to Canton to face the mass struggle was circulated in Canton in mid-January. This was coupled with the rumor that Chiang Ch'ing was coming to Canton to command the struggle against T'ao (on January 18) that precipitated a mass influx of people (said to be a million) into Canton.[66]

The two-month period following the "January revolution" saw an unprecedented upsurge of all kinds of interest groups in China. Youths sent to the countryside and the frontier for permanent settlement streamed back into the cities and demanded the right to reside in the city of their origin. Nonunionized workers demanded a share of the material benefits enjoyed by unionized workers. Apprentice workers asked for a shorter period of training and higher pay. Veterans demanded better treatment. Peasants refused to submit grains to the state and insisted on a lower quota of state requisition. Significantly, national and cross-trade organizations were formed by these groups, validating Oberschall's observation that "participants in popular disturbances and activists in opposition organizations will be recruited primarily from previously active and relatively well-integrated individuals within the collectivity, whereas socially isolated, atomized, and uprooted individuals will be underrepresented, at least until the movement has become substantial."[67] By the end of March 1967 the mass movement in China had certainly become substantial.

During the next year and a half (from April 1967 to the end of 1968) the conflict between the national authorities in Peking and the various groups was crucial. The authorities wanted to reimpose social controls but found it difficult to reverse the almost autonomous movement. The fissure in the social order opened by the "link-up" movement in September–November 1966 and the chasm created by Shanghai's "January revolution" resulted in several different kinds of social deviance—looting, pilfering, random assaults, rape, murder, arson, etc. For example, the breakdown of order resulted in a situation which brought only volunteers to fight a forest fire in Honan province on January 15, 1967—six of them were killed.[68] A report from Kirin in July stated that "reactionary elements . . . resort to the vicious measures of cutting off water and power supplies to strangle the revolutionary people, but also to openly commit homicide, arson, the poisoning of people, and sabotage as well as looting in broad daylight."[69] Because of roving bands of criminals in Canton, "walls were erected at the corners of all main streets, causing . . . obstruction to communication" in August 1967.[70] The bandits were reported to be "large groups of prisoners recently released from jail."[71] Similar reports about crimes never publicized in the media persisted even in March 1968. Railway and other forms of transport in China were paralyzed or interrupted through the early months of 1968 and as a result there was a sudden rise in press reports about thefts, illegal trafficking, black market operations and other speculations. The most seriously affected regions were Peking, Shanghai, Szechwan, Inner Mongolia, Shantung and Kweichow.[72]

The Cultural Revolution contrived by Mao and his colleagues came of age by mid-1967 and its development corresponded closely to naturally induced collective movements. "The history of riots and related outbursts," says Smelser, "is filled with instances of looters, gangs of delinquents, individual criminals, etc., moving in to the scene of disturbance and thereby multiplying the acts of disorder."[73]

The mobilization phase of the Cultural Revolution reached its highest stage with the rising disorders of mid-1967. The leaders of the Cultural Revolution in Peking mobilized the revolution by publicizing elite division, loosening social control, promoting communication between Peking and other cities in China and precipitating the collapse of local Party authorities. After January 1967 the events in China cannot be considered a "mobilization" because the conflicts by then were self-sustaining. The stage was set for group violence.

Notes

1. Harold D. Lasswell and Abraham Kaplan, *Power and Society* (New Haven, 1963), p. 206.

2. This analogy is from Lucian W. Pye, ed., *Communication and Political Development* (Princeton, 1969), p. 27.

3. William Kornhauser, *The Politics of Mass Society* (Glencoe, Ill., 1959), pp. 93–94.

4. Lewis Coser, *The Functions of Social Conflict* (New York, 1956), p. 48.

5. Travel in China, as is known by all specialists in Chinese studies, is difficult for Chinese. As Granquist reports:
   A Chinese who is planning a trip that will last more than two days must report to a police station not only when he leaves but also when he arrives at his destination. Visitors may not live with a family more than three days without reporting to the police, whereupon they are put down as "family members" in the registry. When they have come, from where, how long they intend to stay, and so on. If a visitor does not report to the police within three days of his arrival, he can be certain of being called on during the morning of the fourth day. . . .
   See Hans Granquist, *The Red Guard: A Report on Mao's Revolution*, trans. Erik J. Friis (New York, 1967), p. 49.

6. For a very interesting eyewitness account, see Chin Chien-li, *Pei-kuo Chien-wen-lu* [Odyssey in North China] (Hong Kong, 1973), pp. 403–586.

7. See general discussions of this in Ezra Vogel, *Canton under Communism: Programs and Politics in a Provincial Capital, 1949–1968* (New York, 1971), particularly Chapters 3 and 5. Also see Hai Feng, *Haifeng Wen-hua Ke-ming Kai-shu* [A General Account of the Cultural Revolution in Haifeng County] (Hong Kong, 1969) (hereafter cited by English title).

8. See Ezra Vogel, "From Friendship to Comradeship: The Change in Personal Relations in Communist China," *The China Quarterly*, January–March 1965.

9. For general discussions on this, see Peter Schran, *The Development of Chinese Agriculture 1950–1959* (Urbana and Chicago, 1969); Yuan-li Wu, H. C. Ling and Grace Hsiao Wu, *The Spatial Economy of Communist China. A Study on Industrial Location and Transportation* (New York, 1967).

10. Gordon A. Bennett and Ronald N. Montaperto, *Red Guard: The Political Biography of Dai Hsiao-ai* (Garden City, N.Y., 1972), p. 2.

11. Ibid., p. 20.

12. Neale Hunter, *Shanghai Journal: An Eyewitness Account of the Cultural Revolution* (Boston, 1969), p. 10.

13. Ibid., p. 27. One might argue that this is also true in supposedly liberal-democratic nations in the West. But the main difference is that in the United States and other Western democracies, knowledge about the government is freely and publicly available and there is always a great deal of cynical analysis about the "power structure" of the government in the media. The "know-nothings" in the United States are the result of the public's sense of lack of relevance of politics in their life. In China, few are permitted to be politically aloof. That is why it is significant that many can still be so ignorant of politics.

14. See, for example, Dai Hsiao-ai's lack of knowledge about the upper realm of the power hierarchy in school, in Bennett and Montaperto, *Red Guard*, pp. 16, 18–19. Again, this must be interpreted against the background of Dai's activism and also the regular political indoctrination that all students must subject themselves to.

15. Mao Tse-tung, *Mao Tse-tung Ssu-hsiang Wan-sui* [Long Live the Thought of Mao Tse-tung], Vol. 1 (n. p., 1969), pp. 646–647.

16. Chao Tsung, "An Account of the 'Great Proletarian Cultural Revolution,'" (Part 57), *Tsukuo*, No. 103 (October 1, 1972), p. 20. For a slightly different version of this, see *Chung-kung Wen-hua Ta-ke-ming Chung-yao Wen-chien Hui-pien* [Important CCP Documents of the Great Prole-

tarian Cultural Revolution] (Taipei, 1973), p. 217 (hereafter cited by English title).

17. *Translations on Communist China*, No. 90, Joint Publications Research Service 49826 (February 12, 1970), pp. 13–14 (hereafter cited as JPRS).

18. Edgar Snow, *The Long Revolution* (New York, 1972), p. 39.

19. Anthony Oberschall, *Social Conflict and Social Movements* (Englewood Cliffs, N.J., 1973), p. 64.

20. As some readers may have already noted, I am following Smelser's idea of "value-added" scheme of analysis. See Neil J. Smelser, *Theory of Collective Behavior* (New York and Glencoe, Ill., 1963), pp. 13–20, particularly his remarks about "time sequence," pp. 19–20.

21. This view is held by Chao Chung (also Chao Tsung), whose chronicle of the Cultural Revolution was serialized by the *China Monthly* (formerly *Tsukuo;* since 1973, changed to *Chung-hua Yüeh-pao*) of the Union Research Institute (Hong Kong). Chao's account is perhaps the best and most authoritative historical record of the events in China from 1962 to 1968 (the serial is continuing and is now in its 76th installment). A bulk.of Chao's chronicle consists of reprinting original Red Guard and official documents, accompanied by short background briefing by Chao. Probably more than two-thirds of the documents republished in Chao's account have been translated by the U.S. government in SCMP or JPRS publications. One also finds these documents in the Taiwan publication, *Important CCP Documents of the Great Proletarian Cultural Revolution* (Taipei, 1973). For Chao's view on Nieh's posters, see Chao Chung, "An Account of the 'Great Proletarian Cultural Revolution,' " (Part 13), *Tsukuo*, No. 58 (January 1, 1969).

22. Chao Chung, "An Account of the 'Great Proletarian Cultural Revolution,' " (Part 13), *Tsukuo*, No. 58 (January 1, 1969), p. 26.

23. Their letters are published in *Jen-min Jih-pao* [People's Daily], June 18, 1966 (hereafter cited by English title).

24. For Liu Shao-ch'i's role in the "work teams," see the Taiwan publication *Liu Shao-ch'i Wen-ti Tze-liao Ch'uan-ch'i* [A Special Collection of Materials on Liu Shao-ch'i] (Taipei, 1970), pp. 416–429, 621–628 (hereafter cited by English title).

25. Smelser, *Theory of Collective Behavior*, p. 250.

26. The best composite picture of what the work teams did in Peking is in Chao Tsung (same as Chao Chung), "An Account of the 'Great Proletarian Cultural Revolution,' " (Part 14), *Tsukuo*, No. 60 (March 1, 1969); the various documents that Chao excerpted have all been published in other sources such as in *A Special Collection of Materials on Liu Shao-ch'i*. Also, Victor Nee and Don Layman, *The Cultural Revolution at Peking University* (New York, 1969).

27. See Ma Sitson, "Cruelty and Insanity Made Me a Fugitive," *Life*, Vol. 62, No. 22 (June 2, 1967); Lai Ying, *The Thirty-Sixth Way. The Story of a Young Woman Who Escaped from Red China*, trans., adapted and ed. Edward Behr and Sidney Liu (Garden City, N.Y., 1969) pp. 156–160; Ken Ling, *The Revenge of Heaven: Journal of a Young Chinese* (New York, 1972), p. 45; and Bennett and Montaperto, *Red Guard*, p. 74. Ma Sitson reports that as early as June 1966, an army officer newly appointed to head the Music Academy was dismissed after only one day because he had called in police to break up a fight between students.

28. See the original document by the Central Committee and State Council on September 5, 1966, authorizing the "link-up" movement in *Important CCP Documents of the Great Proletarian Cultural Revolution*, p. 129.

29. "Speech at a Central Committee Work Conference" (October 25, 1966), *Translations on Communist China*, No. 90, JPRS 49826 (February 12, 1970), p. 14.

30. Smelser, *Theory of Collective Behavior*, pp. 154–155, 257–261.

31. Hai Feng, *General Account of the Cultural Revolution in Haifeng*, pp. 14–15.

32. Hai Feng, *Kuang-chou Ti-ch'u Wen-ke Lieh-chen Shu-lueh* [An Account of the Cultural Revolution in the Canton Area] (Hong Kong, 1971), pp. 28–34 (hereafter cited by English title).

33. Hunter, *Shanghai Journal*, p. 44.

34. Ken Ling, *Revenge of Heaven*, pp. 13–15.

35. Bennett and Montaperto, *Red Guard*, pp. 41–48.

36. Hai Feng, *Account of the Cultural Revolution in Canton*, pp. 33–34.

37. Hunter, *Shanghai Journal*, pp. 51–52.

38. Bennett and Montaperto, *Red Guard*, p. 41.

39. Hai Feng, *Account of the Cultural Revolution in Canton*, pp. 31–32.

40. Hai Feng, *General Account of the Cultural Revolution in Haifeng*, p. 16.

41. Hunter, *Shanghai Journal*, p. 53.

42. Ibid.

43. Ibid., p. 40.

44. For descriptions of local demands to form Red Guards, see Hunter, *Shanghai Journal*, pp. 81–82; Bennett and Montaperto, *Red Guard*, pp. 66–71; Hai Feng, *Account of the Cultural Revolution in Canton*, pp. 48–49. Ken Ling's account of the events in Amoy from June to August is confusing *(Revenge of Heaven)*. For example, he writes that the work teams were withdrawn on June 12 (p. 18) but elsewhere in China the

teams were only introduced at that time. He states that the students were excited by the editorial of the *People's Daily* (July 2) which called for "Destruction of the Four Olds," and that that campaign got started on July 18 (pp. 35, 45). Actually that editorial merely republished Mao's famous talk on art and literature of 1942 in conjunction with the purge then going on against the top propaganda officials of the Department of Propaganda of Central Committee. The editorial was entirely unrelated to the "Destroy the Four Olds" movement, which did not begin until after Mao's review of the Red Guards on August 18. Ken Ling also states that the first Red Guard group was formed on July 16, a month before Mao's public review of the Red Guards in Peking (pp. 37, 41), which resulted in the formation of Red Guards elsewhere. Furthermore, Ken Ling also states (this time more plausibly) that the first unified Red Guard organization in Amoy was set up in mid-August but then he states (not so plausibly) that students not of "five-Red classes" were also organizing Red Guards (p. 65). At that time students of nonproletarian background were actually not allowed to organize until October. Later, Ken Ling seems to have erred again when he implies that the "Shanghai Commune" was formed in January 1967, when actually the "Shanghai Commune" was formally announced on February 5 (p. 233).

45. Bennett and Montaperto, *Red Guard*, p. 81.

46. Hai Feng, *Account of the Cultural Revolution in Canton*, p. 55.

47. Hunter, *Shanghai Journal*, pp. 84–85.

48. Bennett and Montaperto, *Red Guard*, p. 100.

49. See the Red Guard publication *Sou-tu Hung-wei-pin*, January 31 and February 22, 1967, as cited in Chao Tsung, "An Account of the 'Great Proletarian Cultural Revolution,' " (Part 18), *Tsukuo*, No. 64 (July 1, 1969), p. 38.

50. Hunter, *Shanghai Journal*, p. 190.

51. Ken Ling, *Revenge of Heaven*, p. 36; Bennett and Montaperto, *Red Guard*, pp. 71–72.

52. Ken Ling, *Revenge of Heaven*, pp. 38–39; Hunter, *Shanghai Journal*, pp. 91–97.

53. Ken Ling, *Revenge of Heaven*, p. 147.

54. Hunter, *Shanghai Journal*, p. 131.

55. Ken Ling, *Revenge of Heaven*, p. 58.

56. *People's Daily*, January 19, 1967. According to Hunter, the takeover of one newspaper, the *Wen-hui Daily*, was approved by Chou En-lai before it was carried out, *Shanghai Journal*, p. 208.

57. *Radio Lhasa*, 1200 GMT, February 20, 1967.

58. Hunter, *Shanghai Journal*, p. 214.

59. Ibid., pp. 215, 220.

60. Hai Feng, *Account of the Cultural Revolution in Canton*, p. 83.

61. Ken Ling, *Revenge of Heaven*, pp. 246–248.

62. *Anhwei Jih-pao*, February 17, 1967; Hunter, *Shanghai Journal*, p. 249.

63. *Red Guard Publications* (Association of Research Libraries), Group VI-1 (Chou En-lai's talk on January 22, 1967) (hereafter cited as RGP).

64. *Radio Canton*, 1105 GMT, January 16, 1967.

65. *Important CCP Documents of the Great Proletarian Cultural Revolution*, p. 91.

66. Hai Feng, *Account of the Cultural Revolution in Canton*, p. 75.

67. Oberschall, *Social Conflict*, p. 135.

68. *Radio Chengchow*, 1200 GMT, July 17, 1967.

69. *Kirin Jih-pao*, July 12, 1967.

70. *Hung-se Pao-tung*, August 22, 1967, trans. in *Survey of China Mainland Press* (Hong Kong: U.S. Consulate General), No. 4026, p. 12 (hereafter cited as SCMP).

71. *AFP* (English broadcast), 2255 GMT, August 13, 1967. Hai Feng disputes this, stating that in late 1967, the people of Canton often resorted to lynching persons caught committing crimes and legitimized their punishment by labelling the victims "released prisoners" (Hai Feng, *Account of the Cultural Revolution in Canton*, p. 181). There is a similar report from Kwangsi about the use of prisoners by the Public Security Bureau for combat among factions; see SCMP, No. 4081, p. 10.

72. *AFP* (English broadcast), 2005 GMT, January 21, 1968.

73. Smelser, *Theory of Collective Behavior*, p. 257.

4

GROUP CONFLICT & VIOLENCE

The conflicts in China spread from late 1966 until the end of 1968 and they became more and more violent. Students of social conflict often distinguish between intense and violent conflicts, but it is logical to assume that prolonged and intense conflict significantly increases the probability of violence.[1] This chapter deals with these aspects of group conflict in China.

Intensity of Conflict

The prolonged and intense nature of group conflict in the Cultural Revolution can be explained by the large number of groups, the divided and equivocal nature of the authorities and the presence of several types of conflict not readily subject to settlement, e.g., induced conflicts, ideological conflicts, intercommunity (noncommunal) conflicts and power conflicts.

Number of Conflicting Groups

The proliferation of numerous Red Guard and so-called rebel groups was one of the most important causes of the intensity of group conflict in the Cultural Revolution. The rebel groups were formed after October 1966, when new groups, workers and others began to join the movement. The rebels were more heterogeneous and radical than the Red Guards. "The title Rebels," says Hunter, "was introduced to identify those who were truly out to change the system. . . . The Rebel policy was to abandon the idea of a purely student movement and take advantage of the growing restlessness of the workers."[2] Even a partial list of these groups testifies to their multiplicity as shown in Table 1. This list is

Table 1: A Partial List of the Number of Organizations in Provinces and Cities during the "Power Seizure" Movement in January–February 1967.

Province	Number of Organizations
Hupei	147
Chekiang	103
Kiangsi	89
Kansu	74
Shansi	70
Honan	69
Fukien	67
Inner Mongolia	46
Szechwan	45
Kweichow	45
Ts'inghai	43
Heilunkiang	39
Tibet	36
Sinkiang	24
Yunnan	23
Liaoning	18
Kwangsi	17
City	
Shanghai	61
Kuang-chou (Canton)	39
Ts'ingtao	23
Peking	12

SOURCE: Except for Liaoning, Ts'ingtao and Canton, the information is from *Yi-chiu Liu-pa Chung-kung-nien-pao* [1968 Yearbook on Chinese Communism] (Taipei, 1969), pp. 281–464. The figure for Liaoning pertains only to "major" organizations in September 1967 and is from *Liao-lien Chan-pao,* September 6, 1967, as translated in SCMP, No. 4091, pp. 7–12. The figure for Ts'ingtao is from *Wen-hui Pao* (Hong Kong), January 31, 1967, as translated in SCMP, No. 3874, p. 11. The figure for Canton is from Hai Feng, *Kuang-chou Ti-ch'u Wen-ke Lieh-chen Shu-lueh* [An Account of the Cultural Revolution in the Canton Area] (Hong Kong, 1971), pp. 198–203. The Taiwan source is consistent with other sources in at least two instances: Canton and Kweichow. In Kweichow, *Wen-hui Pao* (Hong Kong), February 2, 1967, gave the figure of 39, which is close to the "45" used in the list. On Canton, Hai Feng and Taiwan's reports show no difference.

partial both in time and space. The number of organizations at most reflects the situation in January–February 1967 in the capitals of the provinces. The Red Guard or rebel organizations split or merged according to different situations as time went on. Furthermore, the accuracy of this list varies according to the availability of information. Hence, the number of organizations shown in remote provinces like Tibet, Sinkiang, Yunnan and Inner Mongolia is at best a very partial list.

Naturally as the national authority moved to reimpose law and order beginning in late 1967, it forced many groups to merge into larger organizations and also banned many others.[3] For almost a year, however, the rebel groups proliferated and the extent of factional split was unprecedented. For example, Hunter found no less than fifty-seven separate Red Guard headquarters at Shanghai wharves in January 1967.[4] In July, Japanese correspondents reported that hotel employees in Peking were split into two groups and were fighting.[5] The famous Taching Oilfield was divided into a large conservative and a small revolutionary faction in August 1967.[6] Chang Ch'ung-ch'iao reported that the crew of the train which took Mao on an inspection tour in September 1967 split into three factions and that Mao listened to them debate.[7] That report is most significant.

Mack and Snyder have hypothesized that "the larger the number of parties, the more difficult it will be to discover a common solution, in which all parties can achieve at least some gain over previous power positions."[8] The case of the "power seizure" in Shanghai seems to confirm this hypothesis. Chang Ch'ung-ch'iao, the most powerful Party official in Shanghai, recounted the situation:

> In February [1967], after *repeated* meetings, the 38 organizations recognized by all were to announce the seizure of power. To include the 38 means to have the majority of the organizations in Shanghai. All famous organizations joined and this was already better [than other places]. Just as the 38 organizations were ready to draft the document to establish the "Shanghai Commune," we discovered that another 25 organizations were also meeting to establish a "New Shanghai commune." They said: You do not want us to join, so we establish a "New Shanghai commune." Now we faced the problem of two opposing factions. The 38 organizations were the majority and were unified rebels. Those 25 organizations were the minority and were not unified. Each called the other conservative. How do you cope with this type of situation? [Emphasis added.][9]

The Red Guards and rebels combined were a small minority of the total population and there were many separate groups among them, so it is fair to conclude that most of them represented very small organizations. As an extreme example, the "Independent Company of

Canton Ocean Storm" was reported to have but one member, a former journalist who published his own tabloid, *Scout*.[10] From time to time some of the rebel organizations boasted of tens and thousands of members but they were loose and temporary alliances lacking the time and environment to become viable associations. Most of the Red Guards or rebels formed small and sect-like groups solely dedicated to political conflict with each other and the authorities. For example, Ken Ling's description of his group, the so-called 8–29 Revolutionary Rebellion-Making General Headquarters, strongly suggests a "sect-like" organization:

> In time the 8–29 would include children of party cadres and children of enemies of the party, Communist Party and Youth League members and counterrevolutionaries, good students and bad students, and plain gangsters and hoodlums. Factional loyalty would override everything else, and differences in class composition would no longer matter.[11]

Apparently, the only criterion used by Ken Ling's group to recruit members was a willingness to combat other groups or authorities.

Dai Hsiao-ai's description of relationships between group members is almost equivalent to the definition of a sect:

> If two people belonged to different factions, no matter how close their personal relations had been in the past, they would now face each other as enemies. Correspondingly, people from the same faction would treat each other like brothers, even though they came from different units and had never before met. This change in social relations thus had a political origin.[12]

The sect-like nature of most Red Guard and rebel organizations is also reflected in their emphasis on group unity against dissenters. Dai Hsiao-ai, for example, mentioned that he and his colleagues were more worried over the Trotskyite threat from within his group than that posed by outside opponents or simple defectors. "Trotskyites," says Dai, "were the ones who defected in reality without defecting in name." They were internal opponents and "Dai Hsiao-ai and other rebel stalwarts devoted considerable energy to combating their arguments."[13] These descriptions correspond to Coser's analysis of sect-like groups and conflict:

> Groups engaged in continued struggle with the outside tend to be intolerant within. They are unlikely to tolerate more than limited departures from the group unity. Such groups tend to assume a sect-like character; they select membership in terms of

special characteristics and so tend to be limited in size, and they lay claim to the total personality involvement of their members. Their social cohesion depends upon total sharing of all aspects of group life and is reinforced by the assertion of group unity against the dissenter. The only way they can solve the problem of dissent is through the dissenter's voluntary or forced withdrawal.[14]

Such small groups tend to be more radical than large ones and engage in more intense conflict with the outside.[15] Thus there seems to be little doubt that part of the reasons for the prolonged group conflict in China (1966–1968) is the multiplicity of groups and the small size of most of them.

Type of Conflict

Another equally important cause of the protracted and intense conflict in the Cultural Revolution was the expression of suppressed and highly personalized frustrations. The national practice of "settling scores" (or accounts) promoted by the Communist leaders for political reasons before the Cultural Revolution was now used by various groups to conduct their own conflict. For example, during the first stage of the Cultural Revolution students were directed to attack revisionist teachers, and eyewitnesses testified that the radical students were of working and lower class backgrounds. Lower class students unable to meet academic standards held grudges against their teachers and the teachers were mostly from middle class and urban backgrounds.[16] Scapegoat tactics were used by school principals and the work teams in June–July 1966, thus exacerbating conflicts caused by students seeking personal revenge. The teachers who were attacked earlier vented their anger, after July 1966, on the cadres who persecuted them prior to that time.[17] The collapse of regional Party authority after November 1966 led the students who were subjected to discrimination by these cadres to seek personal revenge. Dai Hsiao-ai was amazed by the depth of resentment of teachers discriminated against by members of the Communist Party. In November 1966, Ken Ling witnessed a feud between the two best ping-pong players of China, world champion Chuang Tse-tung and his runner-up Li Fu-jung. Li believed he was forced to take second place to Chuang for political reasons. Ken Ling observed, "The Cultural Revolution brought all this enmity into the open."[18]

Individual enmity was augmented by group enmity. The Red Guards who were exclusively sons and daughters of ranking regional officials are a noteworthy case in point. Their goal was to defend the status and power of their parents, and they, more often than not, initiated violence against other groups.[19] It is interesting to note that students of middle class backgrounds did not exhibit the strong group cohesion shown by the "new class," sons and daughters of high national and regional Party leaders. The special group of Red Guards with strong group consciousness and collective grievances were offspring of regional cadres who were the subject of discrimination and suppression imposed by national leaders and their policy of breaking regionalism. Grievances of this kind have been strong in Kwangtung province. In Haifeng county, for example, the first group of Red Guards was composed of the children of cadres punished by the national leaders in past "anti-provincialism" campaigns. The children wanted revenge and their opponents were the children of northern or outside cadres.[20]

Personalized conflicts, however, are usually dissipated after wrongs are righted and the source of frustration is punished. Induced conflicts are more complex and difficult to resolve. They are "cases where representatives of conflicting groups have ends to be gained (e.g., their own prestige) apart from the ends in dispute between groups."[21] The Cultural Revolution fused highly personalized conflicts and induced conflicts; this was reflected in the presence of many older leaders among student and rebel groups. Both Ken Ling and Dai Hsiao-ai, for example, mentioned that there were veterans in their midst. The radical group at Amoy University in August 1966, according to Ken Ling, was led by "a thirty-eight-year-old military man who had returned to the university for further study."[22] The veterans were active individually in other groups and, in Canton, even organized themselves into a large and separate group named "August 1 Combat Detachment." (August 1 is China's Army Day, in celebration of the Nanch'ang Uprising by the Communists on August 1, 1927.)[23] There were also middle-aged civilian leaders in the Red Guard groups. In Ken Ling's high school group the former leader of the "work team" agitated for an attack on the provincial education minister (a woman). The leader was formerly director of the Provincial Athletic Association and a subordinate of the education minister. Obviously his motive in participating in Red Guard activities was quite different from that of the students.[24] In Canton, according to Hai Feng, a group of Party cadres organized themselves into the "United Council of Criticism of T'ao Chu" and masterminded the radical students' attack on the army. This group was allegedly in league with ultra-left leaders around Chiang Ch'ing in Peking and its goal was to take over as many positions as possible in the Party structure. The "United Council" met strong resistance at the provincial level from the military and intended to use young radicals to purge the army.[25] The most important case of induced conflict was the support given by Chiang Ch'ing and her colleagues to the radical student K'uai Ta-fu of Ts'inghua University in his attack on Wang Kuang-mei, wife of the late Liu Shao-ch'i. In June 1966, Wang went to Ts'inghua University as a member of the work team and disciplined K'uai, who went on a hunger strike while being detained. Two of Chiang Ch'ing's colleagues, Kuan Feng and Wang Li, were dispatched to investigate and they supported K'uai's protest. K'uai was subsequently released and put in charge of the mass trial of Wang Kuang-mei on April 10, 1967. The conflict between Chiang Ch'ing and Wang Kuang-mei obviously involved issues beyond the activities of K'uai Ta-fu.[26] Chiang's colleagues, Kuan Feng and Wang Li, also contacted the "United Council of Criticism of T'ao Chu" in Canton.[27] The presence of these older leaders in the midst of young students greatly complicated the conflict situation. These older men and women had goals quite different from youths who were often puzzled by the aim of the Cultural Revolution. Eyewitness accounts repeatedly mention a sense of loss among the students involved in the Cultural Revolution. In fact, it is safe to say that the entire Red Guard movement was substantially an induced conflict, which is much less amenable to normal settlement than real conflict because of the "coincidence of group and personal values." Moreover, "induced conflicts arise more from imbalance or ambiguity of power relations, whereas realistic conflicts arise more from incompatibility of objectives."[29]

The conflicts caused by regional antagonism added fuel to the already intense personalized and induced conflicts in the Cultural Revolution. The split between national leaders and the consequent purge of powerful regional leaders enabled localist groups at lower levels to assert themselves. This was particularly apparent in Kwangtung, where the central leaders repeatedly suppressed manifestations of regionalism among lower level leaders. In 1967, municipal Party cadres who were punished for localist sentiments in 1957 mounted a campaign of "reversal of verdict," since the higher officials who punished the localists were denounced as "anti-Maoists."[30] In Haifeng, for example, the entire Cultural Revolution was dominated by conflicts between natives and outsiders. The students were split along this line and so was the entire county staff. The local faction naturally was supported by the peasants, who provided the native Red Guards and rebels with food and demonstrated in support of the local group in confronting the civil-military faction representing outsiders.[31]

Local Party officials in various parts of China during the fall of 1966 fanned regional sentiment to keep "outside agitators" out. Amoy Red Guards were greeted in Foochow by slogans like "Foochow belongs to Foochow natives."[32] Former Shanghai mayor Ts'ao Ti-ch'iu was accused of agitating among local residents and he urged them to send telegrams to Peking "to set the record straight," since Peking Red Guards kept the leaders in the capital informed about the situation in Shanghai.

Afterwards, "misguided Shanghai workers, students, and townfolk" harassed the Peking students.[33] The depth of provincial antagonism was shown in the people's spontaneous reactions to each other. Free movement became possible for a large number of people for the first time since 1949 and regional ethnocentrism surfaced spontaneously. Ken Ling and Dai Hsiao-ai repeatedly mention a strong regional consciousness on the part of the students, generally over the gross division between North and South. The "link-up" movement in the fall of 1966 created an upsurge of regional prejudice. Ken Ling describes how the Shanghai people looked down on the students from North China:

> The Red Guards from North China who had gone out on the link-ups with only the clothes on their backs were treated with especial rudeness. One could tell at once that they were northerners from their shabby tunics which were so filthy that they glistened. The salesgirls either refused to sell them things or limited their purchases sharply. The northerners denounced the girls for wanting to sell only to capitalists and threatened to launch rebellion against the First Department Store [of Shanghai].[34]

"The southerners made rebellion for power and position," says Ken Ling, "the northerners for food."[35] Dai Hsiao-ai concurs with Ken Ling. "We felt," says Dai, "the standard of living in Peking was considerably low in comparison with that in Canton."[36] Dai, who came from Kwangtung, shared Ken's contempt for the northerners:

> One group nearby was dirty enough to make one sick. We could tell at a glance they were from Manchuria. Dressed in fur coats, passed down from generation to generation and saturated with filth, they sat idly under the sun picking fleas. We hastily moved to another place, fearing those northern fleas might jump onto us southerners.[37]

Dai's group lived in a peasant house outside of Peking with a group of Shantung Red Guards and was repulsed by the crudity of the Shantung students' fight for food. Dai's group later ate separately.[38] Regional differences and prejudices of this type were reinforced by genuine differences in living standards, customs and language and often provoked spur-of-the-moment fights among students in the "link-up" movement.[39] As the Cultural Revolution developed into violent conflict, in many provincial capitals one usually found a small radical faction consisting overwhelmingly of outsiders (students from Peking and elsewhere) and a large conservative faction of natives warring continuously. In Foochow, the faction named *Ke Tsao Hui* ("Fukien Revolutionary Rebellion-Making Committee") was composed entirely of people from

Foochow, while its enemy, the 8-29 General Headquarters, was in the hands of "outsiders."[40]

Conflict generated by provincialism is difficult to resolve. At a superficial level, it involves clashes over "life styles, standards of behavior and morality, and the denigration or negative evaluation of qualities and attributes"; at a deeper level provincial conflict results from "symbols," i.e., a community identity which involves the individual's "group integrity, moral standing, and self-respect." Conflicts of this type can not be resolved by "dividing the pie"; they tend to be intense and difficult to regulate.[41]

Elite Division & Equivocation

The difficulty of regulating or mediating group conflict in the Cultural Revolution was aggravated by the deepening division of elites at regional and lower levels and the contradictory actions of national and regional leaders. Both types of equivocation on the part of the elite encouraged intransigence on the part of the radicals and embittered the conservatives among the groups in conflict.

The Cultural Revolution, as discussed in Chapter 3, began when the national leaders deprived local leaders of their authority and thus precipitated a student rebellion against local authorities. The national leaders subsequently countermanded measures ordered by the acting civil and military leaders in 1967. For example, during the first six months of 1967, the central leaders issued directives repudiating the actions of Party leaders in Anhwei, Szechwan, Inner Mongolia, Fukien and Chungking city. Beginning in late May, instructions emanating from Peking rebuked military authorities in several provinces for errors in their "support the left" policy. In Foochow, Shantung, Canton and Kwangsi, military authorities were forced to make public self-criticisms.[42] These central directives boosted the morale of the radicals and embittered the conservatives in the rebel groups. One radical group in Chengtu, the "September 16 Rebellion Corps," reported that the corps and its local ally, the "August 26" group of Szechwan University, were subjected to mass arrests by the military authorities in February 1967. Subsequently, the national leaders in Peking issued the "Decision on the Question of Anhwei" on April 1. The Anhwei leaders were ordered to cease condemning the "organizations of the masses" as counterrevolutionary and arresting the members. The directive ordered military authorities in Anhwei to release offenders imprisoned because of their raid on the military headquarters. It outlawed public humiliation of "the revolutionary masses" by the authorities. Five days later the Central Military Affairs Commission transmitted an order to the military units that reinforced measures in the decision on Anhwei and added an injunction against firing at the rebels. The report of the "September 16" group in Chengtu continued:

> After the directive with regard to Anhwei was transmitted to Szechwan and the Ten Articles of the Military Affairs Commission had reached Chengtu, the fighters of our "September 16" corps rejoiced. Together with their comrades in Chengtu they immediately marched in the streets and continued their demonstration for days. They strongly demanded the release of their comrades. They shouted loudly: "The February Suppression Must Be Totally Reversed!" "Resolutely Support the Comrades of 'August 26'!" "Resolutely Support the Hunger Strike of Our Comrades in Prison!" On April 18, our comrades in prison burst open their cage and were released. The "September 16" corps in Chengtu and the "69th Detachment" of a certain factory then set up the Broadcasting Station for Mao Tse-tung Thought. . . .[43]

The rebels had won, but violent conflict ensued soon after. The conservatives who supported the local authorities raided and demolished the rebel broadcasting station on April 23 and drove the rebels out of the city on May 6. The rebels left the city on a train and were ambushed by armed conservatives using machine guns and grenades.

Similar events occurred in Canton. The military authorities broke up several rebel organizations in March 1967, including the veterans' group—the "August 1 Combat Detachment"—and made mass arrests. On April 14, Chou En-lai visited Canton and talked with the warring groups. He repudiated the policy of disbanding and arresting radical groups and leaders. The rebels then agitated for "reversal of verdict" and concentrated their attacks on the military commander, General Huang Yung-shen. Chou's support of the radicals embittered the conservatives and after Chou's departure, on April 22, the first large-scale "struggle by violence" (*wu-tou*) took place. The "Doctrine Red Guards," children of high civil and military officials in Kwangtung, attacked several high school Red Guards with iron implements.[44]

The national leaders also precipitated conflict by equivocating before different groups. The Cultural Revolution enabled students and workers to have face-to-face conversations with national leaders or their representatives for the first time. Equivocation on the part of these leaders created confusion and conflict. For example, two warring groups in Haifeng county sent representatives to the Central Cultural Revolution group seeking support for their views. Both groups obtained approval of the national authority and the result intensified conflict between factions.[45] Other groups found the national leaders were evasive. For example, Chang Ch'ung-ch'iao told the students of Ts'inghua University (October 1966) that a leaflet reported that he favored struggle by violence and he refused to repudiate the report.[46] Similarly, Ch'i Peng-yu, who was entrusted by Chiang Ch'ing to be in charge of the attack on Liu Shao-ch'i, was asked by a group of Peking Red Guards to deny a rumor. Ch'i replied: "I do not want to deny the rumor. I am insignificant so there is no need for me to clarify myself in every instance."[47] On September 5, 1967, Chiang Ch'ing talked to the representatives from Anhwei on the problem of "violent struggle":

> Some comrades say: "It is easy for Comrade Chiang Ch'ing to talk, but the struggle in our place is severe." The struggle here is severe too; only that we did not resort to struggle by violence. Now I want to make myself clear that if someone wants to struggle with me by violence, I will and must defend myself and strike back. . . . (Response from the audience: Learn from Comrade Chiang Ch'ing! Salute to Comrade Chiang!) . . . Comrades, I am not advocating struggle by violence. I support resolutely Chairman Mao's appeal "to struggle with reason, not violence." I only said that when we are attacked by class enemies, we can not do without any arms. . . .[48]

Local leaders were often indecisive; they were confused by the equivocation of their superiors, bewildered by the countermeasures ordered by the central leaders and pressured by subordinate groups. The vacillation of local leaders embittered both the rebels and the conservatives. The former mayor of Shanghai twice reversed himself in dealing with students and workers. On October 27, 1966, he agreed to meet the demands of a group of radicals who were fasting to compel Party authorities to release secret dossiers on the students. He quickly retracted his promise. Hunter reports that by agreeing to the demands of the fasting students, the mayor alienated many conservatives; by retracting, he convinced the radicals of his treachery. The mayor was temporarily saved when the rebels became distracted by the "link-up" movement, but he was not as lucky in December. On December 23, the mayor agreed to the demands of a supposedly conservative workers' organization. Two days later, in a radical rally he retracted his agreement. According to Hunter, "Violence followed almost at once." As expected, the conservative workers' group was particularly active in the hostile conflict between the radicals and the conservatives—they raided radical hideouts and beatings were reported.[49]

The local military commander in Tibet, Chang Kuo-hua, first faced a challenge from the radical "Rebellion Headquarters" *(Tsao Chung)* allied with outsiders, and subsequently supported the conservative group, the "Great United Command" *(Ta-lien-tse)*. Chang felt the pressure in August, when the national leaders took action against the military commander of Wuhan, who had refused to obey the directives from Peking in July. When Chang shifted his support to the radicals in mid-August, intensified armed conflict soon followed. The expanding conflict compelled the national leaders to issue a surprisingly even-handed directive (a rarity in those days) on September 18 and forbade the groups in Tibet to attack Chang.[50]

The leaders in other localities split. Some, for opportunistic or ideological reasons, joined the radicals, who thus acquired inside information from defecting establishment figures. The information strengthened antiauthority attitudes. The presence of former leaders in the rebel ranks justified an even less conciliatory attitude toward the acting authorities. Conflict was thus enlarged and prolonged. The motivation of local leaders was summarized by Hai Feng, who described the county staff in Haifeng county of Kwangtung:

> When the Cultural Revolution had developed to the stage of "dragging out the capitalist power-holder within the Party," the cadres could not but consider seriously their future. They all attempted to avoid being regarded as the capitalist power-holder. Based on their experience in inner-Party struggle, some would be used as targets for the Red Guards to attack. It was either you go or I go. So inside the county Party committee, the officials were selecting what they each regarded as the reliable Red Guard group as their means to attack the others. The Red Guards also needed some high-rank officials to provide them with information and support. Under this kind of circumstance, the various members of the Haifeng county Party committee could no longer maintain their silence or reservation.[51]

Consequently, the Party staff in Haifeng county split into two factions, outsiders and natives, following the main division of the community. The authority of the military establishment in nearby Canton began to crack as early as August 1966. A group of political commissars acquired information suggesting that the two top military commanders of the Canton Military District were corrupt. Eventually this group of former commissars allied with the chief radical Red Guard group—the "Flag Faction" *(Ch'i-pai)* of Canton.[52]

The military commander in Foochow acknowledged publicly that in July 1967, "the differences among the Party committee in the army were known outside and the result was confusion both within and without the army; the spirit of the 'ultra-left' was strengthened accordingly."[53] In his self-criticism the Foochow commander revealed that the military was inconsistent in dealing with a special group of peasants in Fukien in the western part of the province (the base areas of the Communist Party in the late 1920s and early 1930s). The peasants there had developed a strong political identity. During the Cultural Revolution some of the local leaders apparently used the peasants in the "old area" to attack Party superiors, including the former secretary of the Provincial Party Committee. Some, e.g., the former mayor of Foochow, used peasants from the "old area" to protect themselves, thus causing violent confrontations between students in Foochow and the peasants. The military changed its stand on this problem three times and thus aggravated the situation.[54]

The protracted and violent conflict in Kwangsi province was largely caused by a split among Party leaders. The acting Party leader, Wei Kuo-ch'ing (former First Secretary of the Party Committee in Kwangsi Autonomous Region), was supported by a group called "United Command." The other faction (the "April 22" group) was supported by Wu Ching-nan, a former member of the Secretariat of the Party Committee in Kwangsi. The violence reached its height from December 1967 to July 1968, and both Wei and Wu were members of the preparatory group assigned by the national leaders to set up the revolutionary committee for Kwangsi. In retrospect the violence was clearly an induced conflict, since the two leaders used the combating groups to influence the organization of new authority structures—e.g., the revolutionary committee—which was finally formed on August 26, 1968.[55]

In March 1968 a split in Peking caused a similar split in the leadership of Shansi province. On March 24, the Acting Chief of Staff Yang Cheng-wu was suddenly dismissed and so was the commander of the Peking garrison, Fu Chung-pi. A high rank military official, Yu Li-chin, the chief political director of the Air Force, was arrested. The atmosphere in Peking on March 28, according to the French correspondent Jean Vincent, was militant:

> For the second straight day, hundreds of thousands of people marched through the capital chanting "Down with the big ambitious rightwingers Yang Cheng-wu, Yu Li-chin, and Fu Chung-pi," "Down with Soviet revisionism and American imperialism," and "Defend Chairman Mao, Mao Tse-tung's thought, and Mao's revolutionary line."
>
> The walls of Peking's main thoroughfares are covered with long paper banners calling on the people to shed blood if need be to defend Mao, Vice Premier and Defense Minister Lin Piao, and Mao's wife, Chiang Ch'ing. There was also a meeting of thousands of militants in the Workers Stadium, and the sale of activist pamphlets which was resumed . . . continued in Peking's streets.[56]

In Shansi province, 125 miles from Peking, a state of war was seemingly provoked by events in Peking. The vice-chairman of the revolutionary committee, Chang Jih-ching, mobilized "120,000" peasants to "exterminate the proletarian revolutionaries." Chang was rumored to be a follower of the deposed Chief of Staff Yang Cheng-wu, and the national leaders were rumored to have ordered the arming of "8,000" people in Shansi to resist his force. The gist of the matter was the factional dispute between Chang Jih-ching and his immediate superior, Liu Ko-ping, chairman of the Shansi revolutionary committee. The split in leadership in Peking precipitated a split in Shansi which further aggravated conflict among different groups in the province. The militant atmosphere of Peking was emulated in Shansi.[57]

In sum, the intensity of group conflict in the Cultural Revolution was caused by the multiplicity of conflicting groups, the appearance of highly personalized, induced and cultural conflict and the vacillation, partiality and split of the Party and military elites. The type and form of conflict in the Cultural Revolution logically led to group violence. Mack and Snyder hypothesize that "if there are multiple parties, if the issue is one of political power, if power relations are diffuse and unstable, if the conflict is relatively non-institutionalized, if the conflict is direct and immediate, and if limitations (internal and external) are either absent or minimal, then an observer might predict a violent mode of resolution."[58] Conflict in the Cultural Revolution met all the conditions of that hypothesis and group violence was the result.

Group Violence

The violence of conflict "relates rather to its manifestations than to its causes; it is a matter of the weapons that are chosen by conflict groups to express their hostilities."[59] Following the initiation of the Cultural Revolution in the fall of 1966, the conflicting groups steadily progressed from the use of primitive to highly advanced and modern weapons. Japanese reporter Minoru Shibata, who was in China during the height of the armed struggle, in 1967 reported:

> There were varying degrees of armed struggle. In the incident which took place at the Hsinchiao Hotel, where I was staying, the rebels used bludgeons and beer bottles as "weapons"; it was more of a free-for-all. At a slightly more violent stage, iron clubs, chains, swords, and spears were used. In an even more intensified confrontation involving workers, peasants, and the Liberation Army, they resorted to what we call incendiary bombs, and trench mortars, not to mention ordinary rifles. In Shenyang, even tanks were put into action, and some wall posters said: "All kinds of weapons except aircraft are being used."[60]

The wall poster quoted by Shibata was out of date. He later reported that "on August 6 [1967], when a certain group aboard an airplane was about to take off from Shenyang airport for Peking to make a petition, another airplane attacked and destroyed it."[61] On March 15, 1968, top leaders like Chou En-lai, Kang Shen, Chen Po-ta, and Chiang Ch'ing received a delegation from Szechwan province, where violent struggles were being waged. Chen Po-ta asked: "There was artillery fire in Chungking?" The garrison commander of Chungking replied: "Yes, double-barrel anti-air-artillery was used." Chou En-lai interjected: "The first in the nation."[62] Szechwan was possibly the first incident of such struggle initiated by modern weapons.

In retrospect an escalation of the means used in group conflict in the Cultural Revolution was hardly avoidable. Violence of varying degree and kind marked the movement from the outset. The subsequent analysis will discuss five precipitating factors which aroused group violence between 1966 and 1968: (1) institutionalized violence or aggression (or legitimate aggression); (2) violence caused by local authorities in defending themselves; (3) violence caused by the partiality of the army; (4) spontaneous violence caused by withdrawal or equivocation of authorities; and (5) violence resulting from a reimposition of control. These five precipitating factors follow a chronological sequence: June–August 1966; September 1966–February 1967; March–April 1967; May–December 1967 and January–December 1968. The violence in each period precipitated violence in the ensuing period. The sheer physical violence of the first three periods led to greater violence and the use of modern weapons in the fourth period. After that, both primitive and modern weapons were used, though modern weapons were more available in some areas than others.

Institutionalized Violence (June–August 1966)

The participants in spontaneous group violence often exercise restraint to rationalize and legitimize their actions. Even violence "is subject to norms embedded in the culture."[63] So participants in violence often invoke the name of a beloved figure or leader. Chinese Communist leaders (particularly Mao) were experienced craftsmen in mass movement and they appreciated the importance of a rationale for group conflict. They used rationales, or norms, mainly to precipitate and channel group conflict and aggression and only secondarily to restrain their followers. Their interest was to use the "igniting" function of norms, not their "self-steering" functions. The Cultural Revolution began with a systematic program formulated by the national leaders intended to incite aggression against selected groups and generally arouse the people.

The events from June to the end of August 1966, led by the Chinese Communist Party, comprise an authentic case of institutionalized violence. The first target was individual teachers in high schools and colleges singled out for physical and mental torture. Eyewitness accounts agree that the methods used by students on some of their teachers were cruel. Both Dai Hsiao-ai and Ken Ling (particularly the latter) recount how they unthinkingly carried out the orders of school and Party authorities to commit aggression against their teachers. Here is Dai's account:

> The struggle was always very intense. We forced the teachers to wear caps and collars which stated things like "I am a monster." Each class confronted and reviled them in turn with slogans, accusations, and injunctions to reform their ways. We made them clean out the toilets, smeared them with black paint, and organized "control monster teams" *(kuan niu-kui tui)* to see that it was done properly. We would charge them with specific mistakes and not relent until they admitted they were true. . . . They had little rest and were forced to sleep apart from their fellow teachers. We would join into informal groups, raid their quarters, and begin to work on them again. They could not escape us.[64]

According to Ma Sitson,

> Students at one high school actually beat to death every one of their teachers. The woman who lived next to us in the west city was accused of having a radio transmitter and sending messages to Chiang Kai-shek. Red Guards pulled her from her house into the street and killed her. People spoke of heaps of unburied bodies rotting in the mortuaries.[65]

Following the teachers, the families of "black elements" became targets for attack. The Red Guards freely raided their houses and violently attacked individuals and destroyed their property. Neale Hunter's account is informative despite the author's manifest goal to play down violence in the Cultural Revolution:

> . . . Victims of the raids were often paraded past our house wearing tall white dunce caps or forced to stand on a makeshift dais in front of angry crowds. No one ever got hurt in these performances, though the student leaders were always stern and sometimes gave prisoners a shove.
>
> We had only the vaguest idea of what was going on; all we knew was that we did not like it. *The students did not share our*

scruples. They saw themselves as the vanguard of a new era, entrusted with the task of cleansing away every vestige of Shanghai's humiliating past. If their work involved some violence, forcing people to submit to indignities, they felt this was unavoidable. Revolution, they quoted from Mao, is not a dinner party [emphasis added].[66]

The students, of course, did not share Hunter's scruples! They observed a dual standard: "To be kind to the enemy is to be cruel to the people."

"The people about us," writes Berkowitz, "may lessen or eliminate [a person's] aggression and anxiety if they define hostile behavior as being socially proper in a given situation. . . . Adult permissiveness toward aggression may result in such a social definition of aggression for children, the children transferring their 'superego function' to the watching adult."[67] Hunter's students and all the students in China knew that watching adults—Chairman Mao and the media—would assume the "superego function" in June and August 1966. The violence of the Red Guards reached a peak in August and an editorial in the *People's Daily*, entitled "It is Fine" (a quotation from Mao's 1927 report on the peasant movement in Hunan), urged students to continue their violent actions:

> The dust certainly will not fly away by itself if you do not sweep it with a broom. Waving their iron brooms, the thousands upon thousands of "Red Guards" have in only a few days swept clean the countless names and customs and habits representing the ideology of exploiting classes.
> This is a stimulating affair; this is delightful news.[68]

The organ of the armed forces, the *Liberation Army Daily*, approved the actions of the Red Guards with an editorial entitled "They Have Done Right and Well."[69] On October 25, 1966, Marshal Lin Piao, heir apparent to Mao, praised the actions of the Red Guards: "Many reactionary, bourgeois 'authorities' had been made to stink and many hidden counterrevolutionaries were dug out. . . . After this movement, many youths could be cultivated into reliable successors of the revolution."[70] A Red Guard paper reported in December 1966 that Chiang Ch'ing personally called out two educational leaders to stand in front of shouting students in a mass rally.[71]

The degree of violence in this movement varied from place to place and also among student groups of different backgrounds. The most violent groups were "children of party cadres and army officers" and generally the so-called five-Red classes, a group that also included "children of workers, poor and lower-middle peasants and revolutionary martyrs." The most violent groups came from the North:

> Coarse and cruel, they were accustomed to throwing their parents'
> weight around and brawling with other students. They did so
> poorly in school that they were about to be expelled and, presum-
> ably, resented the teachers because of this.[72]

The violent actions of these children of the "new class" bear out the
observation that "violence can assume intense and bizarre forms"[73] when
socially sanctioned and when latent hostility is given free vent. This
institutionalized aggression probably created what Berkowitz calls "a
general arousal" among most youths. According to Berkowitz,

> One must not forget that observed violence is often exciting, and
> this diffuse excitement can also energize the dominant response
> tendencies. . . . The witnessed aggression may also have appetitive
> consequences in which there is a specific preference for further
> aggression-associated stimuli.[74]

On this point, Berkowitz's professional analysis is verified by Ken Ling's
intuition. Ken finally realized the nature of the Cultural Revolution
in August: "We now understood that the previous struggles against
the teachers and the movement to destroy the four olds in society
had been a *mere tempering and a trial of Red Guard courage*. The
Cultural Revolution had only now begun" [emphasis added].[75]

Violence by Authorities (September 1966–February 1967)

Once the people were generally aroused, the leaders of the Cultural
Revolution were content to provide broad guidance. They let the movement, particularly that of students, run its course. The movement
evoked a degree of spontaneity, thus clearly creating a similarity between
group violence in China and that observed elsewhere. One uniformity
of group violence is that violence is initiated more by the authorities
and their agents than by the protesters. The authorities break up peaceful
demonstrations and attack marchers, petitioners and other peaceful
assemblies.[76]

In China this uniform pattern of group violence emerged in September
and became widespread in November. Local civil and military authorities were the target and they were not defenseless like the teachers
and the "black elements." The pattern was repeated everywhere; dramatic provocations by the rebels (who were a minority)—usually the
seizure of a newspaper office or sit-ins in Party headquarters—were
followed by violent confrontations in which the rebels were surrounded
by hordes of angry workers and local residents, often accompanied by
peasants from nearby villages. The rebels were ordered to leave the

buildings and fights ensued when the rebels refused to comply. The groups opposing the rebels were undoubtedly organized by local Party authorities, since they had access to transportation and other facilities.

Shanghai was the focal point in this type of violent confrontation. The best-known incident (also probably the first of its kind) was the fight over the newspaper *Liberation Daily*. On November 30, 1966, some 200 radical Red Guards seized the newspaper because the publisher, i.e., the Municipal Party Committee, refused to circulate the Red Guard paper with its own paper. Two days later, on December 2, the rebels were surrounded by workers (the "Scarlet Guards") and conservative student groups. Hunter's description of the disparity between the numerical strength of the two groups may be exaggerated. The rebels allegedly increased their number to around five or six thousand (how could a single newspaper office accommodate so many?) and their opponents numbered "more than a million."[77] There was undoubtedly a numerical disparity between the two groups (and the surrounding masses had an overwhelming majority). On December 4, the masses conducted violent assaults on the building. The equipment they used made it clear that they had the support of Party authorities in Shanghai—they used, among other things, fire engines and ladders. The report of casualties varied from one account to another, but no deaths were reported.[78]

The pattern of confrontation followed by violence was repeated in almost every "power seizure" beginning in January 1967. For example, the rebels seized the *Fukien Daily* in Foochow on January 24, and on February 6, a group of Red Guards supported by garrison troops stormed into the building, beat up the rebels and destroyed the radio transmitter and other equipment.[79] Earlier, a group of Red Guards from other provinces staged a sudden raid on the residence of the Foochow major Lin Pai but the raiders were surprised and beaten back by a group of peasants lying in wait.[80] A more serious counterattack by local authorities occurred in Ts'inghai province. On February 14, the former provincial Party secretary Wang Chao and the deputy commander of the provincial military district Chao Yung-fu mobilized armed workers and surrounded the *Ts'inghai Daily*, which had been seized by a rebel group ("August 18" Headquarters) in late January. The workers were equipped with search lights, handcuffs and other "instruments of dictatorship." On February 23, the real assault began and several participants were killed. On March 24, the national leaders denounced Wang and Chao and accused Wang of being responsible for the attack. The directive from the capital accused Chao of lying to the national leaders, saying that the rebels were armed and had fired first.[81] Throughout China rival rebel groups resorted to violent conflict over the right to seize power from local Party authorities. One group or alliance of rebels would act first and then would be challenged by another group which would stage a "counterseizure" with inevitable physical clashes.[82]

The escalating violence accompanying clashes among Red Guard groups and between rebels and local authorities caused the national leaders to order the army to intervene to "support the left" on January 23, 1967.

Partiality of the Army (March–May 1967)

When the army intervened, the conflicting groups had already polarized. At one extreme was a minority of radicals, composed of local people (mostly students and workers) and students from Peking and elsewhere. At the other extreme were large groups of workers allied with small groups of conservative students, more often than not the children of ranking regional officials. The conservative groups were covertly supported by local officials. To use troops as a partisan force in response to group violence in general usually aggravates the situation. Oberschall observed another uniformity of group violence: "When the confrontation is not directly between the protesters and the authorities but between two hostile population groups . . . the casualties tend to be higher when the authorities either openly side with one group against the other, or refrain from intervening in the situation." In retrospect, the intervention of the army in January 1967 was the most immediate cause of group violence during the Cultural Revolution.

The national leaders and radical groups all over China were temporarily astounded because the army's partisanship was wrong. Instead of "supporting the left" as ordered, the army allied with regional Party authorities, conservative workers and students (some their own offspring). The embittered radicals consequently staged a series of raids into military headquarters. From the end of January to the first week in February, reports about army-student conflict came from Foochow, Changsha, Shenyang, Hangchow, Canton and elsewhere. The army promptly reacted by making mass arrests and forcibly disbanding many rebel organizations. The minority radicals were thus suppressed, while the conservatives grew under the army's sponsorship. In many areas conservative groups joined with the army to arrest or disband the radicals and that produced other clashes and accumulated hatred on both sides. Violent encounters became inevitable.

The events in Canton were a model of group conflict. Canton endured a phase of physical clashes between radicals and conservatives resulting from "power seizures." The student group (the Provincial Revolutionary Alliance) staged raids on the Party offices, the Public Security Bureau and the radio station on January 22, and proclaimed a "power seizure."

The conservative groups (mostly workers) mounted a counterseizure movement on January 24 and 25 and violence broke out. The radicals believed that the military in Canton was involved in the counterseizure actions and the ill will between the army and the radical students was increased by the agitation of a rebel group within the military, mainly the staff of the Political Department and students of the army literary schools. In February, the suppression of the army rebels by their commanding officer provoked a raid into the military headquarters by external radical groups on February 8. The army and the radicals then engaged in a propaganda war.[84]

On March 15, Canton was officially put under military rule. By that time, the various groups in Canton had polarized into loosely organized groups, the "Flag Faction," representing the radicals (mostly students) and the "Headquarters Faction," representing the conservatives (mainly workers). The "Headquarters Faction" included a militant student group—the "Doctrine Red Guards"—composed of children of high ranking civil and military officials. The army quickly allied itself with the "Headquarters Faction," particularly the "Doctrine Red Guards," to commence a campaign to suppress the radicals. Two radical groups were forcibly disbanded and their leaders arrested, including the large veteran group known as the "August 1 Combat Detachment." The antiradical campaign caused a mass defection of radical students but a determined and embittered hard core remained, supported by the national leaders in Peking. Meanwhile the conservative groups in Canton proliferated rapidly with the army's blessing. Some new groups were formed by defectors from the radical groups. The polarization deepened as the number of splinter groups joining the conservative side increased. The feeling of the radicals was summed up by Dai Hsiao-ai: "We carefully recorded all debts we would someday collect from the conservatives."[85]

The radicals did not have to wait long to "collect their debts." On April 6, 1967, the Central Military Affairs Commission issued a ten-item order to the armed forces that severely restrained the actions of the army including an injunction against firing at "organizations of the masses," whether or not they were revolutionary.[86] The order was a rebuke of the army's actions during the previous two months. Chou En-lai visited Canton on April 14 and personally approved the radical student groups. Following Chou's visit, the radical groups enjoyed a vigorous revival and they demanded an immediate release of their arrested cohorts. The army refused and the radicals staged a hunger strike on May 3. Despite the directive issued by the national leaders, the military was in no mood to switch support to the radicals. The conservatives resented the order from Peking but could still count on the covert support of the army and they thus provoked the first use of lethal weapons. Four days after Chou's departure (April 22) the

"Doctrine Red Guards" attacked a group of high school students with iron bars and knives and serious casualties resulted for the first time. The violent challenge continued in May. Dai Hsiao-ai recalled seeing the "Doctrine Red Guards" training for combat and the use of lethal weapons.[87] Starting in June, a series of violent conflicts took place, and each time the conservatives attacked the minority. Peasants were also mobilized to attack the students. At this stage, the weapons were still the traditional bars and knives. On July 21, the "Headquarters Faction" used rifles to fire at the "Flag Faction" in a sugar refinery near Canton and the use of more modern arms quickly spread to all groups.

The Canton case indicates that the partiality of the army was a precipitating factor which emboldened the conservatives and further polarized the conflicting groups. It also revealed that the use of lethal weapons was initiated by the agents of the authorities who started the violence. The radical minority resorted to hunger strikes and daring raids without the use of weapons.

The Canton model had a nationwide validity. For example, the military in Kweichow summed up its experiences by concluding that "if the military supported the wrong side, then the situation in that area immediately became tense. . . . A flock of complaints and reports about armed conflicts would go forth to the central authority and the local leaders found themselves hemmed in from all sides." According to the Kweichow report, the army erred by "interpreting too many problems from the security angle . . . too much contact with local leaders but too little with the masses and too much emphasis on class background but too little on actual political deeds."[88] The self-criticism of the army in Foochow included the report that in March, it had arrested two thousand rebels and disbanded some eighty organizations. The result was a "further polarization of the two factions of the revolutionary masses."[89] The army in Kwangsi also admitted that it had "supported one faction and suppressed another," disbanded student groups and withheld material support from the radicals. The result was "more mutual antagonism among the two factions in Kwangsi and the "armed struggles became more serious" after that.[90]

In summary, the partiality of the army in March and April embittered the radicals and emboldened the conservatives, whose ranks grew rapidly. The restraining order from the national leaders contributed to the increase of armed conflict beginning in June. The radicals, elated by support from the national leaders, began to regroup, and they initiated other provocative actions. The army adopted a posture of defiant and superficial neutralism. The army did not force the conservatives to disband, since most of them were workers, but the army had once broken up the radical groups. The army's defiant neutralism encouraged the conservatives, who were angered by the dispensation from Peking and particularly by the new activities of the radicals. The army and some of its commanders covertly supported the conservatives. The first outbreak of armed conflict, in Chengtu, should be analyzed against this background.

Spontaneous Violence with Use of Modern Weapons
(May–December 1967)

Several accounts attribute the start of *armed* conflict during the Cultural Revolution to a statement by Chiang Ch'ing (July 14) that the revolutionaries should "attack with reason but defend with arms." The incident in Wuhan (on July 20) in which the local military commander supported a conservative attack and seizure of two emissaries from the leaders in Peking also contributed.[91] Actually, the armed conflict in Chengtu on May 6 and 7 set a precedent for the use of modern weapons. According to Dai Hsiao-ai,

> Late in May, as the general situation around the country grew more unsettled, the first gunshot was heard from the southwest. A conservative workers' organization in Ch'eng-tu (Szechwan Province) known as the Workers' Production Army *(kung-jen ch'an-yeh chun)* opened fire on student Red Guards from Szechwan University's "August 26" group, killing several. Included among the dead was a Ch'eng-tu liaison man from Peking Geology College East Is Red, Li Ch'uan-hua. This incident shook the whole country. When we heard about it in Canton the atmosphere became quite tense.[92]

The incident in Chengtu was the result of the general configuration of physical violence so far described. In this case the means used by the contending groups and the attitude of the army are notable. Modern weapons were used for the first time and throughout the fighting the army maintained a defiant neutralism. The army's defiance was directed toward the national leaders who had earlier reprimanded the army for its antiradical actions.

As in other cases, the violence in Chengtu began with a provocation by the radicals. The conflicting groups in Chengtu were polarized into two factions, one composed of local students and a small group of workers allied with students from outside, the other composed of workers, veterans, cadres and peasants. The second group included the "Production Army," composed of veterans employed in the munitions plant "No. 132 Factory." The bloodshed in May was preceded by repeated clashes between the radicals and the "Production Army" in April. Four thousand radicals were reportedly arrested by local military authorities in April, and the radicals resorted to fasting in protest.[93] The violence in early May occurred in two factories where small splinter groups of workers were allied with radical students from outside. The outbreak of armed struggles was preceded by clashes within the two plants between conservatives (those adhering to "business as usual") and the radical minority. The first incident occurred on May 3 in the Szechwan Cotton Mill. The radicals provoked the conservatives by posting wall bulletins. Scuffles started following the seizure of radical students and workers by conservatives. Both sides called for reinforcements. The conservatives appealed to the peasant organization "Combat Army of Poor and Lower-Middle Peasants." Violent clashes began in the late afternoon of May 3 and continued through the night. The radicals appealed to the military command but when the violence escalated the next morning, there was still no sign of military intervention. The radicals employed traditional weapons, i.e., rocks, clubs, and hammers, and the workers used modern weapons including chemicals of various kinds. No reliable report of casualties was given.[94]

The second clash in Chengtu, however, was bloodier than the one at the cotton mill. The fighting occurred at the munitions plant on May 6. Most of the workers and employees of this plant were demobilized soldiers organized into several groups under the overall title "Production Army." One small group in the plant allied with the radicals. Before the bloodshed on May 6, several violent encounters occurred outside the plant between students and the "Production Army." On May 4 a demonstration by the small radical group in the munitions plant, who had been joined by students from outside, precipitated the fighting. The radical group was protesting the support given by the "Production Army" to workers in the cotton mill. The demonstration was broken up by the "Production Army." During the morning of May 6 the radicals returned to the munitions plant ostensibly to collect wounded comrades and a scuffle broke out. Some students were seized (or at least rumored to be). The radicals called in more reinforcements and made repeated assaults against various buildings in the factory starting not long after nine o'clock. The military command reacted quickly but only with a token effort. At eleven o'clock the military command dispatched a propaganda truck urging both sides to stop and until then the fighting was confined to the use of rocks and clubs. The fighting continued and the radicals relentlessly tried to seize the building. The first gunshot was heard from inside one of the buildings in the afternoon and the shooting then continued. The army intervened forcefully after dark and only after receiving an explicit order from Peking. One account reported 45 killed and 2,800 wounded.[95] If that account is reliable the shooting was apparently limited, since the large number of wounded indicates that most of the fighting employed traditional implements.

The fighting continued until the army moved in at eleven o'clock that night. The "Production Army" reportedly slipped away with rifles and machine guns and, on May 7, together with the "Combat Army of Poor and Lower-Middle Peasants," surged back into Chengtu and surrounded the cotton mill, the waterworks bureau, a machine plant and the radio station, all of which had been seized by radicals during the fighting from May 3 to May 6. Violent clashes between the two factions continued in June.[96]

The conflict in Chengtu during the first week of May was characteristic of physical violence in the Cultural Revolution: it included partiality on the part of authorities, provocative actions by the minority and a counterattack by the agents of local Party authorities (the conservatives). The violence in Chengtu was unique only because modern weapons were used and the army affected neutralism. Because of the total absence of social control, violent encounters from May 3 to May 6 were spontaneous and unmediated. Modern weapons were used because military veterans were skilled in their use and weapons were readily accessible in the munitions plant. Modern weapons were used in other places when these two conditions were present.

The Chengtu incident did not immediately create nationwide use of modern weapons; "seizure of arms" actually began in late August and September. Spontaneous physical violence among different rebel groups in China increased following the Chengtu incident mainly because of a sudden change of attitude on the part of the army, from active intervention to defiant neutralism or covert support of the conservatives after April. Unmediated group conflict and violence were the result.

The violence in Chengtu was accompanied by bloody clashes between radical students and organized workers, peasants and cadres in Kaifeng and Chengchow, in Honan province. The causal factors were similar in each case: conservatives resented the renewed activities of radicals. The radicals unwittingly provoked head-on clashes by seemingly challenging the conservatives in a parade (in Kaifeng) and a rally (in Chengchow). The conservative side had access to modern facilities and was more responsible for the increasing casualties. The workers used fire trucks, bulldozers and cranes, according to a Red Guard report. Cranes equipped with swaying iron balls battered down the walls and windows of a building occupied by the radicals in a bloody confrontation in Chengchow on May 30.[97] Earlier reports indicated that violence was continuous after May 4 and every clash resulted in scores of deaths and hundreds of injuries.[98] Violence in Chengtu and the cities in Honan confirms another uniformity in group violence, i.e., casualties tend to be higher when one side has access to modern weapons and equipment than when there is no weapons disparity.[99] It was in commenting on the Honan situation that Chiang Ch'ing reportedly spoke of the need to "attack with reason but defend with arms."[100]

The typical, unmediated, spontaneous group conflict and violence in Chengtu and Honan were probably endemic in China during May–July. The national leaders issued a directive on July 20:

> Recently in Kiangsi, Szechwan, Chekiang, Hufei, Hunan, Honan, Anhwei, Ningsha and Shansi, a small group of capitalist power-holders, particularly some comrades of county and commune arms departments whose thought has not been reformed well, provoked ignorant peasants to go into cities to attack the revolutionary masses in schools, offices, factories and mines. Some places even used reactionary slogans like "encircling the cities from the countryside" to organize peasants to go into cities to suppress the revolutionary rebels . . .[101]

Against this background of widespread group violence the Wuhan incident of July 20 merely added one more precipitating factor to an already tense situation. Except for the open resistance of the commander of the Wuhan garrison against the direction from Peking, the Wuhan incident conformed, in every detail, to the conflict situation elsewhere. Before the incident on July 20 in which the army openly supported the action of a workers' group in arresting and manhandling two emissaries from Chiang Ch'ing, there were repeated clashes between radical students and the workers' group ("Heroic Division of One Million"). According to one account, "Between April 29 and June 30, more than 2,400 factories and mines in the Wuhan area were forced to stop operations partially or completely. A total of 50,000 workers and peasants . . . were affected."[102] So far as the dynamics of group violence are concerned, the Wuhan incident is significant in that it again verifies the danger of partiality (real or perceived) on the part of authorities in a volatile and tense situation. The attack on the two officials from Peking in Wuhan on July 20 was the result of Chou En-lai's mediation effort from July 14 to 18. Chou angered the army in Wuhan by calling the workers conservative and the students revolutionary and he ordered the army to support the students. The reckless agitation of the two emissaries of Chiang Ch'ing among the radical students provoked the "Heroic Division of One Million" to attack the two emissaries and the students.[103]

Chiang Ch'ing then made an inflammatory statement:

> In accordance with Chairman Mao's teachings, armed struggles must be restricted and civilized struggles must be carried out first. However, you revolutionary faction members are too naive. You must not be deceived. What do you think will happen if the

revolutionary factions put aside weapons, when the enemy has not done so. Look at the case of Wuhan. Revolutionary faction members who did not possess weapons were seized and completely defeated by reactionary organization members who were armed with weapons, weren't they? This is the reason why Vice Premier Hsieh Fu-chih was caught. If the enemy has weapons we must not lay aside our weapons.[104]

The fight between radical students and workers in Wuhan resembled the violence in Honan—no modern weapons were used. The students and workers both used spears, and the workers were supported by modern fire trucks and search lights.[105]

The violence in Chengtu, Honan, Wuhan and Chiang Ch'ing's agitation created an "appetitive effect," i.e., the appetite of other combating groups for violence was increased throughout China. The Cultural Revolution was marked by a wave of "weapon seizures" in August and September. This new movement was national in scope;[106] the extent of group violence employing modern weapons was nonetheless determined by the same conditions which made armed conflict in Chengtu a reality: access to weapons and the presence of veterans. Kwangtung and Kwangsi provinces especially possessed these conditions. There was a large number of veterans present and both provinces, particularly Kwangsi, are located on the railway route by which the Chinese supplied arms to North Vietnam. Furthermore, some Chinese arms for Hanoi were shipped via the Canton harbor facilities. These arms were frequently seized by contending groups in the two provinces.

The first use of modern weapons in Canton occurred the day after the Wuhan incident, on July 21. The events started on July 19 in a sugar refinery where workers had been polarized into a majority conservative faction (the "Headquarters Faction") and a minority radical faction (the "Flag Faction"). The minority faction, together with several students, started posting wall papers inside the refinery and a scuffle ensued. A group of peasants was called in by the "Headquarters Faction" to attack the building where the "Flag Faction" was housed. During the early morning, shots were heard from the "Headquarters Faction" side. The "Flag Faction" then called in reinforcements and violence spread throughout the city as both factions began to seize weapons wherever they could find them. The aloofness of the army and the withdrawal of police (they had staged a walkout on August 8) aggravated the situation. The conservatives acquired weapons from the militia, while the "Flag Faction" was supported by the veterans' organization, "August 1 Combat Detachment." On August 9, it was reported "machine guns and ammunition were hauled off from a freighter loaded with arms aid to Vietnam when the ship was attacked."[107] As the violence progressed it became self-sustaining. One side would demonstrate its strength by occupying and fortifying a building which was regarded by the other side as a threat and a challenge. The opposition then would respond in kind. Each side paraded its acquisition in a show of force and the other responded by parading its weapons. For example, the "Headquarters Faction" and the "Flag Faction" both staged parades and rallies to exhibit their arsenals on September 14 and 15. The "Headquarters Faction" paraded "brand new cannons, rifles, carbines, mortars, submachineguns and hand grenades."[108] Fortified buildings effectively invited armed attacks.

The armed conflict in Canton was not altogether unrealistic; violence reached new heights from mid-August to early September, coinciding with Chou En-lai's mediation with the representatives of both Canton factions in Peking. The combating groups fought to increase their bargaining power and dissatisfaction over the efforts at mediation provoked new violence. A tentative agreement was reached by both sides in Peking on September 1, and that evening the "Doctrine Red Guards" (children of the "new class") attacked the T'ai Ku Warehouse, using artillery and armored vehicles. The "Doctrine Red Guards" replied to the settlement in Peking by retorting: "Premier Chou always listened to the 'Flag Faction'; he would not let us speak. Chairman Mao was also deceived. Our opinions could not be transmitted to the above."[109]

The most violent and protracted armed conflict occurred in Kwangsi, starting in May 1967 and continuing through July 1968. The destruction spread over four cities, three of which are on the main railway connecting China with Hanoi. China and the Soviet Union delivered military aid to Hanoi via the main rail line through Kwangsi and the warring factions made repeated forays into arms caches destined for North Vietnam. The intensity of violence in Kwangsi was caused by the depth of the elite division—civilian and military authorities were polarized, and each sided with a rebel faction. The violence was further intensified because Kwangsi is well removed from the national capital and because of its multiracial background. Kwangsi is the homeland of at least ten minority races. Another factor which contributed to the violence was the availability of arms destined for Vietnam, and the presence of newly demobilized soldiers in sizable force.

Kwangsi replicated the development of group violence observed in other regions of China, but the division of local authorities was much deeper. The two top civilian leaders, Wei Kuo-ch'ing and Wu Ching-nan, split in April 1967. Wei was the top Party official and Wu his deputy. Wei's policy toward the radicals, the so-called April 22 Faction, reflected the attitude of other local authorities in China, i.e., hostility and suppression. Wu went his own way by supporting the radicals against the conservatives, i.e., the "United Command." The radicals, like those in other provinces, were mostly students and the conservatives included students, cadres, veterans, workers and peasants, many of whom were of minority racial origins. Wei and Wu had extensive military backgrounds, so their split also divided the military units in Kwangsi. Wei was allied with the local garrison and Wu was supported by main force units. The main force was mobile; it operated under the direction of national authorities and possessed advanced weapons. The split in the military ranks might also be due to interunit rivalries. The factional dispute also involved the railway workers who, in turn, were polarized.

Armed clashes started in May and reached serious proportions in August 1967. The opposing factions raided freight trains carrying arms to Vietnam and the railway crews assisted the warring factions by redirecting some trains and emptying their cargoes. Chou En-lai reported that some 11,800 crates of weapons and ammunition were lost to the factions during 1967–68.[110] The respective military units also supplied their allies with arms. Violent conflict spread to the major cities in Kwangsi: Nanning, Liuchow, Kweilin and Wuchow; and in November 1967 the national government authorized Wei to organize a revolutionary committee to end the fighting. After receiving this authorization, Wei returned to Kwangsi and precipitated increased violence by conducting a series of campaigns to suppress the radicals. Wei then mobilized the "United Command," composed of newly demobilized soldiers, peasants, police and fire crews, and directed it to repeatedly attack the radicals. Fires destroyed large segments of Wuchow, Nanning and Liuchow. According to one report, a third of Wuchow was destroyed by fire in June 1968 and 2,000 refugees swarmed from Kwangsi to Canton.[111] In April and May 1968, some 1,000 buildings in Liuchow burned and more than 100 persons were killed.[112] The radicals reportedly used explosives to destroy bridges and raided the Kweilin granary to seek food.[113]

Mediation by the central authority was ineffective. On July 3, 1968, the national leaders issued a special directive, "On the Kwangsi Problem," which enumerated the results of the violence.

> First, obstruction of railway traffic; to this day no train can pass through.
> Second, audacity to seize goods intended for aid to Vietnam and refusal to return them.
> Third, repeated raids to the offices and units of the People's Liberation Army, robbing the army of its weapons and equipment and wounding and killing of army officers.
> Fourth, refusal to carry out the "June 13" directive from the central government.[114]

The directive lacked the magic formula needed to bring the conflict in Kwangsi to an end and the violence continued. The central government invited representatives of the various factions to Peking to talk with Chou En-lai and Kang Shen. The delegates were also assigned to special classes. The result was discouraging. Chou and Kang received the whole Kwangsi group on July 25 and Chou berated representatives of the railway crews for breaking five agreements before July 1968. He asked one faction of railway workers from Liuchow: "You must admit that we called you up so many times and sent you so many telegrams. Now that the July 3 directive has already elapsed for some 20 days but the rail traffic is still blocked, we still cannot pass the station of Liuchow. Did you dispense among yourselves the seized arms intended for aid to Vietnam?"[115] Kang Shen's angry statement to the delegation from Kwangsi reveals the intransigence of the warring factions:

> You have been making troubles in Kwangsi for a long time. You have become famous nationally and even internationally. Now that we have invited you comrades to come to the Center . . . most of you have come but *some still will not come.* Some who have come will not attend study classes. Instead they engaged in conspiracy. . . . The problem of Kwangsi is that for two months the rail traffic has been obstructed. Let me ask you this. Do you or do you not want to oppose American imperialism? . . . Do you or do you not want to aid Vietnam? . . . Who is pleased by your seizing the goods intended for aid to Vietnam? . . . You talk about *revolution* but you are counterrevolutionary in deeds. . . .[116]

The situation in Kwangsi worsened in 1968 because both factions sought to increase their strength in the emerging authority structure, i.e., the revolutionary committee. Wei's campaigns of suppression after November 1967 were perceived by the radicals as an attempt to deprive them of legitimate influence. The angry talk between Chou En-lai, Kang Shen and the Kwangsi delegates on July 25, 1968, reveals that the violence was mostly perpetrated by students and ideologues on both sides. One radical representative was a senior member of the Kwangsi Party Institute whose "April 22" organization set the fire in Nanning. Chou concluded the conversation by commenting that most of the delegates were students and that there were too few workers. Chou blamed the factional war on "the bourgeois education" that the students allegedly received before the Cultural Revolution.[117] It is interesting and highly significant to note that Chou attributed the cause of factionalism and conflict to cultural reasons.

Reimposition of Control (1968)

From February to August 1968 violent conflict was renewed and intensified among various groups in at least 13 provinces. Most of the factional strife during this period was associated with the establishment of the revolutionary committees, but there were other causes.

Table 2 indicates the cause of violence in 1968 by comparing the time of reported violence with the dates on which the revolutionary committees in these 13 provinces were created. Table 2 thus shows three possible patterns of violence. First, the violence in Kweichow, Shansi and Ts'inghai does not seem to coincide with the establishment of revolutionary committees—there is a considerable lapse of time between the date on which the revolutionary committee was formed and the date of the reported disturbances. Furthermore, renewed conflict occurred during March 1968 in all three provinces. The unrest in Shansi was linked to the purge of three top-rank army commanders in Peking, which was announced on March 24.[118] This suggests that the conflict between rebel groups in Kweichow and Ts'inghai must have been of

Table 2: Occurrence of Violence in 1968 and the Establishment of the Revolutionary Committees.

Province	Date of the Revolutionary Committee	Reported Occurrence of Violence
Kweichow	February 13, 1967	March 1968
Shansi	March 13, 1967	March, April 1968
Ts'inghai	August 12, 1967	March 1968
Kwangtung	February 21, 1968	May–July 1968
Kiangsu	March 23, 1968	August 1968
Chekiang	March 24, 1968	July, August 1968
Hunan	April 8, 1968	June 1968
Shensi	May 1, 1968	April 1968
Liaoning	May 10, 1968	April 1968
Szechwan	May 31, 1968	March, April 1968
Yunnan	August 13, 1968	July 1968
Fukien	August 19, 1968	June, August 1968
Kwangsi	August 26, 1968	June–July 1968

SOURCE: The dates of the creation of the revolutionary committees are from *Yi-chiu Liu-chiu Chung-kung-nien-pao* [1969 Yearbook on Chinese Communism], Vol. 1 (Taipei, 1970), pp. 26–27. The reports about the violence in different provinces are from the following news items: *AFP*, 0515 GMT, March 14, 1968; *AFP*, 1713 GMT, April 16, 1968; *AFP*, 1220 GMT, June 21, 1968; *AFP*, 0948 GMT, June 25, 1968; *AFP*, 1103 GMT, July 7, 1968; *AFP*, 1544 GMT, August 11, 1968; and *AFP*, 2302 GMT, August 2, 1968.

a similar nature. The discontented Red Guards in the provinces tried to reassert themselves by exploiting the division of the leaders in Peking. The rebels exploited the apparent fissure in the top elite by initiating conflict. The crisis in Kweichow was particularly significant since the fighting there reportedly employed rifles and small arms and Peking authorities dispatched a special mission to investigate.[119]

The second pattern is characterized by the protest movements which followed establishment of the revolutionary committees. Certain groups revolted against the revolutionary committees for one reason or another in Kwangtung, Kiangsu, Chekiang and Hunan. In Kwangtung, the protest movement was conducted by the "Flag Faction" in the city of Canton. As a minority, the "Flag Faction" was systematically discriminated against and underrepresented in the new power structure.[120] The "Flag Faction" had, in the past, compensated for its minority status in each organization by establishing a cross-organizational alliance of radicals. The national government in late 1967 banned all the so-called cross-trade organizations and confined all "mass organization" activities to their unit and profession. In other words, the Peking government returned to the old policy of integration through segregation. The radicals were thus cut off from each other and overwhelmed in their own work units. The actions of conservatives seeking revenge, supported by rehabilitated cadres and army officers, aggravated the situation.[121] The radicals responded by regrouping and renewing their resistance and the pattern was being repeated throughout China. The events led the leader of the Canton "Flag Faction," a college student named Wu Ch'uan-p'in, to meet in Peking with radical leaders from all over the nation. The gathering was denounced by the national leaders as a "black meeting," but it was eventually convened on July 17 on the campus of Peking Aviation College, attended by radical delegates of 20 organizations from Canton, Kweichow, Kwangsi, Ts'inghai, Heilunkiang, Liaoning and Peking. The representatives discussed the establishment of a nationwide "rebels' correspondence network,"[122] but by then the national leaders were no longer interested in conflict mobilization and the meeting produced nothing.

The violent clashes in Kwangtung, Kiangsu, Chekiang and Hunan were futile and desperate actions. In Kiangsu, a group of radicals reportedly established a stronghold in Yencheng and declared: "You have Yenan and we have Yencheng. Let us see who is the winner."[123] In Chekiang bloody clashes between two student groups at the University of Chinhua occurred in July; both sides used machine guns and grenades.[124] In August, "large forces of the Chinese People's Liberation Army have been dispatched to the southern part" of Chekiang to "propagate Mao's thought." The rebels declared that their actions were vindicated by Mao himself.[125] Against this background the general remark by Sidney Waldman on the intransigence of the minority group is relevant.

> When a minority sees that it will not get much of what it wants in any probable resolution of deadlock within some collective decision system, it has little incentive for breaking the deadlock. In these circumstances, one of the few rewards available to the minority is the feeling of righteousness associated with being for the right cause. Such a minority will have no reason to compromise or aggregate interests and thus will have little reason to see the process of aggregation as a useful and necessary one.[126]

The third pattern of violence revealed in Table 2 indicates that it either resulted from a struggle for more power in the emerging revolutionary committee or resistance to the formation of such authority altogether. The Kwangsi pattern (discussed in detail earlier) included six provinces, i.e., Shensi, Liaoning, Szechwan, Yunnan, Fukien, and Kwangsi. These provinces were the last to have revolutionary committees installed and the late formation was an indication of the degree of unrest in that part of China. A foreign reporter noted in April 1968 that the Red Guard posters which reported these disturbances should be treated with caution, but he added:

> Observers found it interesting that the incidents were said to have occurred in Shensi, Liaoning, and Szechwan, three of the nine Chinese provinces which have not yet managed to set up Maoist revolutionary committees. It is also noteworthy that the posters were put up following the distribution by Peking militants of leaflets containing speeches by Premier Chou En-lai and Chiang Ch'ing affirming that revolutionary committees will be set up in all Chinese provinces and regions by May 1.
>   If the reports of fighting are accurate, it will be difficult for the Maoists to set up revolutionary committees in the remaining provinces before May 1 unless the army intervenes massively, as it reportedly did in Kiangsu, Chekiang, and Ningshia.[127]

Only Shensi met the May 1 deadline. Revolutionary committees in Liaoning and Szechwan were set up on May 10 and 31 respectively, and the last two were set up in Tibet and Sinkiang on September 5. The disturbances, at least those in the southern provinces, were likely caused in part by economic deprivations following a general breakdown of law and order and the obstruction of railway traffic.[128]

Before we conclude the discussion on violence and conflict in China during 1968, it should be noted that information about the situation in the provinces is difficult to obtain. A strict ban on the sale of Red

Guard publications was carried out in January.[129] There were few disturbances reported in Anhwei (committee formed on April 18, 1968) and Tibet and Sinkiang (committees formed on September 5). There was considerable conflict and violence in these regions, yet no information concerning the events is available. The existence of intense conflict in these places can only be inferred from oblique references in official documents. For example, the conflict in Anhwei was quite serious, judging from the national leaders' public endorsement of the Anhwei Revolutionary Committee, which stated "the class struggle in Anhwei had been *very* sharp and complicated," that the enemies "madly engaged in desperate struggle and destruction" and that they "either cruelly suppressed the revolutionary rebels or spread rumors, shot poisonous arrows, infiltrated into the organizations of the masses to provoke masses struggling with masses, etc., etc."[130] Similarly, in Sinkiang, a terse order from the national leaders to the rebel groups in September 1967 informed them that "Sinkiang is at the forefront of anti-revisionism, so there should not be too much disturbance."[131]

Violence & Socioeconomic Change

In accounting for the outbreak of violent group conflict in various places, the most immediate causes have been cited, e.g., access to weapons, the presence of groups skilled in combat and the degree of an elite division. The social and economic similarities of cities and provinces where violent struggles and protracted group conflicts took place in 1967 and 1968 are, however, also impressive reasons. Several cities, Fushun, Anshan and Fousin (Liaoning),[132] Taiyuan (Shansi), Hofei (Anhwei), Chengchow (Honan), Wuhan (Hopei), Canton (Kwangtung) and Chengtu (Szechwan), experienced similar circumstances.

The correlation between the occurrence of violence in these cities and Yuan-li Wu's study of the expansion of major industrial centers in China from 1953 to 1958 produces interesting results. Wu classified the major cities of China into four groups according to population growth. Group I cities experienced large absolute increases but small relative changes in population. Group I thus included "large established economic centers that expanded further."[133] "Group II includes cities showing both large absolute and relative growths. Since their absolute population increases are comparable to those of Group I and their initial populations are smaller, their economic development would seem to be more intensive and vigorous."[134] The nine cities mentioned above which experienced violent group conflict between 1967 and 1968 are classified Group II. Group II cities experienced intensive and vigorous economic development in the first Five-year Plan of the Chinese Communist regime.

Five of the nine cities (the three Liaoning cities plus Wuhan and Canton) were highly industrialized and urbanized before 1949, so their rapid development during the 1950s was to be expected, given the new government's strategy of developing the already developed cities first. The new industrial centers in the interior, i.e., Taiyuan (Shansi), Chengchow (Honan), Chengtu (Szechwan) and Hofei (Anhwei) significantly accentuate the correlation between socioeconomic change and group conflict (or violence). For example, in Taiyuan, according to Theodore Shabad:

> Industrialization and territorial expansion raised the city's population from 270,000 at the time of the Communist take-over in 1949 to 721,000 in the 1953 census and 1.02 million in 1957. Industrial growth was achieved in particular through expansion of an iron and steel plant and machine-building and chemical industries, making Taiyuan a major diversified center of heavy industry in China. The iron and steel plant, situated in the northern suburbs of Taiyuan, is an integrated operation with a capacity of about 700,000 tons . . .[136]

Another source reports that the rapid industrial development in Taiyuan was part of a province-wide growth. From 1948 until the end of 1956, the number of people employed in nonagricultural occupations in Shansi increased from 600,000 to 3.3 million. This high rate of growth was made possible by moving plants, skilled labor, technicians and professional manpower from coastal cities into Shansi as part of a plan to redress the unevenness of China's economic development.[137] Shansi was the first city to respond to Shanghai's "power seizure" movement and there were seventy known Red Guard and rebel groups in that area. The dissension in Peking in March 1968 obviously had an immediate effect in Taiyuan, the capital of Shansi.

In Chengchow violent clashes occurred simultaneously with the bloody conflict in Chengtu during the first week of May 1967. Interestingly, Chengchow was also subject to forced draft industrialization in the 1950s. To quote Shabad:

> Because of its situation in the heart of China's cotton belt, the availability of manpower and transport routes, Chengchow was one of the inland cities earmarked in the early 1950s for industrial development with emphasis on textiles and processed foods. The city has four cotton mills, with a combined capacity of more than 400,000 spindles and 15,000 looms, and two textile-machine plants, completed in 1950 and 1958. The food-processing industry includes

a large flour mill and an oil-and-fats factory. New industrial construction, mainly in the western and northern outskirts, led to
a rapid population increase from 595,000 in 1953, to 766,000 in
1957, and to 1.1 million in the late 1960s. Reconstruction of the
Yellow River bridge, north of the city, in 1960 further strengthened
the Chengchow transport position.[138]

The relatively advanced state of industry in Chengchow enabled the
workers to fight the radicals with modern equipment, bulldozers and
cranes, in May 1967.

Two cities in Szechwan, Chungking and Chengtu, experienced intense
and protracted conflict following a similar rapid growth in industry
and population. The population of Chungking declined slightly after
1945, since it was the capital of the Nationalist government during the
war, but "by the time of the 1953 census," the population "had risen
again to 1.77 million, and the official estimate of late 1957 was 2.12
million. In the late 1960s as a result of territorial annexations and
industrial expansion, the population had grown to 4.4 million."[139] The
city built a large and integrated iron and steel complex and the steel
output is estimated at one million tons.[140] Chengtu, a manufacturing
center, "had a population of 857,000 in the 1953 census, rising to 1.1
million in 1957 and an estimated 1.7 million in the late 1960s."[141] In
addition, Chengtu is being developed into a "greater city" with new
industrial centers in the northeastern part of the surrounding area.

In Hofei and Hwainan (or Huianan) in Anhwei province, the rebels
reportedly raided the "main force" units of the People's Liberation Army
and acquired artillery shells,[142] illustrating again that intensity of violence
is related to social and economic change. From 1950, Hofei received
new industry and people from Shanghai and a steel industry was developed in 1958. "The city's population rose from 183,600 in 1953 to 360,000
in 1957, partly through northward expansion of the municipal area,
and was probably close to 500,000 by 1970."[143] Hwainan developed as
a city after 1949, when a coal mine town was merged with a coal harbor.
Its population was 287,000 in 1953 and "may have risen to 350,000
by 1970."[144] Hwainan is now the source of coal and electricity for cities
on the lower Yangtze. The April 1968 directive from Peking notes:
"Anhwei is an important province of coal, steel and food production;
it is a communication center in the Southeast."[145] The rapid industrialization and the influx of population in these cities and provinces
created numerous strains in the society, particularly a lack of integration
of new and old population groups. As a consequence, each of the cities
experienced a high level of free-floating aggression. The violent group
conflict in these localities resulted partly because of the high rate of
socioeconomic change.

The cities in Kwangsi province, however, were neither Group I nor Group II. Wu classified Nanning in Group III and Liuchow, Kweilin and Wuchow in Group IV. According to Wu,

> Group III consists of cities that have registered a large relative growth although the absolute increase in population has been small. These cities are predominantly smaller ones that have experienced rapid growth, but that are nevertheless far from being major market or supply areas. Growing mining towns, railway junctions and other cities with specialized industries or economic functions are also in this category. Finally, Group IV consists of cities that have registered only small increases in population as well as low growth rates. Cities in Group IV are lesser economic centers, although a few fairly important industrial towns may offer limited or specialized employment opportunities.[146]

Nanning, Liuchow and Kweilin are railway junctions and manufacturing centers. Wuchow is a river port and a trade center. Each has a substantial number of newly settled people. The population of Nanning, for example, rose from 195,000 in 1953 to 260,000 by the end of 1957 and to about 400,000 in the late 1960s.[147] It is highly likely that most of the radicals in Kwangsi were from newly settled groups, as evidenced by Chou En-lai's talk with the Kwangsi delegation on July 25, 1968, in which Chou inquired about the background of two radical leaders. One from Nanning, Chu Jen, was a native of Kwangsi who had left to study in Northeast China and returned to Kwangsi in 1960. The radical leader from Liuchow, Pai Chien-ping, was a native of Shantung province. This prompted Chou to ask: "You are a Shantung native. How is it that you are now in Liuchow?"[148] If the background of most of the radical participants in the violence in Kwangsi is represented by these two leaders, then they are "marginal men," affected by what Daniel Lerner calls "psychic mobility,"[149] i.e., their social experience and economic status contributed to their participation in group conflict.

This chapter dealt with two distinct aspects of group conflict—the intensity of conflict and group violence. The conflict in China from 1966 to 1968 was like a hurricane which moved through China and assumed different shapes and forces in time and space. Yet, it is also evident that the Cultural Revolution conformed to many uniformities of group conflict and violence.

The following chapters will analyze conflict in the Cultural Revolution from the vantage point of its constitutive parts—the social groups whose actions produced the hurricane portrayed in this chapter. The frame of reference will, however, give equal weight to the cultural and sociological sources of conflict.

Notes

1. Ralf Dahrendorf, *Class and Class Conflict in Industrial Society* (Stanford, Calif., 1959), pp. 211–212. Lewis Coser concurs with Dahrendorf in *Continuities in the Study of Social Conflict* (New York, 1967), p. 3.

2. Neale Hunter, *Shanghai Journal: An Eyewitness Account of the Cultural Revolution* (Boston, 1969), p. 133.

3. For a description of such a process in Canton, see Hai Feng, *Kuang-chou Ti-ch'u Wen-ke Lieh-chen Shu-lueh* [An Account of the Cultural Revolution in the Canton Area] (Hong Kong, 1971), pp. 301–322 (hereafter cited by English title).

4. Hunter, *Shanghai Journal*, p. 219.

5. *Kyodo* (Tokyo), 1258 GMT, July 28, 1967.

6. *Asahi* (Tokyo), August 7, 1967.

7. Cited in Chao Tsung, "An Account of the 'Great Proletarian Cultural Revolution,'" (Part 58), *Tsukuo* [China Monthly], No. 104 (November 1, 1972), p. 28.

8. Raymond W. Mack and Richard C. Snyder, "The Analysis of Social Conflict—Toward an Overview and Synthesis," *Journal of Conflict Resolution*, Vol. 1, No. 2 (June 1957), p. 230.

9. *Kuang-ying Hung-ch'i*, November 23, 1967, as cited in Chao Tsung, "An Account of the 'Great Proletarian Cultural Revolution,'" (Part 26), *Tsukuo*, No. 72 (March 1, 1970), p. 32.

10. Hai Feng, *Account of the Cultural Revolution in Canton*, p. 331.

11. Ken Ling, *The Revenge of Heaven: Journal of a Young Chinese* (New York, 1972), p. 129.

12. Gordon A. Bennett and Ronald N. Montaperto, *Red Guard: The Political Biography of Dai Hsiao-ai* (Garden City. N.Y., 1972), p. 181.

13. Ibid., pp. 167–168.

14. Lewis A. Coser, *The Functions of Social Conflict* (New York, 1956), p. 103.

15. Ibid., pp. 101–102.

16. See Bennett and Montaperto, *Red Guard*, p. 127; Hunter, *Shanghai Journal*, pp. 56–57; Ken Ling, *Revenge of Heaven*, p. 19.

17. Bennett and Montaperto, *Red Guard*, p. 49; Ken Ling, *Revenge of Heaven*, pp. 167–168.

18. Ken Ling, *Revenge of Heaven*, p. 177.

19. This was particularly true in Peking, where almost all the Red Guards in the initial stage were organized by the offspring of high rank officials; for more on this, see the report by Liu Shao-ch'i's daughter in *Liu Shao-ch'i Wen-ti Tze-liao Ch'uan-ch'i* [A Special Collection of Materials on Liu Shao-ch'i] (Taipei, 1970), pp. 416–429 (hereafter cited by English title); Chao Tsung, "An Account of the 'Great Proletarian Cultural Revolution,'" (Part 18), *Tsukuo*, No. 64 (July 1, 1969), pp. 36–38; Hunter, *Shanghai Journal*, p. 72.

20. Hai Feng, *Haifeng Wen-hua Ke-ming Kai-shu* [A General Account of the Cultural Revolution in Haifeng County] (Hong Kong, 1969), pp. 17, 44 (hereafter cited by English title).

21. C. Kerr, "Industrial Conflict and Its Mediation," *American Journal of Sociology*, Vol. 60 (1954), p. 230, as cited in Mack and Snyder, "Analysis of Social Conflict," p. 220.

22. Ken Ling, *Revenge of Heaven*, p. 65.

23. Hai Feng, *Account of the Cultural Revolution in Canton*, pp. 59, 61–63.

24. Ken Ling, *Revenge of Heaven*, p. 62.

25. Hai Feng, *Account of the Cultural Revolution in Canton*, pp. 89, 203–225.

26. K'uai's case is mentioned in virtually every account. See, for example, *A Special Collection of Materials on Liu Shao-ch'i*, pp. 421, 528; Ken Ling, *Revenge of Heaven*, p. 200; Bennett and Montaperto, *Red Guard*, p. 60; Chao Tsung, "An Account of the 'Great Proletarian Cultural Revolution,'" (Part 14), *Tsukuo*, No. 60 (March 1, 1969), p. 37.

27. Hai Feng, *Account of the Cultural Revolution in Canton*, pp. 208–209.

28. Hans Granquist, *The Red Guard: A Report on Mao's Revolution*, trans. Erik J. Friis (New York, 1967), p. 77; Hunter, *Shanghai Journal*, p. 90; Bennett and Montaperto, *Red Guard*, pp. 52, 65, 67, 141; Ken Ling, *Revenge of Heaven*, pp. 16, 61.

29. Mack and Snyder, "Analysis of Social Conflict," p. 230.

30. Hai Feng, *Account of the Cultural Revolution in Canton*, pp. 125–134; see also *Survey of China Mainland Press* (Hong Kong: U.S. Consulate General), No. 4132, pp. 1–8 (hereafter cited as SCMP).

31. Hai Feng, *General Account of the Cultural Revolution in Haifeng*, pp. 17–18, 48–52, 63.

32. Ken Ling, *Revenge of Heaven*, p. 83.

33. Hunter, *Shanghai Journal*, p. 102.

34. Ken Ling, *Revenge of Heaven*, p. 122.

35. Ibid., p. 125.

36. Bennett and Montaperto, *Red Guard*, p. 92.

37. Ibid., p. 110.

38. Ibid.

39. Ibid., pp. 101, 116; Ken Ling, *Revenge of Heaven*, p. 110.

40. Ken Ling, *Revenge of Heaven*, p. 293.

41. Anthony Oberschall, *Social Conflict and Social Movements* (Englewood Cliffs, N.J., 1973), pp. 50, 62.

42. See the text of these directives in *Chung-kung Wen-hua Ta-ke-ming Chung-yao Wen-chien Hui-pien* [Important CCP Documents of the Great Proletarian Cultural Revolution] (Taipei, 1973), pp. 145–190 (hereafter cited by English title).

43. For the two central directives, see *Important CCP Documents of the Great Proletarian Cultural Revolution*, pp. 75, 152, and the account by the "September 16" group, *Tsao-fan-yu-li*, May 14, 1967, in *Red Guard Publications* (Association of Research Libraries), Group IX-2 (hereafter cited as RGP).

44. Hei Feng, *Account of the Cultural Revolution in Canton*, pp. 121–124, 140–144; I Fan, "The Obscure Situation of Power Seizure in Kwangtung Province," *Tsukuo*, No. 41 (August 1, 1967), p. 23.

45. Hai Feng, *General Account of the Cultural Revolution in Haifeng*, pp. 36–37, 77.

46. *Chung-yang Shou-chang Chiang-hua Hui-pien* [Talks by Central Leaders], November 3, 1966, in RGP, Group VI-1.

47. *Tung-fang-hung*, December 20, 1966, in RGP, Group VII-1.

48. "Speech of Chiang Ch'ing on September 5, 1967," *Tsukuo*, No. 47 (February 1, 1968), pp. 48–49; *Important CCP Documents of the Great Proletarian Cultural Revolution*, pp. 307–308.

49. Hunter, *Shanghai Journal*, pp. 120–122, 191–192; for the latter incident, see also Chao Tsung, "An Account of the 'Great Proletarian Cultural Revolution,'" (Part 22), *Tsukuo*, No. 68 (November 1, 1969), p. 35.

50. *Yi-chiu Liu-pa Chung-kung-nien-pao* [1968 Yearbook on Chinese Communism] (Taipei, 1969), pp. 416–421 (hereafter cited by English title); *Important CCP Documents of the Great Proletarian Cultural Revolution*, p. 174.

51. Hai Feng, *General Account of the Cultural Revolution in Haifeng*, p. 49.

52. Hai Feng, *Account of the Cultural Revolution in Canton*, pp. 40–42, 84–92.

53. *Important CCP Documents of the Great Proletarian Cultural Revolution*, p. 160.

54. Ibid., p. 159.

55. See the documents and Red Guard publications concerning Kwangsi in Ting Wang, ed., *Chung-kung Wen-hua Ta-ke-ming Tze-liao Hui-pien* [A Collection of Documents on the Great Proletarian Cultural Revolution] (Hong Kong, 1972), pp. 71–83, 323–391 (hereafter cited as *Collection of Documents*).

56. *AFP* (English Broadcast), 0412 GMT, March 28, 1968. For a description of the purge, see Chao Tsung, "An Account of the 'Great Proletarian Cultural Revolution,' " (Part 74), *Chung-hua Yüeh-pao* [China Monthly], No. 709 (October 1, 1974), pp. 47–51.

57. *AFP* (English broadcast), 0142 GMT, April 9, 1968.

58. Mack and Snyder, "Analysis of Social Conflict," p. 247.

59. Dahrendorf, *Class and Class Conflict*, p. 212.

60. *Sankei* (Tokyo), September 28, 1967.

61. Ibid.

62. *Ch'iu Peng Lo Chan-pao*, March 1968, in RGP, Group XI-2.

63. Oberschall, *Social Conflict*, p. 328.

64. Bennett and Montaperto, *Red Guard*, p. 39.

65. Ma Sitson, "Cruelty and Insanity Made Me a Fugitive," *Life*, Vol. 62, No. 22 (June 2, 1967), p. 29. For other eyewitness accounts, see Ken Ling, *Revenge of Heaven*, pp. 19–32; Hai Feng, *General Account of the Cultural Revolution in Haifeng*, pp. 24–31. Lest one regard Ken Ling's account as too bizarre, an almost completely identical account appeared in the Red Guard paper *Paoting Hung-wei-ping*, May 27, 1967, in RGP, Group IX-2.

66. Hunter, *Shanghai Journal*, pp. 89–90.

67. Leonard Berkowitz, *Aggression: A Social Psychological Analysis* (New York, 1962), p. 103.

68. *Jen-min Jih-pao* [People's Daily], August 23, 1966, as translated in SCMP, No. 3769, p. 1. One might argue that the editorial approved only the changing of names and enforcing a revolutionary type of "fashion" on the people, not the violence. In fact, the violence against the so-called black elements in June–August 1966 was part of the whole movement and the endorsement of the paper was sweeping. The paper did not make a distinction in Red Guard actions until September 5, when factional fights broke out among the students.

69. *Chieh-fan-chun Pao*, August 23, 1966, trans. in SCMP, p. 2.

70. *Important CCP Documents of the Great Proletarian Cultural Revolution*, p. 342.

71. *Tung-fang-hung*, December 20, 1966, in RGP, Group VII-1.

72.   Ken Ling, *Revenge of Heaven*, p. 19.

73.   Irving L. Janis and Daniel Katz, "The Reduction of Intergroup Hostility: Research Problems and Hypotheses," *Journal of Conflict Resolution*, Vol. 3, No. 1 (March 1959), pp. 96–99.

74.   Leonard Berkowitz, "Words and Symbols as Stimuli to Aggressive Responses," in John F. Knutson, ed., *The Control of Aggression* (Chicago, 1973), pp. 133–134.

75.   Ken Ling, *Revenge of Heaven*, p. 61. One might speculate that if this was Mao's tactic, then he must have learned this psychological phenomenon—aggression breeds more aggression—from his experience in mobilizing peasants to conduct class struggle.

76.   Anthony Oberschall, "Group Violence: Some Hypotheses and Empirical Uniformities," *Law & Society Review*, Vol. 5, No. 1 (August 1970), p. 85.

77.   Hunter, *Shanghai Journal*, p. 164.

78.   Ibid.; also Chao Tsung, "An Account of the 'Great Proletarian Cultural Revolution,'" (Part 22), *Tsukuo*, No. 68 (November 1, 1969), p. 34; *Kung-jen Tsao-fan-pao*, June 1, 1967, RGP, Group IX-1.

79.   *Radio Foochow*, 1030 GMT, February 8, 1967; *1968 Yearbook on Chinese Communism*, p. 388.

80.   *Radio Foochow*, 1030 GMT, February 5, 1967.

81.   *Tung-fang-hung-pao*, April 1, 1967, in RGP, Group X-2; also see *Important CCP Documents of the Great Proletarian Cultural Revolution*, p. 149.

82.   See the incident over the power seizure of the Public Security Bureau of Canton in Hai Feng, *Account of the Cultural Revolution in Canton*, pp. 83–84.

83.   Oberschall, "Group Violence," p. 85.

84.   The account on Canton is entirely based on Hai Feng, *Account of the Cultural Revolution in Canton*, pp. 77–180.

85.   Bennett and Montaperto, *Red Guard*, p. 165.

86.   *Important CCP Documents of the Great Proletarian Cultural Revolution*, p. 75.

87.   Bennett and Montaperto, *Red Guard*, p. 184.

88.   *Chung-hsueh Feng-pao*, May 27, 1967, in RGP, Group VII-2.

89.   *Important CCP Documents of the Great Proletarian Cultural Revolution*, pp. 175–176.

90.   Ibid.

91.   Ken Ling, *Revenge of Heaven*, p. 316; again Ken Ling's dating is erroneous (his calendar put Chiang's statement sometime in May 1967). Also see

Hai Feng, *General Account of the Cultural Revolution in Haifeng*, p. 83; Hai Feng, *Account of the Cultural Revolution in Canton*, p. 150; and *Asahi* (Tokyo), July 24, 1967.

92.   Bennett and Montaperto, *Red Guard*.

93.   Chao Tsung, "An Account of the 'Great Proletarian Cultural Revolution,' " (Part 42), *Tsukuo*, No. 88 (July 1, 1971), p. 28. Chao's source is *Kyoto Shimbun* as reported in an AP news dispatch from Tokyo on May 8, 1967. Given the earlier discussion about the mass arrest by the army in Foochow, Canton and elsewhere, the army's action in Chengtu does not seem to be out of the ordinary. Nor is the fasting, which was a common form of protest by the minority of radicals in China, implausible.

94.   This is based on a reprinted Red Guard source *Shih-i Chan-pao* (Chengtu), No. 17, 1967, as published in Chao Tsung, "An Account of the 'Great Proletarian Cultural Revolution,' " (Part 42), *Tsukuo*, No. 88 (July 1, 1971).

95.   *Hungchi Pao*, Nos. 3 and 4 (May 22, 1967), in Chao Tsung, "An Account of the 'Great Proletarian Cultural Revolution,' " (Part 43), *Tsukuo*, No. 89 (August 1, 1971), p. 35.

96.   *Sankei* (Tokyo), May 8, 1967; *Nihon Keizai* (Tokyo), May 9, 1967; *Asahi* (Tokyo), May 9, 1967; *Tokyo Shimbun*, June 16, 1967.

97.   *Erh-chih Chan-pao*, No. 2, June 3, 1967, as reprinted in Chao Tsung, "An Account of the 'Great Proletarian Cultural Revolution,' " (Part 50), *Tsukuo*, No. 96 (March 1, 1972), pp. 36–37. For available translation, see SCMP, No. 4009, pp. 1–15; see also SCMP, No. 4012, pp. 1–6, for the armed struggle in Honan.

98.   *Sankei* (Tokyo), May 9, 1967; *Asahi* (Tokyo), May 12, 1967.

99.   Oberschall, "Group Violence," p. 86.

100. Hai Feng, *Account of the Cultural Revolution in Canton*, p. 150.

101. *Important CCP Documents of the Great Proletarian Cultural Revolution*, p. 48.

102. *Sankei* (Tokyo), September 29, 1967.

103. Ibid.

104. *Asahi* (Tokyo), July 24, 1967.

105. Ting Wang, *Collection of Documents*, pp. 469, 472, 475.

106. Receiving the delegation from Anhwei on September 5, 1967, Chiang Ch'ing stated: "Now that seizure of arms is nationwide." See her statement in *Important CCP Documents of the Great Proletarian Cultural Revolution*, p. 310.

107. The general account is based on Hai Feng, *Account of the Cultural Revolution in Canton*, pp. 150–152. The raid on the freighter is from *Sankei* (Tokyo), August 13, 1967.

108. *AFP* (English broadcast), 0440 GMT, September 17, 1967.

109. *Tung-fang-hung*, No. 27, in RGP, Group X-1. See also "Incident at the Butterfield and Swire Godown," *Tsukuo*, No. 43 (October 1, 1967); SCMP, No. 4040, pp. 7–16.

110. Ting Wang, *Collection of Documents*, p. 74.

111. *AFP* (English broadcast), 0948 GMT, June 25, 1968. See also Ting Wang, *Collection of Documents*, p. 78.

112. *AFP* (English broadcast), 1646 GMT, August 12, 1968.

113. Ting Wang, *Collection of Documents*, pp. 76, 81.

114. *Important CCP Documents of the Great Proletarian Cultural Revolution*, p. 187.

115. Ting Wang, *Collection of Documents*, pp. 73–75.

116. Ibid., pp. 71–72.

117. Ibid., pp. 72, 82.

118. *AFP* (English broadcast), 0412 GMT, March 28, 1968; Chao Tsung, "An Account of the 'Great Proletarian Cultural Revolution,' " (Part 74), *Chung-hua Yüeh-pao*, No. 709 (October 1, 1974), pp. 47–51; *AFP* (English broadcast), 0142 GMT, April 9, 1968.

119. *AFP* (Spanish broadcast), 0515 GMT, March 15, 1968.

120. Hai Feng, *Account of the Cultural Revolution in Canton*, pp. 355–366.

121. Ibid., p. 333.

122. Ibid., pp. 384–386. Chou En-lai and Kang Shen confirmed that this meeting occurred in their July 25 conversation with the delegation from Kwangsi; see Ting Wang, *Collection of Documents*, pp. 79, 81.

123. *AFP* (English broadcast), 1544 GMT, August 11, 1968.

124. *AFP* (English broadcast), 1103 GMT, July 7, 1968.

125. *AFP* (English broadcast), 1544 GMT, August 11, 1968.

126. Sidney R. Waldman, *Foundations of Political Action. An Exchange Theory of Politics* (Boston, 1972), pp. 186–187.

127. *AFP* (English broadcast), 1713 GMT, April 16, 1968.

128. *AFP* (French broadcast), 2302 GMT, August 2, 1968.

129. *AFP* (English broadcast), 1843 GMT, January 19, 1968.

130. *Important CCP Documents of the Great Proletarian Cultural Revolution*, p. 184.

131. Ibid., p. 149.

132. In a meeting with the delegation from the Northeast on September 28, 1967, Chou En-lai mentioned that "struggles have been severe" in these three industrial and mining centers. See RGP, Group X-1. The whole document is also reprinted in Chao Tsung, "An Account of the 'Great Proletarian Cultural Revolution,' " (Part 58), *Tsukuo*, No. 104 (November 1, 1972), pp. 25–33.

133. Yuan-Li Wu, H. C. Ling and Grace Hsiao Wu, *The Spatial Economy of Communist China. A Study on Industrial Location and Transportation* (New York, 1967), p. 42.

134. Ibid.

135. Ibid., pp. 223–224.

136. Theodore Shabad, *China's Changing Map. National and Regional Development, 1949–71* (New York, 1972), p. 235.

137. *1968 Yearbook on Chinese Communism*, p. 301.

138. Shabad, *China's Changing Map*, p. 121.

139. Ibid., p. 220.

140. Ibid.

141. Ibid., p. 221.

142. Chiang Ch'ing's remark to the Anhwei delegation on September 5, 1967. See *Important CCP Documents of the Great Proletarian Cultural Revolution*, p. 309.

143. Shabad, *China's Changing Map*, p. 146.

144. Ibid., p. 144.

145. *Important CCP Documents of the Great Proletarian Cultural Revolution*, p. 184.

146. Yuan-li Wu, *Spatial Economy of Communist China*, p. 42.

147. Shabad, *China's Changing Map*, pp. 194–195.

148. Ting Wang, *Collection of Documents*, pp. 72–73, 81.

149. Daniel Lerner, *The Passing of Traditional Society* (New York, 1958), pp. 47–52.

PART TWO
CONFLICTING GROUPS

5

STUDENTS & YOUTH

The previous discussions showed that the students and youth on mainland China spearheaded group conflict from 1966 to 1968 and were the most powerful force in the derived phase of the movement. Other groups, encouraged by the social fissures opened up by the students, joined in the conflict during the derived phase. The behavior of students, however, gave the Cultural Revolution its changing goal and scope. Initially, the students responded to the remote and idealistic symbols of "destruction of the old," "prevention of capitalist restoration" and "dragging out China's Khrushchev" emanating from Peking. The students thus became unconscious participants in induced conflicts and they enthusiastically joined in their leaders' scapegoat tactics by attacking teachers and outcast groups. Later, the students participated in "power seizures" and turned against local authorities as ferociously as they did the teachers and the "black elements." The students, consciously or not, exploited the elite's induced conflicts to their own advantage. They openly clashed with the authorities, including the previously revered army, and engaged in rampant factional warfare.

The behavior of the students, particularly their sudden change from docility to open rebellion, took many Chinese by surprise, including

Mao. Two alien residents in China were amazed at the transformation of their students. Rene Goldman observed the "Hundred Flowers" campaign in 1957 and described the intense student criticism at Peking University *(Pei-ta)*: "The events at *Pei-ta* considerably surprised foreign students in the university, who had hitherto thought their Chinese fellow students too indoctrinated to be capable of criticism."[1] Nancy Milton, a participant in the Cultural Revolution, taught English at the Institute of Foreign Languages in Peking and similarly described the actions of her students:

> I found my Chinese students to be remarkable young people, real products of socialism in their selflessness and honesty, their kindness and hard working disciplined qualities, their concern for the people of the whole world. At the same time I also found them to be perhaps too obedient, unwilling and sometimes unable to argue out their ideas. Most of them had been raised in a very secure society.[2]

During the Cultural Revolution, Milton found that her students became "effective public speakers, organizers, political analysts, and writers."

The students' behavior, e.g., aggression, violence, factionalism and fickleness, can be explained in terms of adolescent psychology. Youths from 15 to 22 years of age face an inner battle of "identity" versus "role confusion." Most youths carry an almost unbearable burden—they must integrate the lessons of childhood, their rudimentary skills and professional interests with the demands of anticipated adulthood, which requires that they seriously consider the opinions of others. The need to combat "role confusion" frequently results in clannish adolescent behavior—young people are often "cruel in their exclusion of all those who are 'different.'" They are often inclined to "appoint perfectly well-meaning people to play the roles of adversaries." And they are vulnerable to ideological appeal. The adolescent, says Erikson, has

> an ideological mind—and, indeed, it is the ideological outlook of a society that speaks most clearly to the adolescent who is eager to be affirmed by his peers, and is ready to be confirmed by rituals, creeds, and programs which at the same time define what is evil, uncanny, and inimical.[3]

The interaction between "the ideological outlook of a society" and a youthful search for identity tacitly acknowledges the role of public institutions in "working out" adolescent psychology. Erikson explicitly argues that socioeconomic-political factors are directly related to the resolution of identity crises faced by youths. He says:

> To be adult means among other things to see one's own life in continuous perspective, both in retrospect and in prospect. By accepting some definition as to who he is, usually on the basis of a function in an economy, a place in the sequence of generations, and a status in the structure of society, the adult is able to selectively reconstruct his past in such a way that, step for step, it seems to have planned him, or better, he seems to have planned it.[4]

In other words, the value system and institutions of society either facilitate or inhibit the young adult in his search for identity. The study of adolescent behavior is closely related to an understanding of the collective socioeconomic and political order.

The behavior of Chinese students during the Cultural Revolution can be only partly explained in terms of the universal tendencies recognized by adolescent psychology. China's political culture and public institutions suggest other explanations. The actions of students and youths on mainland China between 1966 and 1968 were largely determined by its political and social institutions.

Political Institutions & Chinese Youth

The new political culture described in Chapter 2 was almost tailor-made to suit the psychological needs of Chinese adolescents. The young generation in China was taught a double standard of behavior toward comrades and enemies and most young people were dedicated to a transcendental ideology. Chinese adolescents thus had a natural tendency toward clannishness, a readiness to identify fellow human beings as mortal enemies and their actions were legitimized by the society's ideological outlook and government authorities. The aggression of young students against their teachers and other outcast groups in China during June–August 1966 must be considered in that light. By committing acts of cruelty against defenseless individuals, Chinese youths invoked the new ethos of double standard. For example, Dai Hsiao-ai described the cruelties he and other students inflicted upon two formerly respected teachers and then stated:

> Most of us felt that these two teachers were good in their work and were extremely surprised when they were accused of their crimes. We found it difficult to believe that they could have done such things; I was disillusioned.
>
> However, we never once doubted their guilt. We trusted the Party and did not feel it could have made a mistake. *While we*

respected them before, our feelings changed to hatred as soon as they were denounced as "monsters and ghosts." *We felt that this is our duty and we showed them no mercy* [emphasis added].[5]

Ken Ling significantly describes his participation in the raid on the house of a teacher, a former friend, in similar terms:

One of the homes we raided—that of a former junior middle school teacher of mine—was a familiar place. I had frequently come here in summer when I went swimming. . . . Everything was familiar—the piano, the go chess set, the reclining chair under the trellis with grapevines, the tung tree that rustled in the wind. And yet it was not the same, because it was now the home of an enemy. Previously, I would have felt deeply sorry if I had accidentally broken a small vase, but now smashing the piano would not have bothered me a bit. *Yet I harbored no grudge against this teacher; I now came in a different capacity and had to act accordingly* [emphasis added].[6]

Ken Ling further describes the authority of a female Red Guard leader nicknamed "Piggy" in these terms: "Her clear demarcation between love and hate—boundless love for her comrades and boundless hatred for the enemy—was the basis of her absolute authority to which her schoolmates willingly submitted themselves."[7]

The behavior of Chinese students just described occurred during the period of the centrally directed induced conflict. Later, young people on mainland China exploited the conflict to their own advantage by challenging local authorities. This phase of youthful rebellion revealed that there was an interaction between the universal applicability of adolescent psychology and the particular social, economic and political order of China. The students' choice of targets and their preferred mode of conduct was clear evidence of that interaction. The main attack was directed against excessive political regimentation.

The revolt against regimentation was first manifested by a sharp increase in spontaneous communications among students and the creation of voluntary organizations. The catchword after August 1966 was "link-up" *(ch'uan-lien)*, calling for direct interaction with other students. For example, some students in China felt they were excessively segregated by the Communist Party, so radical students at Ts'inghua University acted first to "link up" the different agencies on campus.[8] Students throughout China sought out colleagues in other schools to exchange information and experiences.[9] The nationwide "link-up" movement, particularly the mass influx to Peking, soon followed. In the meantime, students from Peking set up liaison stations to communicate with students from other towns in almost all the provincial capitals. The "link-up" movement "broke down the situation of mutual self-closure and segregation under the Chinese Communist rule and promoted the mutual understanding and communication among the people." The movement "shook the foundation of the Communist regime."[10]

The segregation of students prior to the Cultural Revolution can not, however, be entirely attributed to the Communist regime. According to Dai Hsiao-ai, students at his school tended to "cross class lines and to identify themselves on the basis of their linguistic and regional background."[11] The intense feeling about the lack of genuine communication was apparently generated by the government's general control of public communication and movement. More specifically, students in the "link-up" movement probably also reacted to the high-handed actions of the "work teams" immediately before the Cultural Revolution. At Peking University,

> Political and social activity had been strictly supervised under the old order, and the University Party apparatus had established a regime under which students were expected to report any of their fellow students' rebellious thoughts to higher authority or face the prospect of having a black mark placed in their permanent records. At times students appear to have been afraid to enter into friendships and talk openly about their thoughts and feelings . . .[12]

After it was made known that the university president had been dismissed by the higher authority on June 2, 1966,

> Students talked in excited groups and chanted slogans under trees and buildings draped with colored paper streamers. The atmosphere seemed festive rather than tense. . . . Columns of demonstrators paraded around the wall surrounding the University grounds. Students at dormitory windows shouted slogans in unison and sang revolutionary songs.[13]

The student revolt against government regimentation significantly resulted in a rejection of the Young Communist League and the subsequent organization of sect-like groups. Before the Cultural Revolution, the League was a central clearinghouse, a link between schools and groups. The League sponsored fraternizing activities with the army and other social groups. Members of the League maintained surveillance over student activities and led small group discussions in the schools. Yet even activists like Dai knew little about the inner workings of the League, and the majority of its members knew even less.[14] The regimentation of youth by the League and other state-run organizations (e.g., the Student Association) was so effective that "the adolescents in Communist China have little time or opportunity to form a distinct subculture, even if they wished to. Youths are under constant supervision of the Party apparatus, school authorities and parents, in both work and study."[15] This comprehensive political regimentation may have had certain "positive" functions for Chinese students. Erikson notes, "At no other time as much as in adolescence does the individual feel so exposed to anarchic manifestations of his drives; at no other time does he so need oversystematized thoughts and overvalued words to give a semblance of order to his inner world."[16] Yet too much pressure of this kind produces a "hostility of suffocation" in people subject to regimentation. The "hostility of suffocation" refers to "the resentful awareness that [a person's] strivings toward new information, independent judgment, and self-expression are being thwarted."[17] Lifton adds that such resentment "when encouraged by external conditions . . . can emerge suddenly and unexpectedly."[18] That is precisely what happened in the Cultural Revolution—the hostility of China's youth toward authority emerged suddenly and unexpectedly.

The way the Young Communist League stopped functioning in the Cultural Revolution is particularly noteworthy. The national organization was not apparently the subject of a formal "power seizure"; the students simply ignored it and formed their own groups. It is remarkable that a once powerful organization could be rejected so easily by its members. That rejection undoubtedly reflects the depth of alienation felt by Chinese youths. Mao Tse-tung said: "For seventeen years since the liberation, our separation from the masses has been serious. The Youth Association, Women Association and the central organ of the Young Communist League are all empty frames . . ."[19]

In August 1966 it was reported that all of the national officers of the League were to be suspended and the members were promised "a Paris Commune type of general election by secret ballots" of new League officers.[20] No such election took place.

The student revolt against regimentation was also evidenced by the initial attack on officials in charge of agitation-propaganda-education. Those officials were, of course, immediately responsible for the life of students. The special target of attack was probably affected by the purge of top educational and propaganda officials earlier in 1965 and 1966, but eyewitness accounts leave no doubt that the attack on regional propaganda officials was spontaneous.[21] The attack on the agitation-propaganda authorities was closely related to the nationwide movement led by students to seize the mass media, particularly the newspapers. The radicals occupied the newspaper *Liberation Daily* on November 30, 1966, and the first violent conflict between radical students and workers occurred shortly thereafter. Two major Shanghai dailies were formally taken over by the radicals on January 3 and 5, beginning the nationwide seizure of newspapers and radio stations. The selection of the mass media as one of the primary targets by the rebelling students is significant in that this also took place in the Hungarian revolution of 1956.[22] Two reasons seemingly underlie the attack on the media. The newspapers remind the Chinese people daily of the totalitarian order and its policy of regimentation. The Shanghai Party secretary asserted that "the press is an instrument of the dictatorship of the proletariat."[23] Thus, the press in China is categorized with the police, the army and the court as instruments of proletarian dictatorship. The police and the court represent sheer coercion, the controlled media coercive persuasion. The gap between the substance of the media and the reality has been a constant provocation to the people in China. Hence, the media bore the brunt of the rebel attack. Also, the rebels needed an instrument to propagate their cause and win more comrades. Even so, the regimented media left a mark on the rebels. The monolithic media structure and the massive doses of propaganda probably evoked an exaggerated image of the media's power so the rebels naturally wanted control of this powerful instrument for their own use.

The revolt against the official monopoly of the mass media logically developed to the stage where the students published their own papers and the Red Guard wall posters and tabloids soon followed. The effect of rebel publications can be deduced from Chou En-lai's roundabout statement to student delegates from northeastern provinces in September 1967:

> You do not read official newspapers anymore. You read only the tabloids. I acquired a bundle of tabloids from Kwangtung and all they talked about was power seizure and power seizure. This is also true in Canton, Nanking and Shenyang. They get disseminated quickly. Now I said they were disseminated quickly. I did not say that they had authority. The intellectuals published these sensational papers. But Chairman Mao's words are the most authoritative. These petit-bourgeois things, once they get circulated, they are accepted. So everyone now wanted to seize power; some even suggested to seize power from the army.[24]

More Red Guard publications were reportedly published in Szechwan than anywhere else in the nation; in the city of Chungking alone, there were 30 publications in 1968.[25] Japanese correspondent Shibata reported that these tabloids "usually disclosed the near truth" and the "wall newspapers always reflected the true outline of events."[26] An

American scholar reported that the Red Guard papers "yielded new insights into the sources of social conflict, the methods of social control, and the dynamics of social organization."[27]

The student rebellion against political control was also indicated by their reaction to the so-called background materials, i.e., personal dossiers compiled by Party authorities. The dossiers were one of the first sources of contention. Before July 1966 the students were supervised by "work teams" which compiled dossiers on students, especially those who offended the team leaders. The background materials obviously threatened the future careers of students and thus were resented. The existence of the dossiers probably inhibited genuine communication among students prior to the Cultural Revolution.[28] Chou En-lai stated that the background materials must be destroyed, "otherwise they would have serious consequences for one's posterity."[29] The radical leaders around Mao were aware of the students' sensitivity and were eager for student support to carry out an induced conflict, so they ordered the destruction of student dossiers on October 5, 1966.[30] The students, however, did not trust the Party authorities. They took the matter into their own hands; a group of them raided the Shanghai Party headquarters to search for the dossiers, which they failed to find. Subsequently they demanded that the authorities hand them over. The demands were refused and radicals throughout the city staged simultaneous hunger strikes.[31] Similar incidents apparently occurred elsewhere, since the subject was repeatedly discussed by student representatives and the national leaders in Peking.[32] The numerous clashes between students and local authorities over the dossiers led the national leaders to issue a supplementary ruling on November 16 which reiterated the October order to destroy the dossiers compiled by the work teams. The order specifically forbade physical violence, on either side, as a means of settling the matter.[33]

The student group which most accurately expressed the purpose of the revolt against the system created by the Communist Party after 1949 was known as *Shen-wu-lien* ("The Great Union of Hunan Proletarian Revolutionaries"). It was formed in October 1967 and composed of some 20 groups in Hunan province. During its brief existence (it was outlawed by Party authorities as "counterrevolutionary" in January 1968), *Shen-wu-lien* published three penetrating analyses of Chinese politics: "Our Program," "On Some Problems of the Great Proletarian Cultural Revolution in Hunan" and "Whither China?" These documents, especially "Whither China?," dealt with (1) the nature of the existing political system in China; (2) the nature of the Cultural Revolution; (3) the nature of the masses in the Cultural Revolution; and (4) a program for the total restructuring of Chinese society and politics.[34]

Shen-wu-lien quoted Lenin's 1923 statement that

our state apparatus is to a considerable extent a survival of the past and has undergone hardly any serious change. It has only been slightly touched upon the surface, but in all other respects it is a most typical relic of our old state machine.[35]

Shen-wu-lien believed ninety percent of the senior cadres had become a special class, the "Red capitalists." Their relationship with the people created class distinctions between the ruler and the ruled, the exploiter and the exploited and the oppressor and the oppressed. *Shen-wu-lien* regarded Chou En-lai as "the chief representative of China's 'Red capitalist' class," responsible for setting up the revolutionary committees in the provinces to reestablish the rule of this new class. *Shen-wu-lien* also believed that part of the army had changed allegiance to become "a tool of suppressing revolution."

According to *Shen-wu-lien*, the Cultural Revolution should have been instigated for "the overthrow of the rule of this new bureaucratic class, thorough destruction of the old state machine so as to realize social revolution, a redistribution of power and assets and [to] establish a new society—Chinese People's Commune."[36] *Shen-wu-lien* stated that the Cultural Revolution was near its goal twice in 1967, once during the "power seizure" movement in January and again in the "weapons seizure" movement in August. The "weapons seizure" logically followed the "power seizure," since the "January revolution" did not touch the "critical question of all revolutions—the army." Both movements sought to "redistribute power and assets," yet they failed, according to *Shen-wu-lien*, because of Mao's policy of "reformism." In the end,

the political power structure . . . changed superficially. The old provincial Party Committees and provincial Military Districts have been changed into "Revolutionary Committees" or "Revolutionary Preparatory Groups." Old bureaucrats are still managing "the new political power." The contradiction between the broad masses on the one side and the old Provincial Party Committees and Military Districts on the other has not been basically solved. The contradiction between the people and the new bureaucratic class has remained; it is now manifested in the contradiction between the new bureaucratic class and *Shen-wu-lien.*[37]

The failure of the two revolutionary movements, says *Shen-wu-lien*, performed a positive function, since it convinced the youths that reformism would not suffice—ultimately the people would destroy the revolutionary committees. Furthermore, *Shen-wu-lien* reported that it had acquired new allies since September 1967—the contract laborers "who had deep understanding of China's social contradictions, thus compensating intellectual youths' deficiency of not fully understanding social contradictions."[38]

Shen-wu-lien also produced a penetrating analysis of its followers and the public at large which indicated that the masses were only interested in changing their personal status. Mass criticism was thus limited to the exposure of individual faults and seldom touched the class origins of reaction and the "bureaucratic machine serving reaction." The response of the masses was merely spontaneous and sensory, lacking the guidance of a revolutionary theory. At the same time opportunism was widespread even among revolutionaries:

> The bourgeois headquarters in the Provincial Revolutionary Preparatory Group has resorted to the dual policy of buying off [the masses] and suppression [of the masses] and has achieved illustrious success in buying off. Opportunism has spread among class ranks and become a dangerous illness. . . . The split in the revolutionary camp has never been so deep as it is today.[39]

The ultimate goal of *Shen-wu-lien* was utopian—"to establish a new society without bureaucrats like the Paris Commune: Chinese People's Commune." But it also declared that the group intended "overthrowing the new bureaucratic class, reducing the three differences [i.e., the differences between city and the countryside, workers and peasants and mental and manual laborers] and establishing a political party for the 'ultra-left.'"

On January 24, 1968, the leaders of the Central Cultural Revolution Group declared *Shen-wu-lien* counterrevolutionary and ordered its immediate dissolution. Kang Shen, a specialist in intelligence work and a member of the Cultural Revolution Group, voiced the concerns of the leaders: "The theory of *Shen-wu-lien* is not the work of a high school student, not even a college student. There must be a counterrevolutionary black hand behind it."[40] The concerted effort made by the national leaders to discredit *Shen-wu-lien* included a mass meeting of one hundred thousand men in Changsha (capital of Hunan) on January 26, 1968.

The Red Guard publications which condemned *Shen-wu-lien* asserted that its leadership consisted of five disgruntled former Party officials of senior rank, two of their children, one apprentice worker in a film studio and a college student.[41] The organizer of *Shen-wu-lien* was reported to be a student in the Department of Electrical Engineering at Hunan University. Most *Shen-wu-lien* documents were supposedly written by an official who was the Party representative in the Provincial

Bureau of Agriculture and Land Reclamation *(Nung k'en chu)* in Hunan prior to the Cultural Revolution—in other words, a man who had access to large numbers of displaced youths and unemployed workers sent to rural areas to set up new farms. Furthermore, the official's wife was reportedly a former deputy director of the Hunan Federation of Trade Unions (she committed suicide later).[42] *Shen-wu-lien* claimed that it had acquired allies among underprivileged workers. In other documents, *Shen-wu-lien* mentioned contacts with youths who resettled in the countryside.[43] The politics of these displaced people will be discussed later, but the potential for the mobilization of these groups must have influenced the official decision to dissolve *Shen-wu-lien* and the mass campaign to discredit it which followed.

Shen-wu-lien was not, however, an isolated, provincial movement, since it had natural allies who shared its sense of alienation. In Kwangtung the group named "August 5 Commune" *(Pa-wu kung-she)* made pronouncements which closely corresponded to those of *Shen-wu-lien*, attacking the army, the revolutionary committee and championing the cause of underprivileged groups (e.g., youths in the countryside and transient workers).[44] In Heilunkiang, the "Red Rebel Corps" echoed *Shen-wu-lien* in its attack on the army and the Provincial Revolutionary Committee.[45]

The statements by *Shen-wu-lien* testify to the rebellion by Chinese youth against regimentation and to the fragile identity bought with "oversystematized thoughts and overvalued words" which is conducive to the solution of identity crisis.[46] Those statements rebut the view that "the indoctrinated individual of another era or country may feel quite at peace and quite free and productive in his ideological captivity."[47] That sense of peace and freedom is quite artificial, as the behavior of indoctrinated youth in China has shown. It was soon shed, once the conditions of ideological captivity disappeared. Once such a group is rid of ideological constraints the result is rage and violence because the identity they thought they had disappears. Dai Hsiao-ai puts it bluntly: "I had concluded that China's Communist society was a lie. It wasn't the injustice so much as it was the way that the leaders denied its existence and instituted policies which made the injustices worse."[48] In the Cultural Revolution, students and youths in China sought to regain a sense of identity by resorting to factionalism and violence which paradoxically were sanctioned by the new political culture.

The behavior of students during the Cultural Revolution cannot be entirely explained by reference to the universal patterns of behavior assumed in the study of adolescent psychology.[49] The actions of Chinese youths between 1966 and 1968 clearly indicate that they found certain aspects of the existing sociopolitical order intolerable.

Social Status & Student Activism

It has already been shown that political institutions in China directed Chinese youth toward certain objectives. Their behavior was also influenced by the social status of individual students from 1966 to 1968. In particular, student politics reflects (1) the importance of class; (2) the rising prominence of young women in politics; and (3) the importance of career considerations.

The reduction of regimentation and the disappearance of nationalized associations like the Young Communist League bared class divisions in Chinese society. There were two elite groups, both were of the so-called five kinds of red (i.e., children of workers, poor and lower-middle peasants, the revolutionary cadres, army personnel and martyrs). One group comprised of children of high ranking civil and military officials (an elite within an elite) almost entirely controlled the first Red Guard organizations. They organized the so-called United Action Committee composed of "mostly sons and daughters of the members of the CCP Central Committee, the State Council, the NPC [National People's Congress], the PLA [People's Liberation Army], the CCP Central Committee Military Affairs Commission, and the National Defense Ministry, and those who are related to them."[50] It is interesting to note that this young elite belonged to the new aristocracy in every way, yet the members still identified themselves as genuine rebels. The actions of this young elite in the Cultural Revolution stemmed directly from their high social status. They established the ascriptive and exclusionist criteria which limited membership of the initial Red Guards to "five kinds of red." Their slogan expresses a class arrogance: "If your father was a reactionary, you're no good; if your father was a revolutionary, you're automatically a good fellow." At the beginning of the Cultural Revolution their actions reflected their past behavior—they took control of the movement. There was no doubt in their mind that they were a superior breed. Liu Shao-ch'i's daughter admitted that she and other offspring of high ranking Party and state officials socialized among themselves and were "alienated from the masses."[51] They acted as assistants to the "work teams" and after the teams were withdrawn and the students from genuinely lower class background rebelled, the young aristocrats quickly organized to defend their class interests. Some of them went to the special prep schools in Peking and agitated their younger brothers and sisters to defend their status. The daughter of the chairman of the Federation of Trade Unions told the students of the high school attached to Ts'inghua University that "at Ts'inghua, some said that in the new revolutionary committee, the seats for the children of cadres will be limited to two." The student body was instantly aroused and Red Guards from this school stormed onto the campus of Ts'inghua.[52] This group's ascriptive ideology was finally repudiated by the radical leaders around Mao and the young elites openly rebelled against the national leaders in Peking. Their slogans were frank: "Down with the Cultural Revolution Group of the Party Central Committee!" "Long Live Liu Shao-ch'i!" "Let the Children of Revolutionary Cadres and Revolutionary Armymen in the Whole City Unite!" The mentality of this youthful elite was revealed in a letter written by a member of the United Action Committee:

> Since most of the United Action Committee members are from the families of top-ranking officials, they are all bright, highly intellectual, and politically oriented. On the other hand, Chiang Ch'ing's intellectual level is very low. To begin with she is still under the influence of bourgeois ideology.[53]

The violent actions of these young aristocrats resulted in their arrest and Mao finally ordered their release in April 1967.[54]

The elite status of the second group was more apparent than real. They were the children of "revolutionary martyrs" and true proletarians. This group of students came into conflict in Peking and the provincial capitals with the aristocrats who were proletariat in name only. Ken Ling provides a very telling example of this conflict. While in Peking in the autumn of 1966, he and his colleagues visited a special school "for children of Peking high ranking cadres, where only children of persons above and including the civilian rank of bureau director or department head and the military rank of general were permitted to attend." The school was "for the children of 'limousine class' cadres." Ken Ling reports,

> We discovered that the Red Guards in this school had been split into two factions. The majority faction, composed entirely of the children of ministers, generals and other prominent officials, has been responsible for torturing the teachers. Now that their fathers were exposed to struggle, they were in an increasingly dangerous position and no longer had anyone to shield them.
>
> Their opponents, the minority faction called the 5–16 Red Guards, had been the underdogs of the school—mostly orphans, the children of "revolutionary martyrs," who received financial support from the Ministry of National Defense. . . . Every Saturday afternoon they had stayed behind at school while limousines entered the school grounds to take their schoolmates home for the weekend. "That's why they built the school gate so wide. To accommodate the big cars," one of the reception personnel said bitterly.[55]

A similar division among the "five kinds of red" also occurred in Amoy. There, the "General Headquarters" was dominated by students of military and cadre parentage and headed by the daughter of the Municipal Party Secretary. The children of the "true proletariat" joined other Red Guard groups.[56] At the Shanghai Foreign Languages Institute, the same class division among students was reported by Neale Hunter. The small group of radicals were of proletarian origin. The children of cadres were organized by their parents into a different group.[57] Dai Hsiao-ai was of true proletarian origin and he opposed the ascriptive ideology espoused by the young elites in Peking.[58]

Youths of true proletarian backgrounds must have experienced multiple contradictions in their lives. They received some preferential treatment from the government after 1949, especially in educational opportunities, yet they remained lower class when compared to the children of Party and state officials. The social status of the proletarian children was supposed to be higher than that of the city youth from middle-class families. Children of proletariat families were, however, intellectually inferior to most middle-class students in their midst. The offspring of true proletariats must have felt a strong sense of "relative deprivation." According to Dai Hsiao-ai, these students were quite resentful of not being given equal access to higher institutions.[59] While in school, they sometimes were ashamed at not being able to keep up.[60] They became the real radicals in the Cultural Revolution and were, in a sense, a rootless group, since their education set them apart from their parents' generation and status.[61] They found it also difficult to attach themselves to their benefactors, the local Party authorities, who were more interested in elevating their own class status than actively promoting the interest of the proletariat. In the meantime the official status of the proletariat children set them apart from middle-class students. It was the proletariat students who probably gave the youth movement in the Cultural Revolution its adolescent characteristics, i.e., fickleness, violence and ambivalence toward authority (rebellion against local authorities but obedience to national authorities). Accounts by Dai Hsiao-ai, Ken Ling and Neale Hunter agree that the radicals were newly educated youth of working class and peasant backgrounds.

Very little is known about the youth of the old middle class in China. They did not seem to have a strong group consciousness. Hunter, however, mentions that middle-class students at the Shanghai Foreign Languages Institute were conservatives at first, who rallied around the school and Party authorities.[62] Most probably the lack of strong group identity among this class of students was due to the ambivalent policy of the Communist Party toward the offspring of former bourgeoisie. The Party's official ambivalence was epitomized in the statement often quoted during the Cultural Revolution: "One's class background is of basic but not total importance; political deeds must be emphasized too." The ambivalence toward middle-class youngsters was reflected in the inconsistency of Chinese leaders in assessing the class composition of students at Ts'inghua University. On June 15, 1966, T'ao Chu stated that only forty percent of the students at Ts'inghua were of "true proletarian" origin and the rest were of "exploiting class" backgrounds. On August 5 Chou En-lai spoke at Ts'inghua University and stated that "the majority of students at Ts'inghua are young and a very large number of them are of workers' background."[63] This inconsistency, calculated or not, must have made some middle-class students conservative in the hope that their "political deeds" would overcome their origins. Many of them probably became "adapters" like Ken Ling, for example, whose first reaction to the Cultural Revolution was private and opportunistic. He decided to join the attack on the teachers in June 1966 because "if I was to enter the university, I needed 'political capital,' which I could acquire only by disregarding my conscience."[64]

The Cultural Revolution brought the political activism of young women in China to the forefront for the first time since 1949. The first wall poster at Peking University was by a young female teaching assistant named Nieh Yuan-t'ze. Under the influence of either Nieh or Mao's wife, Chiang Ch'ing, young women suddenly assumed leadership roles in the student movement between 1966 and 1968. At Ken Ling's school—the Amoy Eighth Middle School—the chairman and the deputy chairman were both women. The deputy came from "a mason's family and often boasted that for three generations her family had never had a roof over their heads." The chairman "was twenty years old" and "had not yet graduated."[65] The Red Guard organization sponsored by the Municipal Party Committee in Amoy was headed by the daughter of the Party secretary. The leader of "Amoy University Red Guard General Headquarters" was a woman.[66] The opening speech at the first citywide Red Guard rally in Amoy was delivered by a woman.[67] And Dai Hsiao-ai recalled that in the first "link-up" attempt between the students from his school and the workers in a nearby factory, half of the student contingent were female.[68] In Haifeng county, the daughter of the county Party secretary boldly counterattacked those who criticized her father in wall posters.[69] According to Ken Ling, many of the girls in his school "had stepped outside the school gates for the first time during the Cultural Revolution and become coarse and wild."[70]

What accounts for the sudden rise of women's political activism between 1966 and 1968? In retrospect, the mental characteristics and behavior of young women in China were similar to those exhibited by the offspring of the true proletariat described earlier. Like the latter, young women in China were subjected to "rank disequilibrium" after 1949. They were mobilized by the Communist Party to assume activist roles in politics but their real opportunities in the new roles were limited. Latent activism among young female students began to surface in 1957. The most prominent student leader in the "Hundred Flowers" movement was a woman, twenty-one-year-old Lin Hsi-lin, of China's People's University.[71] The Cultural Revolution upset many social norms and the young women of China rose in rebellion, led by Chiang Ch'ing and Nieh Yuan-t'ze. Ken Ling and Ma Sitson both testified that female Red Guards did not avert violence. Lewis Coser's observation that "in revolutionary violence women and the young play a very pronounced role" was borne out in the Cultural Revolution. Coser suggests

> . . . that situations of normlessness differ significantly from the normatively structured situations. . . . In the latter case women, having internalized the acceptance of their lower status, tend to experience relatively low relative deprivation. The matter is quite different, however, when normative restraints and traditional expectations have been shattered . . . the revolution turns absolute deprivation into relative deprivation by raising the hopes of the underdogs in the sex hierarchy. Moreover, and perhaps above all, a revolutionary situation provides the occasion for women to indeed act like men. It offers opportunities for the assertion of equality which were previously unavailable.[72]

In addition to social class and sex, the third most important factor which accounts for the different degree of student activism in the Cultural Revolution was career considerations. The frustration over limited career opportunities must have influenced the conspicuous activism of students from specialized schools and those in the fields of science and technology. Their activism was manifested in a readiness to revolt, their participation in factional conflicts and by the extent of movement to other areas. The first alliance of Red Guards in Peking, for example, was formed and led by a student from Peking Technical University *(Kung-yeh Ta-hsueh)*.[73] In Kwangtung, the first student to contact Peking and challenge the provincial Party authority was from South China Technical College.[74] The first Red Guard leader to organize the "power seizure" movement in Canton was a student in the Department of Physics at Chungshan University.[75] The celebrated "Wuhan Incident" which involved a direct clash between the regional authorities and the leaders of the Cultural Revolution Group found Red Guards from specialized schools playing a prominent role on the side of the Cultural Revolution Group. Specifically those Red Guards were students from Central China Technical College *(Hua Chung Kung Hsueh Yuan)*, Central China Agricultural College *(Hua Chung Nung Hsueh Yuan)*, Wuhan Measurement and Draft College *(Wuhan Tse-hui Hsueh Yuan)* and Central China Agricultural School *(Hua Chung Nung Hsueh)*.[76]

The leader of the *Shen-wu-lien* group was a student in electrical engineering.

The two most prominent Red Guard groups involved in the "link-up" movement were associated with the Peking College of Aviation Red Flag *(Pei Hang Hung Ch'i)* and the Harbin Military Engineering College *(Ha-chun-kung)*. These two schools were highly specialized and they were closely associated with the military bureaucracy. Thus it can be inferred that students of these two schools were from correct class backgrounds with a natural sense of legitimacy. Peking College of Aviation was reported to be under the direct supervision of the Military Affairs Commission of the Party Central Committee.[77] Harbin Military Engineering College, in Chou En-lai's own words, is "under the charge of the National Defense Science Committee." Chou candidly described the reactions of members of this school in 1968, following the new alliance ordered by the Party leaders:

> *Ha-chun-kung* (Harbin Military Engineering College) which gave a proud performance during the initial period of rebellion, formed an alliance recently and lost two thirds of its members after their return home. . . . This is bourgeois oscillation.[78]

The most revealing correlation between the career frustration of students and attendance at specialized schools was shown in the "power seizure" movement in Peking in January 1967. Students from specialized schools attacked the bureaucratic hierarchy of the respective professions. Thus students from the Petroleum College seized the Ministry of Petroleum; students from the Chemical Engineering College attacked the Ministry of Chemical Engineering; students from the Light Industry College seized the First Ministry of Light Industry; students from the Peking Steel College attacked the Ministry of Metallurgy; and students from Dairen Merchant Marine College sought to seize the Ministry of Communications and Transportation.[79]

Most students in the specialized schools and departments were probably of the true proletariat who shared a strong sense of "class righteousness." They doubtless also shared an intense sense of frustration, given their limited job opportunities. Most of the major studies on the Chinese economy have touched on the problem of limited social mobility for young people so it needs no extensive elaboration here. John Emerson, for example, after studying employment in China, concluded: "The inability of the urban economy to provide employment for a rapidly growing urban labor force has proved to be one of the most intractable problems confronting the regime."[80] According to Leo Orleans, "Over 10 million youths enter the labor force ages annually and must be absorbed into the economy. Even during the period of rapid industrial growth, the regime admitted that the cities could not effectively absorb much more than 1 million persons into the urban economy annually."[81] The effect of the lack of employment opportunity on the young Chinese is best shown in "Letters to the Editor" in the journal *China Youth (Chung-kuo Ch'ing-nien)* since 1964 and by the testimony of those who fled China.[82]

The students in technical schools were frustrated because of "anticipatory downward mobility" but the youths who were sent to settle in the countryside and the frontier regions had already been subjected to that fate. Significantly, they contributed to the intensity and violence of group conflict in the Cultural Revolution.

Since 1955, millions of Chinese youths in their late teens have been sent from cities to the countryside, mountainous regions and frontiers.[83] They consist mainly of youths who came from the countryside originally to continue their education in an urban area, yearly graduates of high schools and colleges not qualified to further continue their educations who cannot find gainful employment in the cities and the accumulated group of unemployed city youths.

The psychology of these youths is easy to analyze. They are ashamed at not being able to qualify for higher education or obtain desired jobs. Family ties are still strong in China and some of these youths must have felt guilty for disgracing their families. They also resented the authorities for not giving them a second chance. As if this were not enough, the government handled the problem in a typically bureaucratic manner. In selecting youths to be sent to the countryside, local Party officials were apparently given set quotas to fulfill. In filling their quotas, the officials issued false promises and coerced the parents of the selected youths.[84] Some cadres falsely painted rosy pictures of the villages to which youths were supposed to be sent. Other cadres promised families preferential treatment in the form of extra rations. Still others promised that the youths would eventually be returned to the cities. Chou En-lai, for example, mentioned that T'ao Chu, former director of the Party's Central-South Bureau, agreed to keep the urban residential registration of those youths sent to the countryside.[85] Most of the young people went to rural areas under duress, ashamed of themselves, resentful of authority, and very insecure about their futures.

When these youths arrived at their destinations, they faced a hostile human and natural environment. They were unwanted in the countryside, since they were an economic burden to the villagers, who were mostly quite poor. Besides, the rural cadres and residents entertained antiurban and antiintellectual sentiments which were vented on the unwelcome youths. The government allotted an initial allowance for each youth to cover their expenses in moving to the countryside. These funds were sent first to Party cadres in the countryside to be collected after arrival to ensure that the youths would go to the designated villages. In many cases, village cadres withheld the funds or refused to give the full amounts. The rural cadres frequently underpaid youths from the cities on the grounds that they could request help from their parents. Government officials apparently sought to discourage this kind of discrimination with an urgent notice published on October 8, 1967:

> The personnel assigned to the countryside should be treated politically and economically on an equal basis with the old commune members and old workers and staff members; there must not be any discrimination, any reduction in work-points, any harassment, persecution or attempt to drive them back to cities and towns.[86]

Young women often faced an added problem—coercive overtures from male cadres.[87]

The unwanted and persecuted youth in the countryside were deprived of their urban roots, and soon were ready for a violent revolt. The Cultural Revolution provided the opportunity. The government circular quoted above indicated that many youths were told by rural cadres to return to the cities, presumably in fear the youths would turn on the cadres. But the youths hardly needed persuasion; they took advantage of the "link-up" movement to stream back to the cities in droves. There, they formed organizations with unwieldy titles like "Shanghai Intellectual Youth-Who-Returned-from-the-Mountains-and-Villages Defending Truth" and "National Revolutionary Red Rebel Corps of Youth-Who-Have-Gone-to-the-Mountains-and-Villages." They took their case to the people and their messages reflected their despair. A former Canton resident reported how a large crowd gathered before a wall bulletin written by thirteen such youths:

> Someone read with a low and heavy voice the concluding remarks of the bulletin: "Why are our lives not worth two pennies? Arise ye starvelings from your slumbers. Arise ye suffering people of the whole world!" These two lines are the beginning of the song *Internationale*. But the real meaning of these words now touches people's hearts and finds enthusiastic responses.[88]

The militant factions of the Red Guards responded most enthusiastically to the despair of the returned youths. The response was probably motivated by expediency, because the Red Guards needed allies and fighters to help their "struggle by force." Since the youths returning from the countryside were the most radical group and most ready for violent action, they were wooed by all the factions. The students provided them shelter and food and they then demanded that the Party allow them to stay in the cities permanently. Ken Ling described one such case:

Every year hundreds of thousands of Shanghai youths were forced to don uniforms and join the Liberation Army Sinkiang Production and Construction Corps and serve as peasant soldiers in Sinkiang. After the Cultural Revolution began, these youths used it as an opportunity to return to Shanghai and organize a large force called Shanghai Intellectual Youth-Who-Returned-from-the-Mountains-and-Villages Revolutionary Rebellion-Making General Headquarters. (Later, when we passed through Shanghai on the return trip from Peking, we were to see them encamped in front of the city hall, demanding permission to return permanently to Shanghai and a guarantee of residence registration and jobs.)[89]

Twice in 1967 (on February 17 and October 8) the Party Central Committee issued public decrees ordering youths back to the countryside.[90] According to Chou En-lai, there were more than 30,000 returned youths in cities like Canton, Nanking, Changsha, Wuhan, and Shanghai, but that number dwindled to 10,000 after October 1967.[91] Chou probably understated the number of such youths, but it is apparent that a substantial number ignored the government's orders. The returned youth in Canton effectively opposed the Party authorities by first threatening and later conducting a sit-in demonstration in front of China's trade fair, where hundreds of foreign businessmen visited yearly.

Some of the youths in Shanghai resorted to wishful thinking in desperation, and the strategy of "protracted stay." The *Wen-hui Daily* of Shanghai reported:

Some people may think "that they can get a job in Shanghai or at least go to Kiangsi, Anhwei and other places to take part in agricultural labor if they insistently stay a few years in Shanghai." This is impossible. They must not listen to the rumor started by the handful of class enemies . . . .[92]

Other returnees turned to petty crimes. Some obtained free train tickets from the authorities to return to the frontier of Sinkiang, and "sold tickets and swindled money from parents with children in Sinkiang under the pretext of bringing things . . . to their children."[93] Yet there were sympathetic youth groups and other organizations in the cities willing to shelter the returned students so they lingered. Canton was still grappling with the problem of the returned youth in July 1968. The municipal government accused the youths of

selling weapons to some mass organizations, participating in struggle by force, committing robbery and rape, storming into military compounds and public security offices and prolonged occupation of public offices, factories and schools.[94]

Some youths were finally forced to go back to the countryside and they apparently resorted to passive resistance. This letter of March 12, 1968, from an irate commune member of a suburban village near Shanghai is an example:

> The . . . prevalence of anarchism and laxity of labor discipline is the most outstanding question confronting our Hsinghua Farm. . . . In January last year, besides growing cotton, the farm members basically did nothing. Even if they attended to their work, they came off duty very early. Some youths did not go to work but stayed in their dormitory to sleep and play poker. Some . . . simply went to loiter about in the city and stayed there for a long time. At present, this situation hasn't changed much. The water conservation projects, big and small, on the farm are built by contractors and seldom by our own effort.[95]

Meanwhile, the ranks of youths in the countryside and frontier were rapidly replenished and augmented. In late 1967, the government halted the Red Guard movement by resuming the flow of "intellectual youths" to the countryside. The *People's Daily* reported (May 4, 1970) that "several millions of graduates from junior and senior middle schools" had been sent to the countryside in the past year; the number was reported to be four times the number sent from 1961 to 1966. The authorities then decided to answer the pleas of those youths, at least symbolically. Mao issued a directive (May 6, 1970) which forbade rural cadres from forcing girl students into marriage. The directive also banned the withholding of rations and the conduct of struggles against the youths.[96] The isolation of youth in the countryside was alleviated somewhat when the government began organizing officials, schoolteachers and parents into "comforting corps" and "liaison stations" to visit the youths. "Reporting Study Corps" were organized in the countryside and young people went to the cities to report about their life and study in remote areas.[97] Whether these well-intentioned efforts achieved their desired result is a moot point. Chou En-lai made perhaps the most cogent and definitive statement about the whole matter:

> Going to the mountain areas and countryside is an idea of Chairman Mao, whose aim is to direct our attention to the rural areas and to the masses, to change the abnormal and uneven state of the semi-colonial economy, to effect the transition to socialism and then achieve a more balanced development.[98]

Communist China will have to cope with the continuing danger resulting from radical politics of youths sent to the countryside, until Mao's goal is achieved.

Pattern of Conflict

The actions of students and mainland Chinese youths during the Cultural Revolution confirm three concepts relating to group conflict.

First, the events tend to validate Dahrendorf's basic premise that "group conflict is probably most easily accessible to analysis if it be understood as a conflict about the legitimacy of relations of authority."[99] The student rebellion from 1966 to 1968 revolved around the "legitimacy of relations of authority." Most of the radical students' grievances were in response to political regimentation, and they demanded far wider and more meaningful political participation. They demanded changes in communication patterns between the leaders and the youths and also among youths themselves. Specifically, the students wanted less "mediation" in communication. The youths also demanded fundamental administrative reforms and a genuinely egalitarian distribution of goods and services (in the words of *Shen-wu-lien*, a "redistribution of assets and power").

Second, the reactions of Chinese youth conformed to the five sources of group conflict elaborated by Oberschall, i.e., (1) dislocations resulting from processes of social change; (2) resistance to change on the part of those who benefit from a status quo; (3) the entrenchment of new vested interests; (4) gaps between ideals and reality; and (5) the dilemma of social organizations which results from an inability to achieve simultaneously incompatible values and goals.[100] The first source of conflict was exemplified in the reactions of the children of the true proletariat and students sent to the countryside. The second and third sources of group conflict were apparent in the behavior of the "young aristocrats" in Peking and elsewhere, i.e., the offspring of high ranking Party and state officials. *Shen-wu-lien* and the young female Red Guards represented student resentment of the gap between ideals and reality. Finally, the dilemma of a society trying to achieve contradictory goals was seen in the Communist Party's ambivalence toward middle-class students and youth from working class and poor peasant backgrounds.

The actions taken by youth during the Cultural Revolution eloquently validate the observation that there are many uninstitutionalized conflicts hidden under Communist China's centralized system. There is likely to be a chronic recurrence of unsettled issues. The actions taken by the students between 1966 and 1968 almost completely repeated student activities in the "Hundred Flowers" campaign of 1957, except for the breakdown of social control and nationwide waves of violence. The formation of small groups with fancy names, publication of tabloids, "link-up" trips ("light fires" in 1957), petitions to higher authorities, the seizure of news media and demands for the destruction of personal dossiers were all present in 1957.[101] The penetrating social criticism of *Shen-wu-lien* during 1968 was preceded by Lin Hsi-lin's public speeches in 1957.[102] The activism of students in science and technology was also conspicuous in 1957.[103] Even the methods used by local authorities to resist students from 1966 to 1968, i.e., the organization of workers and peasants to coerce students, were first used in 1957. The Cultural Revolution was unique only in the appearance of new conflict groups, e.g., those formed by students returned from the countryside and the alliance between students and radical workers. "Authoritarian regimes," says Oberschall, "are more likely to minimize, ignore, and suppress their shortcomings. Thus problems become magnified over time."[104]

Notes

1.   Rene Goldman, "Peking University Today," *The China Quarterly*, July–September 1961.

2.   NCNA, April 24, 1967, as in *Survey of China Mainland Press* (Hong Kong: U.S. Consulate General), No. 3927, pp. 25–26 (hereafter cited as SCMP).

3.   The remarks on adolescent psychology are all from Erik H. Erikson, *Childhood & Society* (New York, 1963), particularly pp. 261–263.

4.   Erik H. Erikson, *Young Man Luther. A Study in Psychoanalysis and History* (New York, 1962), pp. 111–112.

5.   Gordon A. Bennett and Ronald N. Montaperto, *Red Guard: The Political Biography of Dai Hsiao-ai* (Garden City, N.Y., 1972), p. 39.

6.   Ken Ling, *The Revenge of Heaven: Journal of a Young Chinese* (New York, 1972), pp. 32–33.

7.   Ibid., p. 100.

8.   This is revealed in the statement by Liu Shao-ch'i's daughter in her self-criticism of February 1967; see the entire text in *Liu Shao-ch'i Wen-ti Tze-liao Ch'uan-ch'i* [A Special Collection of Materials on Liu Shao-ch'i] (Taipei, 1970), p. 418 (hereafter cited by English title).

9.   Dai Hsiao-ai, for example, reports that communication with other students elsewhere in the city was the reason why he and other students began to question the authority of the school principal; see Bennett and Montaperto, *Red Guard*, p. 41. Hunter also reports about the students of Futan University in Shanghai who broke into the Drama Academy "to make liaison," in Neale Hunter, *Shanghai Journal: An Eyewitness Account of the Cultural Revolution* (Boston, 1969), p. 85.

10. Hai Feng, *Haifeng Wen-hua Ke-ming Kai-shu* [A General Account of the Cultural Revolution in Haifeng County] (Hong Kong, 1969), pp. 33–34 (hereafter cited by English title).

11. Bennett and Montaperto, *Red Guard*, p. 5.

12. Victor Nee and Don Layman, *The Cultural Revolution at Peking University* (New York, 1969), pp. 58–59.

13. From Reuters correspondent in Peking as quoted in Nee and Layman, *Cultural Revolution at Peking University*, p. 59.

14. Bennett and Montaperto, *Red Guard*, p. 18.

15. Lucy Jen Huang Hickrod and G. Alan Hickrod, "The Communist Chinese and the American Adolescent Sub-culture," *The China Quarterly*, April–June 1965.

16. Erikson, *Young Man Luther*, p. 134.

17. Robert J. Lifton, *Thought Reform and the Psychology of Totalism. A Study of "Brainwashing" in China* (New York, 1969), p. 421.

18. Ibid., p. 411.

19. The text of Mao's speech is reproduced in *Yi-chiu Ch'i-lin Chung-kung-nien-pao* [1970 Yearbook on Chinese Communism], Vol. 2 (Taipei, 1971), pp. VII:46–49.

20. *Red Guard Publications* (Association of Research Libraries), Group VI-1 (hereafter cited as RGP). The publication reproduced Li Fu-ch'un's speech to the officers of the League on August 15, 1966.

21. See Ken Ling, *Revenge of Heaven*, pp. 28–30; Hunter, *Shanghai Journal*, pp. 34–37; Hai Feng, *General Account of the Cultural Revolution in Haifeng*, pp. 44–45.

22. Paul Kecskemeti, *The Unexpected Revolution* (Stanford, Calif., 1961), pp. 107, 111.

23. Hunter, *Shanghai Journal*, p. 135.

24. Chou's talk with the delegates from three northeastern provinces on September 28, 1967, in RGP, Group X-1; also in Chao Tsung, "An Account of the 'Great Proletarian Cultural Revolution,'" (Part 58), *Tsukuo* [China Monthly], No. 104 (November 1, 1972), p. 32.

25. *Ch'iu Peng Lo Chan-pao*, March 1968, in RGP, Group XI-2.

26. *Sankei* (Tokyo), September 20, 1967.

27. *Chinese Sociology and Anthropology*, Vol. 2, No. 3-4 (Spring–Summer 1970), p. 131.

28. Nee and Layman, *Cultural Revolution at Peking University*, pp. 58–59.

29. *Hung-t'ieh-tao*, February 11, 1967, in RGP, Group VII-1.

30. For the text of this order, see *Chung-kung Wen-hua Ta-ke-ming Chung-yao Wen-chien Hui-pien* [Important CCP Documents of the Great Prole-

tarian Cultural Revolution] (Taipei, 1973), pp. 59–60 (hereafter cited by English title).

31. Hunter, *Shanghai Journal*, p. 120.

32. See Chou En-lai's statements on October 22, 1966, while receiving the representatives of 18 colleges and special schools in RGP, Group VI-1, and Ch'i Peng-yu's talk with the Second Headquarters of Peking College Red Guards on December 20, 1966, in *Tung-fang-hung*, December 20, 1966, in RGP, Group VII-1.

33. *Important CCP Documents of the Great Proletarian Cultural Revolution*, pp. 34–35.

34. My account of this group is based on the five sections of documents on *Shen-wu-lien* printed in *Tsukuo*, No. 83 (February 1, 1971), No. 84 (March 1, 1971), No. 85 (April 1, 1971), No. 86 (May 1, 1971), and No. 87 (June 1, 1971). For English translations of these documents, see SCMP, No. 4136, pp. 15–17, and No. 4174; see also *Chinese Law and Government*, Vol. 3, No. 4 (Winter 1970–1971), pp. 315–347.

35. For Lenin's original statement, see *Lenin: Selected Works*, Vol. 3 (New York, 1967), p. 769.

36. *Tsukuo*, No. 87 (June 1, 1971), p. 39.

37. Ibid.

38. Ibid., No. 86 (May 1, 1971), p. 46.

39. Ibid., No. 84 (March 1, 1971), p. 40.

40. Ibid., p. 41.

41. Ibid., pp. 45–46.

42. Ibid., p. 41.

43. Ibid., No. 86 (May 1, 1971), p. 42.

44. Hai Feng, *General Account of the Cultural Revolution in Haifeng*, pp. 329–332.

45. "Dark Clouds Rolling Over Heilunkiang," *Tsukuo*, No. 81 (December 1, 1970), pp. 41–42 (Chinese text).

46. Erikson, *Young Man Luther*, pp. 134–135.

47. Ibid., p. 135.

48. Bennett and Montaperto, *Red Guard*, pp. 218, 208.

49. For such an approach, see David Raddock, "Innocents in Limbo: China's Youths Recall," *Current Scene*, Vol. 10, No. 6 (June 10, 1972), pp. 12–16.

50. *Sankei* (Tokyo), October 7, 1967.

51. *A Special Collection of Materials on Liu Shao-ch'i*, pp. 417–429.

52. *Ts'inghua Ta-hsueh Ta-tze-pao Hsun-pien* [A Collection of Posters at Ts'inghua University], October 10, 1966, in RGP, Group VI-1.

53. *Tsukuo*, No. 84 (March 1, 1971), pp. 45–46.

54. *Chieh-fang Chuan-jen-jui*, May 29, 1967, in RGP, Group IX-1.

55. Ken Ling, *Revenge of Heaven*, p. 187.

56. Ibid., p. 65.

57. Hunter, *Shanghai Journal*, pp. 72, 114–115.

58. Bennett and Montaperto, *Red Guard*, p. 126.

59. Ibid., p. 127.

60. Hunter, *Shanghai Journal*, pp. 56–57.

61. In a speech in 1966, T'ao Chu, who briefly was the director of the Propaganda Department of Party Central Committee that year, stated that "originally some children from the countryside were quite good but once they acquired junior or senior high school education, they did not want to stay in the countryside anymore; needless to say, those who had gone to the university were even worse." See Hai Feng, *Kuang-chou Ti-ch'u Wen-ke Lieh-chen Shu-lueh* [An Account of the Cultural Revolution in the Canton Area] (Hong Kong, 1971), p. 13 (hereafter cited by English title).

62. Hunter, *Shanghai Journal*, p. 114.

63. RGP, Group VI-1.

64. Ken Ling, *Revenge of Heaven*, p. 17.

65. Ibid., pp. 40, 18.

66. Ibid., pp. 65, 237.

67. Ibid., p. 38.

68. Bennett and Montaperto, *Red Guard*, p. 54.

69. Hai Feng, *General Account of the Cultural Revolution in Haifeng*, p. 17. Note that another book by Hai Feng, *Account of the Cultural Revolution in Canton*, unmistakably showed the prominence of girls in the Red Guard movement in the pictures inside the cover.

70. Ken Ling, *Revenge of Heaven*, p. 146.

71. Dennis J. Doolin, *Communist China: The Politics of Student Opposition* (Stanford, Calif., 1964), pp. 14–15.

72. Lewis A. Coser, *Continuities in the Study of Social Conflict* (New York, 1967), pp. 69–70.

73. *Hung-wei-ping* (Peking), No. 11 (November 25, 1966).

74. Hai Feng, *Account of the Cultural Revolution in Canton*, pp. 30–31.

75. Ibid., pp. 55, 76–81.

76. *Yi-chiu Liu-pa Chung-kung-nien-pao* [1968 Yearbook on Chinese Communism] (Taipei, 1969), p. 351 (hereafter cited by English title).

77. Wang Hsueh-wen, *Chung-kung Wen-hua Ta-ke-ming Yu Hung wei-ping* [The Chinese Communist Cultural Revolution and the Red Guards] (Taipei, 1969), p. 554.

78. *Hsiao-ping* (Canton), No. 22 (February 17, 1968), trans. in SCMP, No. 4134, p. 1.

79. *Chi-tien Chan-pao* (Peking), February 12, 1967; February 28, 1967.

80. John Philip Emerson, "Employment in Mainland China: Problems and Prospects," in *An Economic Profile of Mainland China.* Studies prepared for the Joint Economic Committee, U.S. Congress, Vol. 2 (February 1967), pp. 458–459.

81. Leo A. Orleans, "Communist China's Education: Policies, Problems, and Prospects," in *Economic Profile of Mainland China*, p. 515.

82. Tung Chi-ping and Humphrey Evans, *The Thought Revolution* (New York, 1966).

83. For a comprehensive and perceptive discussion of this problem, see Pi-chao Chen, "Overurbanization, Rustication of Urban-Educated Youths, and Politics of Rural Transformation," *Comparative Politics*, April 1972, and "The Political Economics of Population Growth: The Case of China," *World Politics*, Vol. 23, No. 2 (January 1971). Reports about the total number of youths sent to the countryside are extremely inconsistent. The highest figure is given by the Youth League paper *Chung-kuo Ch'ing-nien Pao* (December 9, 1964), which reports that 40 million youths were sent to the countryside. Yet an NCNA report (September 25, 1966) gives the total number of over a million "intellectual youths" sent to the countryside from 1962 to 1966. The usually reliable *Current Scene* cites a Chinese press report which stated that the 1955–1965 total was about one million persons, Vol. 7, No. 18 (September 15, 1969).

84. See the case of an 18-year-old girl who died in mysterious surroundings as reported by a Red Guard newspaper translated in *Chinese Sociology and Anthropology*, Vol. 2, No. 3–4 (Spring–Summer 1970), pp. 140–148.

85. Chou's speech to the representatives of Canton rebel groups in Peking on November 14, 1967, repr. in Hai Feng, *Account of the Cultural Revolution in Canton*, p. 287.

86. *CCP Documents of the Great Proletarian Cultural Revolution, 1966–1967* (Hong Kong, 1968), pp. 561–562 (hereafter cited as *CCP Documents*); see also the story of an overseas Chinese youth in *Chi-nung Hung-ch'i*, No. 2 (October 7, 1967), trans. in SCMP, No. 4067, pp. 12–13.

87. The Central Committee issued a directive on May 6, 1970, forbidding "compulsory marriage" forced on girl students sent to the countryside by rural cadres; see Shu Huei, "New Crisis and New Trend of the CCP's 'Send-down' Movement of Young Intellectuals," *Chung-kung Yen-chiu* [Study on Chinese Communism], Vol. 4, No. 11 (November 10, 1970), p. 25.

88. Hai Feng, *Account of the Cultural Revolution in Canton*, p. 53.

89. Ken Ling, *Revenge of Heaven*, pp. 127–128.

90. *CCP Documents*, pp. 301–302, 560–563.

91. Chou's talk is reprinted in Hai Feng, *Account of the Cultural Revolution in Canton*, p. 287.

92. Ibid., p. 381.

93. *Wen-hui Pao*, February 25, 1968; trans. from SCMP, No. 4146, p. 16.

94. Ibid.

95. Original document reprinted in "A Selection of Recent 'Notices' of CCP Central Committee and Kwangtung Province," *Tsukuo*, No. 55 (October 1, 1968), p. 37.

96. *Wen-hui Pao*, March 12, 1968; trans. from SCMP, No. 4153, p. 13.

97. Shu Huei, "CCP's 'Send-down' Movement," p. 25.

98. Shu Huei, "Send-down Work of Chinese Youth," *Chung-kung Yen-chiu*, Vol. 6, No. 3 (March 10, 1972), pp. 25–26.

99. Ralf Dahrendorf, *Class and Class Conflict in Industrial Society* (Stanford, Calif., 1959), p. 176.

100. Anthony Oberschall, *Social Conflict and Social Movements* (Englewood Cliffs, N.J., 1973), p. 36.

101. See Roderick MacFarquhar, *The Hundred Flowers Campaign and the Chinese Intellectuals* (New York, 1960), pp. 135–163; Chin Chien-li, *Pei-kuo Chien-wen-lu* [Odyssey in North China] (Hong Kong, 1973), pp. 422–438.

102. Doolin, *Communist China*.

103. Rene Goldman, "The Rectification Campaign at Peking University: May–June, 1957," *The China Quarterly*, October–December 1967, p. 150.

104. Oberschall, *Social Conflict*, p. 70.

6

WORKERS & PEASANTS

The reactions of the Chinese working class to the Cultural Revolution showed a standard pattern and some significant deviations. The standard pattern of worker behavior conformed to Lipset's concept of "working-class authoritarianism." According to Lipset, the working classes emphasize immediate problems and are concerned with personal and concrete goals. They are less likely to participate in political activities than the middle classes; "antiintellectualism" is strong among the working classes, and they tend to be more liberal (or leftist) on economic than political issues. The political orientation of the working classes is rigid and intolerant. Ordinarily the working classes are capable of diffuse and strong commitments to an organization but in time of distress, especially when they suffer severe deprivations, they are prone to respond to chiliastic social movements.[1]

The Cultural Revolution occurred when there was no major economic crisis in China, certainly not in the urban areas. Thus most Chinese workers were initially unenthusiastic about the Red Guards and the struggle against a "capitalist restoration" in China. Students went to the factories to link up with workers but the results were limited. Dai Hsiao-ai attributed that failure partly to the lesson of the "Hundred

Flowers" campaign of 1957 and partly to the mentality of workers in general: "A considerable number of workers were nearly illiterate. Others thought first of their families, fearing that their political mistakes might react unfavorably upon their sons' and daughters' future lives." Even the opposition sentiments of the activists mainly concerned personal and concrete matters. According to Dai,

> We saw that there were opposition sentiments among a part of the workers. Some were burdened with family difficulties to which the factory leadership had paid no heed. Some had been working in their unit for many years with little adjustment in wages. In other cases, a worker's wife had formerly worked at Tsangku but at some point was "transferred down" to a rural village; not only did they have to live apart after that, but their standard of living had dropped since only one of them could earn a wage. Still other workers bore a grudge against the warehouse leadership for its bureaucratic style of work, staying always in their office and hardly ever descending into the shops to labor along with the workers.[2]

The workers whose resentments were personalized were mobilized by Dai and others, yet political mobilization in the factories faltered as soon as the students left. Ken Ling, in his characteristically blunt (also bragging) way, said: "On many issues it had become apparent that there was a basic difference between the students and workers—the students wanted power, but the workers wanted money."[3]

As group conflicts widened after August 1966, workers left their normal work and joined in the movement, but their general behavior remained conservative.

By and large, the workers in mainland China responded to parochial issues. Ken Ling reports that after some students desecrated a famous local temple in Amoy, "angry workers from several factories left their jobs and went together to the Amoy University student dormitories wielding clubs and threatening to kill those Red Guards."[4] During the first wave of group violence, discussed in Chapter 4, workers were often mobilized by local Party authorities to surround and attack the Red Guards from outside. In Canton, the first confrontation between workers and Red Guards occurred in December 1966 over the suspension of the local newspaper *Hung-wei Pao*. When news about the seizure of the newspaper spread, the local labor unions mobilized thousands of workers to march toward the newspaper office shouting the slogan "Protect the Leaders of Central-South Bureau, the Party Center and Chairman Mao!"[5] Chairman Mao's opinion of the working class, however, is not entirely complimentary and since he is an experienced mass leader, his views coincide with Lipset's. Mao stated in August 1967:

> The workers, peasants and soldiers did not have direct contacts with the counterrevolutionary revisionists. In addition these counterrevolutionary revisionists waved red flags in their anti-red flag activities. . . . So, they [the workers] are easily deceived. . . . The intellectuals are always a step ahead of workers and peasants though the former are prone to vacillations . . .[6]

The demands of workers were particularistic or, as Lenin put it, the workers showed only a "trade union consciousness." Workers in mainland China joined the rank of rebels after the "power seizure" movement of January 1967. They initiated the so-called wave of economism by demanding and receiving extra pay from factory managers to go on shopping sprees. The workers also developed what the official media called a guild mentality. The workers spontaneously established guilds in Shanghai and elsewhere representing distinct trades and advocating "narrow, selfish economic interests." Only members of the same trade were admitted.[7] These guilds or unions apparently persisted. Chou En-lai spoke to the workers in Canton (September 1967) and mentioned that the "idea of guild" prevailed in the city because of its large number of handicraftsmen. Chou also mentioned that such guilds and workers' factions existed in Tientsin, Peking and Tsingtao.[8] In this connection, a Japanese correspondent made an interesting observation concerning the motivation of activist workers in Wuhan during the July 20 (1967) incident (note he translated the "Heroic Division of One Million" as "One Million Brave Soldiers"):

> The rebels claimed that the "One Million Brave Soldiers" was a mercenary organization. However, no one would have risked his life in a resistance only for the sake of money. I am of the opinion that they probably could not tolerate the social disruption under the cultural revolution and that they feared the possibility of another period of austerity.
>
> Following the failure of the great leap forward policy, workers saw no improvement in their living standard for nearly 10 years. Then came the economic adjustment policy which attached importance to material incentives and adopted an extra quota allowance system. However, the cultural revolution movement deemed this policy "revisionism." A strong antipathy toward the cultural revolution must have been latent in the Wuhan population, including a large number of industrial workers. It may have been that, owing to such antipathy, workers in Wuhan supported the old cadres and stepped up their resolute activities to defend their own organization.[9]

In their numerous and, later, violent clashes with the radical students, workers responded to an antiintellectual bias. Besides physically assaulting the students, they protested the favoritism of national leaders for the students. Chou En-lai told a group of Peking students (September 1967) that "Shanghai criticized us for making contact with and favoring too many students and that we have not done well among workers. This criticism is correct."[10] Chang Ch'ung-ch'iao, leader of the revolutionary committee in Shanghai, reported that "some old workers are dissatisfied, saying that the state has nourished the students for so many years but all they know is fighting civil war."[11] Kang Shen, an intelligence expert in the Party Central Committee, revealed that Chen Tsai-tao, the military commander of the Wuhan District who led the rebellion against the Central Cultural Revolution Group in July 1967, resorted to antiintellectual slogans to mobilize the troops and the worker-dominated "Heroic Division of One Million." Chen reportedly told his men: "The Central Cultural Revolution Group wants only intellectuals and students; they do not want workers and peasants." Chen was brought before the leaders and Red Guards in Peking supposedly to repent but he remained defiant: "I am a crude man; I know only a few characters." Kang also mentioned that such antiintellectual appeals precipitated clashes between students and workers in Szechwan and Honan.[12] Chapter 4 relates that armed and violent clashes between workers and students took place in these two provinces during May 1967.

The notion that workers are not as responsive to ideological polemics as students follows logically from their antiintellectual bias. "It has been the working-class rank and file," says Lipset, "which has been least disturbed by Communism's ideological shifts and least likely to defect."[13] Some evidence suggests that the large and conservative groups of workers that appeared all over China between 1966 and 1968 were less factional than those of the radical students. In Canton, for example, the student-dominated "Flag Faction" *(Ch'i-pai)* included several workers' groups. But the worker-dominated "Headquarters Faction" *(Tsun pai)* was comprised mainly of two large workers' groups, the "Red General Headquarters" *(Hung-tsun)* and the "District Headquarters" *(Ti-tsun)*. The allies of the workers' faction are revealing—the *Chu-yi Pin* (Doctrine Red Guards) was composed mostly of children of senior Party officials and military officers. The "Headquarters Faction" was also allied with the "Alliance of Poor Peasants in the Suburbs." Furthermore, an eyewitness to the factional fights in Canton observed that the worker-dominated "Headquarters Faction" was more unified than the opposing, student-dominated "Flag Faction," which was severely ridden with factional infighting.[14]

Pattern of Activism among Workers

There were different groups of workers in China and though the data are severely limited, some patterns of varying activism among the workers are evident which constitute deviations from the standard pattern.

The discussion of the pattern of violence thus far notes that small groups of radical workers allied themselves with radical students. Those workers were all rebels out to change the system, and so they became the target of attacks from the majority and groups of conservative workers. Information about the radical workers is virtually nonexistent except that most of them were apparently young (as testified by Dai Hsiao-ai) and there were two groups. One group was attached to the printed media, particularly newspapers. The first working-class rebels in Shanghai were employees of the *Wen-hui Daily*,[15] and some employees of the *Canton Daily* were also among the first to join the radical students in the "power seizure" movement.[16] The other group belonged to the movie studios, notably the "East Is Red" group from the Pearl River Film Studio. The employees of this studio responded to the antiestablishment movement almost as soon as the students started it in June 1966. The "East Is Red" group became one of the most radical in Canton,[17] and Dai Hsiao-ai reported similar developments in Shanghai. During his "link-up" trip to Shanghai in December 1966, Dai visited some film studios and wrote:

> The workers had become the masters of the movie studios. One young worker exultantly told the students come to *ch'uan-lien* ("link up") that in the past they had worked very hard to build scenery so the directors and actors could film scenes in comfort. Now they had turned the tables and were supervising the intellectuals in labor. *In cinema circles, it seemed, the Cultural Revolution was not as mild as among students* [emphasis added].[18]

The unusual political activism (either in the radical or conservative sense) among workers in the mass media may be explained in terms of Lipset's discussion of the political activities of certain working-class groups. According to him, certain occupational activities of workers are highly conducive to the acquisition of political skills. "Leaders who come from the working class generally do so by way of the trade union-office—the one position directly available to a worker in which he can learn political skills."[19] Lipset's observation concerning printers is even more relevant: "Printers—the first literate group of manual workers—were pioneer organizers of trade union and labor parties in many countries, another reflection of the impact of occupational activities on intellectual and organizational skill."[20] The social and intellectual position of printers in China is identical to that of the media workers—some newspaper workers *were* printers. For example, the leaders of the "East Is Red" group in the Canton studio were literate and some were high school graduates, including one veteran who worked in the "special effects" division. Thus the media workers were a special group whose literacy equipped them with political skills and motivation. Moreover, as Dai Hsiao-ai's comments suggest, the *perceived* hierarchical relation in the media between intellectuals and workers was particularly sharp. The media workers obviously had a sense of "relative rank disequilibrium."

Political activism, however, does not mean radicalism exclusively—it may suggest militant conservatism as well.

Whether in the conservative or radical sense of political activism (though more in the former), the textile workers were particularly active during the Cultural Revolution. The foregoing discussion on the pattern of violence noted that the first two cases of violent and armed conflict between conservatives and the radical students (in 1967) took place in the cotton mills of Chengtu (Szechwan province) and Chengchow (Honan province). The students allied with a small group of radical textile workers in both cities and were confronted by militant and hostile conservatives. One of the first factories in Peking to create a Red Guards unit (quickly suppressed) was "No. 3 State Spinning Mill."[21] In Shanghai, the first rebel group of workers to challenge the Municipal Party Committee was formed in the "No. 17 State Cotton Mill," led by Wang Hung-wen, who subsequently became a member of the Politburo though when he led the worker revolt he was a lower echelon factory employee. On November 9, 1966, Wang induced his followers to create the Shanghai Workers' Rebellion Headquarters and the next day that group commandeered a train to travel to Peking "to file a complaint," thus creating the famous "Anting Incident." The train was stopped at Anting, where the rebels and local Party authorities engaged in a lengthy negotiation.[22] Wang's group, however, quickly turned to the national leaders and collaborated with the newly constituted political authorities in Shanghai. Wang, like other veterans, was politicized by the army and discontented with his civilian career. As a lower-level official in the cotton mill responsible for political surveillance and plant security, he was equivalent to the leaders of working class origin who build their careers by way of the trade union office, as suggested by Seymour Lipset.

After the "power seizure" movement began, the textile industry was seriously disrupted so that there was a marked decline in production during 1967.[23] Violent clashes among workers and between the Red Guards and conservative workers occurred in the cotton mills in Peking, Shanghai and elsewhere. The unusual political activism of the textile workers in China was due to largely socioeconomic factors, specifically including the dislocations caused by social change and the vulnerability of the textile industry to short-term downswings in agricultural production. These are the two most important sociological sources of group conflict.

The Chinese textile industry received a tremendous push from the government after 1949. It is not an exaggeration to say that in light industry the Communist leaders gave first priority to investments in textiles. A recent statement about the new textile industry of China is not mere propaganda:

> In these twenty years, the workers have rescued the dying textile industry of the old semi-colonial days and built it into a huge modern socialist industry. Production of cotton yarn and cloth has increased more than fourfold, a faster rate of increase than any other country in the world. In the past, all textile machines were imported. Today, the country not only manufactures all the textile equipment needed for the industry's rapid development, but also helps a dozen countries in Asia, Africa and eastern Europe establish and maintain modern mills. . . .

To achieve such a feat, the above statement continues, certain developments were necessary:

> Besides putting the old textile bases into full use, China has built new bases across the entire nation in a large-scale, planned way, expanding mills and building new ones. . . .
> In the past, textile mills were concentrated in the big cities along the coast. Today, every province except Taiwan, all municipalities and autonomous regions have modern textile enterprises. These are generally located in areas where cotton, wool, flax, hemp and silk are abundant and local conditions justify it. . . . Inland cities like Sian, Chengchow and Shihchiachuang, for example, are in cotton-producing areas but had few textile plants before the liberation. Today these cities are cotton, dyeing, printing and knitting bases.[24]

Students outside of China concur with this official statement concerning the Chinese economy. A Japanese expert called China "a contender in world textile industry with awesome potentiality" in 1967.[25] Alexander Eckstein's study not only confirms this spectacular growth in the Chinese textile industry but also points out the real goal—export:

> The value of textile shipments . . . rose from $40 million in 1952 to a peak of $550 million in 1960. As a result, textiles displaced farm products as China's leading export. It is significant that even

amidst the general decline in exports, textile deliveries were maintained at a high level—even after 1960 when shortages of raw materials forced a curtailment in mainland textile production. [These shortages resulted especially from a decline in cotton output.] One can safely conclude, therefore, that domestic textile consumption must have been curtailed so that Soviet loans could be repaid and that foreign exchange, so vitally needed for financing grain imports, could be earned.[26]

All this means that there was probably a significant increase in the number of urban workers in textile mills after 1949—most of them young; female workers probably constituted a substantial number of them. Furthermore, new mills were developed by transferring many old mills on the coast to the interior. The logical result was social dislocation. The new and youthful textile workers undoubtedly received more political indoctrination than their older cohorts and were probably influenced more by the new political culture, which tended to glorify conflict. Furthermore, Eckstein's statement above suggests that the textile industry was subject to frequent downswings in cotton production. According to Robert Field,

> The output of textiles suffered a particularly sharp decline because cotton acreage was diverted to grain production during the agricultural crisis of 1959–61. The production of cotton cloth fell so sharply in 1961 and 1962 that the annual ration had to be lowered to an estimated 2 meters per person as compared to about 6.3 meters in 1957. By 1966, production was well above the 1957 level, but it fell again in 1967–68 because of work stoppages in textile plants. In 1969, it recovered dramatically and went on to regain its previous peak level of 1970.[27]

This means that textile workers in China felt insecure; in bad years many of them probably were released to become the "support-the-agriculture-workers" who participated in various radical actions from 1966 to 1968. According to the Chinese government, China had a bumper cotton harvest in 1966—the best in the seventeen years "since the liberation."[28] The Cultural Revolution threatened to disrupt the excellent cotton harvest. The statement made by a Japanese correspondent about the workers in Wuhan is equally valid with respect to the textile workers: "They probably could not tolerate the social disruption under the cultural revolution and . . . they feared the possibility of another period of austerity." The textile workers "supported the old cadres and stepped up their resolute activities to defend their own organization."[29] This was the reason for the militant conservatism of the textile workers in Chengtu and Chengchow and the bloody conflict involving workers and students in May 1967. One Red Guard publication hinted that the militant struggles at various cotton mills were the result of "the 'revisionist' policy (i.e., material incentives) of China's Khrushchev (i.e., Liu Shao-ch'i)."[30] In sum, the leftism of the radical students threatened the large number of cotton mill workers with a sudden deprivation in the midst of a good year.

Next to the textile workers, the most active workers groups, in terms of militant conservatism and internal polarization, were comprised of workers in new steel plants, munitions plants and mines (particularly in Northeast China). In the two new steel cities, Wuhan and Taiyuan, workers were split into a radical minority and a majority composed of aggressive conservatives. The Wuhan conservative group, the "Heroic Division of One Million," consisted of "iron-steel workers."[31] In Taiyuan, it was reported that "tens of thousands of workers" laid siege to "the revolutionary rebels, causing work stoppage in many enterprises . . ." which "created *terrifying* communications accidents and other things" [emphasis added].[32] The conservatism of the steelworkers is understandable; Hai Feng noted they "are employed by the only employer of the land—the state—and they have been given an exalted (though, in reality, empty) title; their material life is superior to peasants and other non-salaried classes, so they are conservative, contented and feel superior."[33]

The political activism of the munitions plant workers in connection with the incident in Chengtu suggests that many of them were demobilized soldiers. Their political activities will be discussed later. A revealing report about this group of workers came from Peking. On September 22, 1967, "Peking streets were congested all day . . . with demonstrations celebrating great alliances achieved" and "newspapers were flooded with stories on great alliances." The subject of this jubilation was

> the news that the two rival organizations in the Seventh Machine Building Ministry (munitions industry ministry)—the "new 915 revolutionary rebel headquarters" and the "916 revolutionary rebel combat corps,"—each boasting a membership of 10,000, joined together in a great alliance on 21 September. These two organizations, probably the largest in Peking, have opposed each other in everything and have often clashed. *Peking Daily* devoted conspicuously large space to this important news.[34]

Chou En-lai received a rebel delegation from three northeastern (formerly "Manchuria") provinces on September 28, 1967, and commented on "the severe fighting" in the mining towns of Wushun, Fushin, Pengch'ih, and Dairen.[35] In March 1968 a report from another northeastern province, Heilunkiang, mentioned "a number of instances of anarchist tendencies" among coal miners.[36] The role of coal miners in connection with the violent struggles in Anhwei was mentioned earlier. According to Lipset, mining is an "isolated occupation" which requires miners to live in one-industry areas. Thus ingroup interaction in mining communities is high and so is political activism. In the Western democracies this results in group voting and interest articulation,[37] while in China the general structure of politics directed the activism of miners to factionalism and group conflict.

The general conservatism of workers during the Cultural Revolution sharply contrasted with the hostile and extreme behavior of a specific group known commonly in China as "contract or temporary workers," the underprivileged proletariat.

The Underprivileged Proletariat

The Central Committee circular of February 17, 1967, dealing with the disruptive activities of the underprivileged proletariat, is revealing:

> The system governing the employment of temporary workers, contract workers, rotation workers and piece workers is rational in some cases, but is very irrational and erroneous in some other cases. The Party Central Committee is studying ways to reform these systems according to the actual situation. Before the Party Central Committee arrives at a new decision, the established methods are to be followed as usual. . . .[38]

The temporary workers, contract workers and pieceworkers were primarily young migrants from the countryside and unemployed urban residents. As China suffered periodic downswings in agricultural production, many workers were released from their jobs and sent to the countryside to become part of a displaced group euphemistically entitled "support-the-agriculture-workers." Some joined the so-called rotation workers, who were either former workers in factories or farmers in communes. They thus were part of the worker-peasant system which "provides for the use of seasonal or part-time labor from rural communes to replace permanent workers in industrial enterprises. . . . Displaced workers, in turn, have been assigned to agricultural production teams in the countryside."[39] The rationale for the worker-peasant system was primarily economic:

> In economic terms, the hope, seemingly, is to maintain production levels while reducing the national wage bill and the cost of fringe benefits by diminishing the number of permanent industrial

workers. This is theoretically possible because temporary and contract laborers (two types of worker-peasants) remain members of
their parent communes; they do not become members of trade
unions and thus are not eligible for free medical care, unemploy-
ment and retirement pay, or for other benefits given to permanent
industrial workers.

The worker-system also limits or reduces the State's burden of
providing food to urban areas. Financially, it is presumably intended as a means of utilizing resources for increased capital
investment rather than for immediate consumption.[40]

In ordinary times, underprivileged workers in China were preoccupied
with immediate concerns for their livelihood; as one of their organizations pointed out:

> . . . they are always afraid that they may be dismissed because
> of mistakes in their working methods and technical operations.
> This kind of mental pressure prevents the contract worker from
> making progress in politics and the rationalization of his thought.
> His mind can only revolve around such things as work, livelihood,
> and dismissal.[41]

The intellectual quality of some of the publications produced by temporary workers (e.g., the one just quoted) suggests that part of this transient
group were unemployed intellectuals or high school graduates.[42] The
alienation and resentment of dispossessed workers can be easily imagined.

According to a Red Guard publication, the system of using temporary
workers was first adopted in the Northeast, the most industrialized
region of China, in 1954 (upon initiation of the first Five-year Plan).
The system became nationwide and permanent after 1955 and the ranks
of temporary workers were greatly inflated during the "Great Leap
Forward" of 1958. By the end of 1958 there were close to twelve million
such workers, "about 26.6 per cent of the total workers and employees
in China,"[43] with a sense of alienation and resentment stemming mainly
from economic discrimination. They were not eligible for the welfare
benefits that regular members of the labor unions enjoyed, and even
their title implied that they had no sense of security. Even while employed, the temporary workers were separated from ordinary workers,
and they lived in bare and primitive quarters reminiscent of those
occupied by many migrant farmers in the United States.[44] The social
and physical isolation increased the group consciousness and the resulting political activism of the most extreme kind was only to be expected.
The hostile outburst of the underprivileged workers during the Cultural
Revolution was helped partly by demobilized soldiers in their ranks.[45]

When the Party authority broke down in 1967, these workers organized several groups and demanded an end to their underprivileged status. The most active organization was the "National Rebel General Corps of Red Laborers," which reportedly sent representatives to Peking in December 1966 for an audience with Chiang Ch'ing (Madame Mao). Chiang allegedly condemned the contract worker system as "capitalistic and reactionary" and ordered labor union officials in Peking to provide housing and food for the representatives.[46] As the news (or rumor) of Chiang's order spread, temporary and contract workers in the major cities demanded restitution from local unions and Party officials.

The system of temporary and part-time workers was, however, an integral part of the government's long-range policy of compulsory saving so Party authorities in Peking quickly outlawed the rebel groups. The circular of February 17, 1967, ordered dissolution of the "National Rebel General Corps of Red Laborers" and invalidated all agreements between local unions and temporary workers. It also forbade the formation of independent organizations but allowed temporary workers to join the "local revolutionary mass organizations or those of their enterprises and units." Contradictorily, the Central Committee order granted temporary workers "political rights *equal* to those enjoyed by permanent workers, staff members and other functionaries" [emphasis added]. The Central Committee order did not mention giving *economic rights* to temporary workers equal to those enjoyed by permanent workers.[47]

The circular from the Central Committee had no immediate effect, and in late February 1967 it was reported that the "National Rebel General Corps of Red Laborers" joined with organizations of returned students, demobilized soldiers and workers on state farms to break into the exclusive residential area occupied by high ranking Party officials (e.g., Mao and Chou) in Peking-Chungnanhai.

> National Rebel General Corps of Red Laborers . . . incited the temporary workers and contract workers in other parts of the country to storm into Peking to make trouble. They not only collaborated with other reactionary organizations to storm into Chungnanhai, but also attacked other organs of the Party Central Committee. They kidnapped cadres of the State at will, encircled and attacked cadres of residents' committees and seized power everywhere. They assumed the name of the Party Central Committee several times to summon rallies at T'ienanmen Square. They vigorously enforced economism and clamored for "transfer to the permanent establishment and back pay since 1958." *They took extreme measures in doing everything* [emphasis added].[48]

In Shanghai, a group of "support-the-agriculture-workers" forcibly occupied the office of the new revolutionary committee on February

24, 1967, and called in "large numbers of their counterparts from Kiangsu, Anhwei, and other provinces and adjacent areas of Shanghai." Their statements "denied the great achievements scored over the past 17 years . . . saying that the living conditions of the workers are as poor as those under the rule of the Kuomintang."[49]

The protests and disruptive activities of underprivileged workers continued into 1968. According to a Red Guard bulletin, the Central Committee issued another circular in early 1968 which reaffirmed its injunction of 1967 and forbade temporary. workers from forming independent organizations or demanding permanent worker status.[50]

The underprivileged proletariat in mainland China, like the youths sent to the countryside, cannot expect an immediate alleviation of their plight. On the contrary, there will be more of them in the future. In 1968, the government announced a long-range plan to disperse ten to twenty percent of all city-dwellers to the countryside (15–25 million), "among them are Party cadres and civil servants, teachers and health workers, the urban unemployed and temporary workers, and students."[51] The official policy will continue to enlarge the worker-peasant system, at least in the part of China's industry that depends upon unskilled labor, e.g., in mining and lumbering. The political activism of workers in isolated occupations like mining and forestry may render the new policy of the Communist Party especially vulnerable to potentially hostile outbursts by underprivileged workers.

Peasants

The reactions of peasants to the Cultural Revolution followed a standard pattern, with some deviations, closely resembling that of the workers. For example, most peasants were unable or unwilling to discard their usual role as subjects. Many of them remained receptive to the direction of Party cadres in the countryside and no peasant-movement leader emerged during the Cultural Revolution. Neither was there a proletarian-movement leader, yet there were numerous youth-movement leaders. In Canton, for example, the prevalent attitudes of suburban peasants were expressed in terms like "To oppose the Party secretary is to oppose the Communist Party," "Rebellion is not necessarily justified" or "The rebels may not be able to dominate."[52]

Throughout China, Party cadres mobilized peasants to attack the students and this situation led the Party Central Committee to issue a formal injunction on September 11, 1966, restraining this type of activity. Mao Tse-tung sent a personal directive to Party leaders, saying in part: "The situation is similar in Tsingtao, Sian, Changsha, etc., with workers and peasants being organized against students. To go on like this cannot solve problems."[53]

The local Party officials and the military apparently found it easy to arouse and organize peasants to attack students throughout 1967. For example, the two anti-Red Guard workers groups in Canton—the "District Headquarters" and the "Red General Headquarters"—together with their Allied Doctrine Red Guards mobilized suburban peasants to ambush truckloads of Red Guards from Chungshan University, shouting: "The time for revenge has come. All those who are university students or who are from *Chung-ta* (Chungshan University) Red Flag should be shot . . ."[54] Similar incidents occurred in the northeastern province of Heilunkiang in May and June 1967. The military commander in Heilunkiang organized workers and peasants to assault students of Petroleum College and Harbin Military Engineering College and on one occasion peasants from eight counties were called in to attack students.[55] Finally, the Party Central Committee issued another circular (in July 1967) to prevent peasant-student clashes. That circular reveals the extent of the antiintellectual struggle of the peasants:

> For a time of late, a handful of those in authority taking the capitalist road in Kiangsi, Szechwan, Chekiang, Hupeh, Honan, Anhwei, Ningsha and Shansi—especially a few comrades who have not satisfactorily transformed themselves ideologically in the local militia departments of some provinces, municipalities, administrative districts, county and communes—have instigated some peasants who do not understand the actual situation into going into cities to participate in armed struggle, and encircle and attack the revolutionary mass organizations of factories and mines, organs and schools. *Some places have even advanced the slogan of "encircling the cities with the countryside"* and other reactionary slogans, and organized the peasants to go into cities to suppress the revolutionary rebels . . . [emphasis added].[56]

The militant conservatism of the peasants mentioned in this report is one of the major sources of the violent conflicts after May 1967, which is analyzed earlier. During this period the army took the attitude of "defiant neutralism" and cadre-led peasants resorted to violence in their clashes with the students.

The peasants and workers were both initially passive toward the Cultural Revolution. Young students assumed leadership over the rebel groups organized in villages. For example, the first such group—the so-called Friends of Red Peasants *(Hung Nung-yu)*—was organized by seven youths in a suburb of Canton. During the slack months of rural production, from November 1966 to February 1967, this group enlarged its membership to 7,000 and established branches in other villages. The civil-military authority of Kwangtung soon reacted by forming a royalist peasant group to intimidate the rebels. The ranks of the "Friends of Red Peasants" then dwindled from 7,000 to a little more than a hundred by April 1967. The Red Guard unit that reported the tragic fate of the "Friends of Red Peasants" issued a pathetic appeal to the peasants around Canton:

> The . . . masses of old poor and lower-middle peasants should wash their heads clean of outdated but deep-seated ideas. They should actively partake in the great political struggle, without fear of disrupting the order of production and of losing labor points. . . . Be sure that the . . . naivete of your class sentiments is not preyed on by the power-holders . . .[57]

Toward late 1967 violence increased in the cities and many middle- and lower-echelon Party officials migrated to the countryside to assume the leadership of peasant associations.[58] Undoubtedly these émigrés had a score to settle with the radical students and they probably played an active role in organizing peasants to participate in the violent conflicts after May 1967.

Like the workers, the peasants in the Cultural Revolution responded readily to parochial symbols, particularly in the southern provinces (e.g., Kwangtung), where regionalism remained strong, and in the interior provinces of central China (e.g., Kiangsi and Anhwei). Many peasants in Kwangtung, for example, found it impossible to attack local Party officials partly because, as one Cantonese put it, "most of the cadres here are members of the Party or the League and *have been born and brought up here*" [emphasis added].[59] A. D. Barnett's study indicates that many of the lower-level Party cadres were actually recruited from poor peasants in the locality.[60] A lengthy broadcast emanating from Hofei in February 1967 outlined the tactics used by local authorities to impede the work of radicals—one method was a traditional appeal to clan connections. The activation of traditional sentiment made the work of the "revolutionary alliance" difficult, according to the report from Anhwei.[61] After the establishment of the Kiangsi revolutionary committee in January 1968, a provincial broadcast reported there were "sectarian disputes" in the countryside. The traditional social structure apparently persisted in that Communist stronghold, so the archaic clan warfare was revived in 1968. The traditional sectarian disputes then included the use of modern arms as the villagers joined in seizing weapons and ammunition.[62]

There were, however, exceptions to the standard pattern of parochial response among the peasants in China. The process of social change in the suburbs of Shanghai, Peking and parts of Shansi elicited a type of political conflict more characteristic of the cities. Specifically, the process involved a challenge of local authorities—real struggles against rural Party officials occurred in the villages around Shanghai. One report points out that even cadres "who had made some ordinary mistakes" were targets of attack, and there was talk that "every cadre may be a target."[63] Another report stated that Shanghai peasants subjected "high cadres, low cadres and work team members to indiscriminate struggles and parading through the street," but that the county Party secretary was not attacked.[64] The Red Guard journalist who made the report obviously felt that attacks against cadres below the county Party secretary level were not enough. Yet, compared to the standard parochial pattern of behavior exhibited by the villagers elsewhere, the peasants of Shanghai were quite radical. Similar struggles occurred in the Hoching (also Hotsin) region of Shansi, where a new railway and bridge (across the Yellow River) were built after 1949. The *People's Daily* reported in February 1968 that the peasants in Hoching dismissed "virtually at random almost all those holding positions of responsibility" in 1967. As a result, there was a lack of leadership in production in 1968.[65]

A particularly interesting account from Fengnan county near Peking reported that a group of peasants associated with the Chinese "aquatic system" seized the offices of the local newspaper and radio station and refused to transmit communications from Peking. The peasants must have been led by radicals, since they demanded a reversal of the verdict made during the "Four Clean-up" movement prior to the Cultural Revolution.[66] This group of peasants seemingly had an isolated occupation (i.e., the "aquatic system") which facilitated ingroup communications and gave rise to political activism. This group came closest to adopting the urban pattern characterized by the seizure of the mass media. Yet the locality may also have been related to the unusual activism of these poor and lower-middle peasants. Fengnan lies in a triangular area near three industrial and metropolitan cities, Peking, Tientsin and Tangshan. It is closest to Tangshan, which has steel and cement industries and a large power plant which uses coal mined locally. The armed conflict in Peking demonstrated the aggression of the peasants—the confrontation between the "Red Flag Commune" and miners in January 1968 resulted in several deaths. The peasants from the commune were apparently motivated by economic factors, since it was reported that the peasants seized the miners' provisions.[67]

The peasants and workers also reacted identically by making particularistic and materialistic demands. Chinese peasants during the Cultural Revolution almost uniformly demanded and, in many places, realized a gross reduction in the government's squeeze on them. Peasants refused to turn their grains over to the state and denied local authorities the right to withhold part of their produce for reinvestment. The peasants in some places demanded a redistribution of grains and other goods already requisitioned by national and local authorities. The particularistic demands of the peasants were strongest in the cities where group conflict was most intense or violent. More specifically, peasants near the two focal points of political radicalism, Shanghai and Peking, made the most extreme demands for redistribution of collective produce. The peasants of Wuhan and near cities in Kwangsi also made radical material demands. The economism of peasants was widespread and persistent in Chekiang, where the post–revolutionary committee violences occurred. *Wen-hui Pao* reported that "large numbers of peasants" were incited by cadres to raise questions on "year-end distribution (of income)" and to demand distribution of "accumulated funds and grain in reserve." Hundreds of peasants left the countryside and flowed into Shanghai[68], and all this was done in the name of "immediate elimination of the differences between the city and the countryside."[69] Letters printed in the *People's Daily* in Peking alleged that production teams in the suburbs

> will not discuss the real situation of their teams. . . . They have even distributed seeds, fodder and production capital intended for use in the coming year. They also refuse to deliver the required public grain to the state, or return loans, or pay rent for tractors, water and electricity bills. They incite the public by saying that in the past, too much had been deducted and stored; now is the time to redistribute it.[70]

Around Wuhan, it was reported that the peasants redistributed public grains among themselves and were also allowed "to cut down trees indiscriminately." Local cadres supposedly instructed peasants: "The Great Proletarian Cultural Revolution means extensive democracy; we can do whatever we want. It does not matter if you cannot fulfill the state procurement quota. If the upper levels demand that you fulfill it, you can rebel against them."[71] The government became concerned over the independent actions of the peasants and the breakdown of local leadership in February and March 1967 and ordered the Air Force to drop leaflets over villages near Wuhan, Hofei (Anhwei) and Nanning (Kwangsi) informing the peasants of directives from the national government exhorting them to do their duty.[72] This method of communication might have been designed to catch the attention of the peasants through the novelty of the airdrop, it may imply that the government had lost control over the media or it may indicate that the rural radio stations were deliberately shut down to prevent rebel factions from using them for partisan purposes. A more reasonable explanation might be that the peasants made their communities inaccessible in order to stop the shipment of grains or to simply prevent the violence in the cities from spilling over to the villages. It has already been noted that railway traffic was suspended for months in Kwangsi. The passengers of the "No. 606 express" from Peking to Nanning reported that the train was detained north of Liuchow on May 30, 1968, by armed local militia for a week and that some of the passengers were killed. Looting was apparently not the main purpose, but the armed peasants complained that the train had come from Kweilin, where "the situation was complex and chaotic" and that it "had come from an area of armed conflict."[73] The peasants were simply trying to immunize their area from the conflicts outside. Their actions may have been a reflection of traditional peasant resentments over the presence of railways in their fields or the superstitious belief in geomancy. Such resentments were formerly suppressed by the authorities—now it was permissible to assert them.

There are two possible reasons why the particularistic demands of the peasants were more radical near cities where group conflict was most intense. First, the breakdown of law and order caused by conflicts in the cities lowered the risks. According to Oberschall, the ratio of risk to reward is proportional to the degree of activism among various conflicting groups.[74] Second, groups of peasants in almost all these areas participating in conflicts were probably organized by the local authorities. Thus the radical demands of the peasants represented their conditions used in bargaining with the cadres who desired their participation. A circular published in July 1967 by the Central Committee specified that "all kinds of so-called 'preferential treatment' granted to commune members participating in armed struggle are null and void." The local authorities in areas of violence needed the peasants so they had to agree to more stringent conditions. This does not contradict the point made earlier that the peasants wanted to isolate themselves from struggle in the cities. The peasants who went to the cities to fight were, of course, prepared to protect themselves against retaliation by their opponents.

During the Cultural Revolution both workers and peasants tended to follow a standard pattern of behavior in response to conflict. However, both groups exhibited varying degrees of political activism or deviations from the standard that can only be attributed to sociological and economic factors.

Notes

1.　Seymour Martin Lipset, *Political Man. The Social Basis of Politics* (Garden City, N.Y., 1963), pp. 87–126. I am aware of the criticism of Lipset's concept of "working-class authoritarianism" by Miller and Riessman [S.

M. Miller and Frank Riessman, " 'Working-Class Authoritarianism': A Critique of Lipset," *British Journal of Sociology*, Vol. 12, No. 3 (September 1961)]. The two British scholars, however, merely disputed Lipset on whether these behavioral traits of the working class can be regarded as "antidemocratic"; they did not take issue with Lipset on the manifestation of these characteristics. Their dispute is not relevant to my analysis here.

2. Gordon A. Bennett and Ronald N. Montaperto, *Red Guard: The Political Biography of Dai Hsiao-ai* (Garden City, N.Y., 1972), pp. 53–55.

3. Ken Ling, *The Revenge of Heaven: Journal of a Young Chinese* (New York, 1972), p. 243. Though the descriptions of workers' attitudes by the two former Red Guards may reflect their contempt for workers, their accounts are largely corroborated by official media reports and the activities of workers later on.

4. Ibid., p. 56.

5. Hai Feng, *Kuang-chou Ti-ch'u Wen-ke Lieh-chen Shu-lueh* [An Account of the Cultural Revolution in the Canton Area] (Hong Kong, 1971), pp. 65–66 (hereafter cited by English title).

6. *Yi-chiu Liu-pa Chung-kung-nien-pao* [1968 Yearbook on Chinese Communism] (Taipei, 1969), pp. 773–775 (hereafter cited by English title).

7. *Wen-hui Pao*, March 11, 1967, translated by NCNA (March 14, 1967) in *Survey of China Mainland Press* (Hong Kong: U.S. Consulate General), No. 3902, p. 19 (hereafter cited as SCMP). See also SCMP, No. 3904, p. 15.

8. Hai Feng, *Account of the Cultural Revolution in Canton*, p. 256.

9. *Sankei* (Tokyo), September 30, 1967.

10. Chou's speech is reprinted in "Recent Speeches of CCP Leaders," *Tsukuo* [China Monthly], No. 46 (January 1, 1968), p. 42 (Chinese text).

11. Chang's speech is reprinted in "Selected Statements of Chang Ch'ung-ch'iao," *Tsukuo*, No. 56 (November 1, 1968), p. 42 (Chinese text).

12. Reprinted document in "Recent Speeches of CCP Leaders," *Tsukuo*, No. 46 (January 1, 1968), p. 44 (Chinese text).

13. Lipset, *Political Man*, p. 113.

14. Hai Feng, *Account of the Cultural Revolution in Canton*, p. 139.

15. Neale Hunter, *Shanghai Journal: An Eyewitness Account of the Cultural Revolution* (Boston, 1969), p. 135; Chao Tsung, "An Account of the 'Great Proletarian Cultural Revolution,' " (Part 23), *Tsukuo*, No. 69 (December 1, 1969), pp. 29–30.

16. Hai Feng, *Account of the Cultural Revolution in Canton*, p. 93.

17. Ibid., pp. 56–61.

18. Bennett and Montaperto, *Red Guard*, p. 123.

19. Lipset, *Political Man*, p. 198.

20. Ibid., p. 199.

21. *Mainichi* (Tokyo), November 5, 1966.

22. Chien Ta-chin, "Leading Personnel of New CCP Shanghai Municipal Committee," *Tsukuo*, No. 84 (March 1, 1971), p. 43; Tao Yuan-chang, "The New Members of the Politburo of the Chinese Communist Party," *Chung-hua Yüeh-pao*, No. 697 (October 1973), pp. 53–54.

23. I Fan, "Industry, Communication and Transport of Communist China in 1967," *Tsukuo*, No. 48 (March 1, 1968), pp. 24–25; Robert Michael Field, "Chinese Industrial Development: 1949–70," in *People's Republic of China: An Economic Assessment* (Washington, D.C., 1972), p. 68.

24. Fang Wen, "Rapid Growth in China's Textile Industry," *China Reconstructs* (Peking, November 1969), p. 7.

25. I Fan, "Industries of Communist China in 1968," *Tsukuo*, No. 61 (April 1, 1969), pp. 17–18.

26. Alexander Eckstein, *Communist China's Economic Growth and Foreign Trade. Implications for U.S. Policy* (New York, 1966), p. 116.

27. Field, "Chinese Industrial Development," p. 68.

28. I Fan, "Cotton Production in Communist China," *Tsukuo*, No. 81 (December 1, 1970), p. 3.

29. *Sankei* (Tokyo), September 30, 1967.

30. I Fan, "Industry, Communication and Transport of Communist China in 1967," p. 24.

31. *Sankei* (Tokyo), September 29, 1967.

32. *Radio Peking*, 1230 GMT, January 24, 1967.

33. Hai Feng, *Haifeng Wen-hua Ke-ming Kai-shu* [A General Account of the Cultural Revolution in Haifeng County] (Hong Kong, 1969), p. 69.

34. *Asahi* (Tokyo), September 23, 1967.

35. *Red Guard Publications* (Association of Research Libraries), Group X-1 (hereafter cited as RGP).

36. *Radio Harbin*, 1130 GMT, March 1, 1967.

37. Lipset, *Political Man*, pp. 104–105, 200–201.

38. *CCP Documents of the Great Proletarian Cultural Revolution, 1966–1967* (Hong Kong, 1968), p. 305 (hereafter cited as *CCP Documents*).

39. *Current Scene*, Vol. 6, No. 5 (March 15, 1968), p. 1.

40. Ibid.

41. *Labor War Bulletin*, February 3, 1968, trans. in *Chinese Sociology and Anthropology*, Vol. 1, No. 4 (Summer 1969), p. 57.

42. Ken Ling reported just such a case. An elder brother was briefly imprisoned for criticizing the regime while in high school (in 1957?) and he was not allowed to enter any university and became a contract worker for a construction company; see Ken Ling, *Revenge of Heaven*, pp. 223–226.

43. *Liu Shao-ch'i Tsai Lin-shih-kung, H'e-t'un-kung Tze-tu-chung-ti-he-tsai-liao* [The Black Materials on Liu Shao-ch'i's Role in the System of Temporary and Contract Workers], RGP, Group X-1.

44. *Sou-tu Hung-wei-pin*, January 10, 1967, in RGP, Group IX-2.

45. Ibid.

46. This alleged meeting was reported by a Red Guard organization of the Institute of Economy in Peking *(Chin-chi Hsueh-yuan)* in its publication dated January 4, 1967; this report is reprinted in Chao Tsung, "An Account of the 'Great Proletarian Cultural Revolution,'" (Part 22), *Tsu-kuo*, No. 68 (November 1, 1969); also reported in *Current Scene*, Vol. 6, No. 5 (March 15, 1968), p. 9.

47. *Current Scene*, Vol. 6, No. 5 (March 15, 1968), p. 16.

48. *Ti-yu Chan-hsin*, trans. in SCMP, No. 3913, p. 5.

49. *Radio Shanghai*, 2310 GMT, February 26, 1967.

50. *Kuang-t'ieh Tsung-ssu* (Canton), No. 28 (February 1968), trans. in SCMP, No. 4129, p. 2.

51. *Current Scene*, Vol. 7, No. 18 (September 15, 1969), p. 14.

52. Hai Feng, *Account of the Cultural Revolution in Canton*, p. 139.

53. *CCP Documents*, pp. 73–76.

54. Combined issue of *Kuang-chou Hung-ssu* and *Wuhan Hsin-hua-kung*, No. 18 (August 21, 1967), trans. in SCMP, No. 4017, p. 7.

55. Reprints from Red Guard publications in "Dark Clouds Rolling Over Heilunkiang," *Tsukuo*, No. 81 (December 1, 1970) (Chinese text).

56. *CCP Documents*, p. 475.

57. SCMP, No. 4030, p. 21.

58. Ting Wang, ed., *Chung-kung Wen-hua Ta-ke-ming Tze-liao Hui-pien* [A Collection of Documents on the Great Proletarian Cultural Revolution] (Hong Kong, 1972), p. 32 (hereafter cited as *Collection of Documents*).

59. *Hung-se Pao-tung* (Canton), Nos. 12–13 (July 8, 1967), trans. in SCMP, No. 4030, p. 17. In the original translation, the League is translated as "Corps".

60. A. D. Barnett, *Cadres, Bureaucracy, and Political Power in Communist China* (New York, 1967), pp. 348–349.

61. *Radio Hofei*, 1040 GMT, February 2, 1967.

62. *Radio Nanchang*, 2350 GMT, February 10, 1968.

63. SCMP, No. 3878, p. 12.

64. *Pei-chin Ping-lun*, April 1967, in RGP, Group VI-1.

65. *AFP* (English broadcast), 2119 GMT, February 13, 1968.

66. *Radio Peking*, 1733 GMT, March 10, 1967.

67. *AFP* (English broadcast), 1245 GMT, January 31, 1968.

68. SCMP, No. 3878, p. 3.

69. *Wen-hui Pao*, January 20, 1967.

70. *Jen-min Jih-pao* [People's Daily], January 23, 1967.

71. *Radio Wuhan*, 1100 GMT, February 4, 1967.

72. *Radio Wuhan*, 1400 GMT, March 8, 1967; *Radio Nanning*, 2230 GMT, February 27, 1967; and *Radio Hofei*, 0330 GMT, March 9, 1967.

73. Ting Wang, *Collection of Documents*, pp. 372–379.

74. Anthony Oberschall, *Social Conflict and Social Movements* (Englewood Cliffs, N.J., 1973), pp. 157–172.

7

VETERANS

Throughout the foregoing discussion the role of veterans in group conflict in China was mentioned repeatedly. Yet scholars outside of China rarely expect veterans to engage in antiauthority outbursts, since they played an important role in consolidating the power of the Communist Party during the early years of the Communist regime.[1] Even later, the government used veterans to help carry out radical collectivization in the countryside.[2] Thus, on the surface at least, the veterans were the most indoctrinated group in China and were an important and effective auxiliary of the Communist power structure. In reality, there must be many malintegrated and discontented veterans whose activities were not reported prior to the Cultural Revolution. The totalitarian system had yet another masking feature.[3]

According to one report, the Chinese Communist government demobilized 6.5 million soldiers from 1959 to 1967.[4] The old guerrillas who fought the Japanese, the Chinese Nationalists and, later, as volunteers in Korea were either scattered or organized into large Production and Construction Corps *(Shen-t'san Chien-she Pu-tui)* to settle on China's remote frontiers. The largest and most famous was the Production and Construction Corps of the Sinkiang Military Region which incorporated about 500,000 demobilized soldiers and other groups in 1967.[5] Similar work corps were sent to border provinces like Heilunkiang, Inner Mongolia, Kansu, Ts'inghai and Tibet. The remainder of the demobilized soldiers were given civilian jobs and scattered all over China.

A recent account by a former veteran in China testified that the government was faced with the typical problems of disgruntled veterans. Soldiers who were discharged individually often could not get along in the larger society. They felt they were the object of discrimination on the part of civilian employers who, in turn, considered the former soldiers to be arrogant and difficult to manage. There were repeated instances of group protest; for example, veterans from Szechwan sent a delegation to see Chou En-lai to seek better treatment. Veterans employed in the steel mills of Wuhan staged strikes and demanded higher pay and better living conditions.[6] It cannot be determined whether the veterans in the Wuhan steel plants were the same workers who joined the rebels in the July 1967 incident, since three worker organizations sided with the radical students during the violence there.

Whenever possible, the government tried to relocate veterans in remote frontier regions. Former veteran Chin Chien-li was discharged from an antiair artillery company in 1955 and with a group of other veterans from Canton passed a nationwide college and university entrance examination. All were then assigned to the University of Lanchow in the Northwest—a fate similar to that experienced by veterans in the Production and Construction Corps. Significantly, Chin reported that in the "Hundred Flowers" campaign of 1957, *all* nine veterans at the university joined student critics and later were condemned by the government as rightists. Their special status and subsidies from the government were cancelled and none was able to subsequently clear his name. Chin's only hope was to leave China after a stay in prison and a second exile in the Northwest.[7] Chin's experience was probably extreme; nonetheless, many individually discharged veterans were undeniably discontented. Other cases of political rebellion on the part of veterans have already been discussed (e.g., in accounts by Ken Ling and Dai Hsiao-ai).

Veteran groups in the Cultural Revolution were known for their independent and cohesive organization, their tendency toward violent actions no matter which side they were on and their demands for material improvements. For example, the veterans' group in Canton (i.e., the "August 1 Combat Corps") was led by a 30-year-old veteran named Mu Ching-wei, who was a former employee in a public health agency. The corps was first established in January 1967 with 5,000 members. After they took part in the "power seizure" movement of January 22, 1967, there was a sudden and massive increase in the membership from 5,000 to 80,000, of which 30,000 were located outside of Canton. Most members worked in factories and transport sectors which presumably employed a substantial number of veterans over the years, but the corps was also an authentic "cross-trade" organization because it admitted many nonveterans. The leaders, however, were veterans, the admission policy of the corps was cautious, and the membership criteria included: (1) admission of advanced workers, peasants and students; (2) priority to workers; (3) rejection of "black elements"; (4) rejection of "royalists"; (5) rejection of "those in power"; (6) admission of middle-echelon cadres subject to mass debate; and (7) observation of the national leaders' decree of January 13 concerning strengthening of public security.[8]

The veteran group in Shanghai seems to have been similarly well organized. Neale Hunter reports that the Red Guard Army as it was known was a national body, unaffiliated with any other group until late January 1967, when law and order broke down in Shanghai. The Red Guard Army came under fire from Peking and was reportedly accused of "competing with the Liberation Army"; at that time the group tried to strengthen its legitimacy by allying with radical students and workers.[9]

The political orientation of veterans during the Cultural Revolution indicates that those who were demobilized in groups, e.g., those transformed into a production corps, tended to become mostly royalist, i.e., they became anti–Red Guards and supporters of local Party authority. Those who joined the Red Guards or formed their own rebel groups to participate in "power seizure" movements were mostly discharged and reassigned individually. The soldiers discharged in groups presumably suffered less sense of "atomization," since the members of production corps hardly left the army. The individually discharged soldiers were more likely to have a sense of alienation and atomization—especially those who resettled in small towns and the countryside—and their integration into the larger society was particularly difficult.

Information about the activities of veterans is scant but it is significant to note that reports of violent clashes between veterans and radical students came from Heilunkiang, Sinkiang, Inner Mongolia, Ts'inghai, and Kiangsi. Four out of the five areas had large concentrations of veterans in the Production and Construction Corps (the exception was Kiangsi). From 1966 to January 1967, for example, three veterans groups, the "Red Flag Army" (*Hung-chi Chun*), "The Honorable Demobilized Soldiers" (*Jung-fu-chun*) and the "Combat Ready Army" (*Chan-pei Chun*, in Harbin, capital of Heilunkiang), clashed repeatedly with Red Guards from Peking and the students of Technical University (*Kung-yeh Ta-hsueh*). On January 23, 1967, the local garrison was ordered to disarm and disband "The Honorable Demobilized Soldiers."[10] Peking declared the two veteran organizations in Inner Mongolia to be "royalist" and "illegal revolutionary organizations" [i.e., "The Red Defense Army of

Workers and Employees" *(T'se-kun Hung-wei-chun)* and "Red Flag Army" *(Hung-chi Chun)*].[11]

The most violent clash between veterans and leftist students occurred in Sinkiang on January 26, 1967. A Red Guard unit reported that the leftist students were attacked by a fully armed veteran group, the "August 1 Field Army" *(Pa-i Yea-chan-chun)* with a strength of 10,000. The clash reportedly left scores of dead and wounded and 500 students missing in action.[12] It is significant to note that the clash occurred in Shih-ho-tze (northwest of the capital Urumchi), a town built entirely by the Production and Construction Corps of Sinkiang.[13] By 1967 this corps no longer consisted entirely of demobilized soldiers; reportedly there were about 280,000 uprooted youths in the area, 70,000 from Shanghai who had taken the opportunity provided by the Cultural Revolution to storm back to the cities.[14] The situation made it likely that a major incident would follow the clash of January 26, 1967.

The authorities in Peking reacted quickly. The Party Central Committee joined with the State Council and the Military Commission of the Party Central Committee to issue a regulation placing the Production and Construction Corps of Sinkiang under military control. The regulation stated that the corps in Sinkiang

> is not an ordinary force of land reclamation but a production force equipped with arms. Situated in the border area and in the front line of the struggle against revisionism and imperialism, it shoulders the heavy combat task of guarding the frontier of the mother country.[15]

The regulation allows the corps to participate in the Cultural Revolution, but no group of the corps was allowed to link up with any outside organization. Within the corps, each member unit could conduct its own cultural revolution but without interfering with other units. The open debates and criticism allowed in other organizations were not permitted in the corps. The regulation was seemingly effective but some Red Guard bulletins reported that groups of demobilized soldiers in Sinkiang had "taken to the hills" with weapons and equipment.[16] The reports cannot be authenticated.

The militant and aggressive conservatism of the veterans was related to their *collectivity* and the collectivity of the Production and Construction Corps was of secondary importance. For example, there was no corps in Chengtu when the bloody clashes between veterans and radical students took place in May 1967. The munitions plant in Chengtu was itself a collectivity of veterans. Another factor which possibly contributed to the conservatism of veterans was the recency of their demobilization. Presumably, newly demobilized soldiers retained a strong proauthority bias and would participate in antiradical conflicts. Seven hundred recently demobilized soldiers were on the conservative side in the bloody clashes in Kwangsi, and they acted collectively.[17] There is no reliable information concerning the composition of the veteran group involved in the Kiangsi fighting except that the veterans reportedly organized peasants to attack radical students.[18] It is worth repeating that localism in Kiangsi was strong. Royalist actions of the veterans in Kiangsi may have stemmed from an antioutsider sentiment similar to that in Canton, where some veterans made an alliance with native cadres who vented their grievances against the central authorities' antiregionalism policies during the Cultural Revolution. These two local groups united to clash with Red Guards from outside.[19]

The instances which found large and exclusive veteran groups aggressively defending local authorities contrast with those in which veteran-led associations in Canton, Shanghai, Peking and possibly Wuhan joined with radicals in attacks against local authorities. The Canton group, the "August 1 Combat Detachment," earned the name "the Steel August 1st" *(Kan Pai-i)* for valor and aggressiveness.[20] Dai Hsiao-ai testified that the veterans in Canton taught the radicals how to use mortars in armed conflict with the conservatives.[21] The violent actions of veterans in Canton led to the suppression of the "August 1 Combat Detachment" by the military in March 1967. Military officials charged the detachment with assorted crimes ranging from raids on Party offices and military campuses to rape.[22] Hunter reports that the Shanghai "Red Guard Army" was initially an independent and exclusive group, but it allied itself with radical students and workers to challenge the power structure led by Chang Ch'ung-ch'iao and to legitimize its activities.

The Red Guard account suggests that the veteran group in Peking named "The Red Flag Army of Chinese Workers and Peasants" was the group most opposed to the established authority. This group was armed and equipped with trucks; it joined with other organizations (probably with contract and temporary workers and returned students) to break into the exclusive residence of high ranking Party officials (the Chungnanhai in Peking). The "Red Flag Army" raided the State Council and, when its leader was arrested by the Public Security Bureau, it laid siege to the bureau, demonstrated in the street and scattered leaflets appealing for public sympathy. The "Red Flag Army" sent "liaison" officers to various localities to set up branches and sometimes they reportedly assumed responsibility for representing the national leaders.[23] The suggestion (mentioned earlier) that the steelworkers in Wuhan who allied with the radical students were veterans was based on Chin Chien-li's account of strikes by the veterans. Hai Feng reported that radical students in Canton agitated (in July 1967) for a reversal of verdict on the "August 1 Combat Detachment," which was condemned by the army in March. A Wuhan group named "Guerrilla Detachment to Canton from Wuhan Steel September 13th" joined the "August 1" group to support the students and the veterans group of Canton.[24] The "Guerrilla Detachment" was an organization of veterans.

The radicalism of the veterans groups in Shanghai, Peking and Canton can be explained by noting that they were organized by individuals dissatisfied with their role in civilian life. The leader of the "August 1 Combat Detachment" in Canton, for example, was extremely discontented with his position as an employee in a public health agency. And there are other instances when individual veterans joined with the radical students—e.g., Ken Ling reported that a "thirty-eight-year-old veteran" at Amoy University assumed the leadership of a radical Red Guard organization.[25] A veteran was the leader of the "East Is Red" organization of the Pearl River Film Studio in Canton, which was allied with the radical students and later condemned by army authorities in March 1967. Wang Hung-wen, a discontented veteran at a Shanghai cotton mill, began as a rebel and his group was the first to oppose the Shanghai Municipal Party Committee. Wang was later co-opted into the power structure.

These unhappy veterans had a score to settle (so they thought) with the authorities and they recruited like-minded colleagues to engage in radical politics. If the accusatory accounts of the activities of these individuals are credible, it can be assumed they entertained grandiose schemes for themselves. For example, the aforementioned leader of the Canton "August 1 Combat Detachment" claimed that his group "ranked above the local Party Committee" and even above "the Cultural Revolution Group" in Peking.[26] The leader of the "Red Flag Army" in Peking wanted to control the militia system so as to be equal with the Ministry of National Defense.[27] Initially, however, the demands of the veterans were largely economic, e.g., the first delegation from the Canton veteran group to Peking requested permission to operate their own businesses. Their request was apparently granted but the salary the veterans should have in their own business enterprise became a matter of dispute.[28]

The radicalism of the individually organized veteran groups also arose because the national leaders failed to recognize them. The Party leaders were extremely reluctant to condemn student groups regardless of how violent some of them were (for example, the groups in Kwangsi), but they seldom hesitated to outlaw the veteran groups. Both Mao and Lin Piao explicitly forbade the veterans from setting up their own organizations in February 1967.[29] Throughout February 1967 more and more veterans participated in factional fights and the Party Central Committee issued formal and informal notices banning the veteran organizations. An order was issued on February 15 which forbade veterans to organize the so-called Red Defense Army, enter into army units to link up or distribute leaflets.[30] Yet, in December, delegations of veterans appeared in Peking and elsewhere petitioning for reassignment. Some apparently asked to reenlist in the regular army but that request was reportedly rejected by Chou En-lai on December 4 during a meeting with a group called "The Visiting Team of the Transferred Cadres from the Armed Forces" *(San-chun Shang-fang Kan pu)*.[31] In retrospect the injunctions of the national leaders had little effect, since the veterans were a very active group either on the side of local authorities or on the side of radical students in the violent conflicts that took place after May 1967.

The veterans, like other groups, were polarized into a majority of conservatives and a minority of radicals. Because of their political and combat skill, they aggravated group conflict during the Cultural Revolution. The presence of veterans in the students groups created induced conflicts that accounted partly for the protracted group violence from 1966 to 1968.

Notes

1. See, for example, repeated reference to the role of veterans in the new administration of Canton after 1949 in Ezra F. Vogel, *Canton under Communism: Programs and Politics in a Provincial Capital, 1949–1968* (New York, 1971). This is also evidenced in Dai Hsiao-ai's biography.

2. Franz Schurmann, *Ideology and Organization in Communist China* (Berkeley, Calif., 1968), p. 451.

3. For some revealing information about the problems of veterans, see Chin Chien-li, *Pei-kuo Chien-wen-lu* [Odyssey in North China] (Hong Kong, 1973) (hereafter cited by English title).

4. *Yi-chiu Liu-ch'i Chung-kung-nien-pao* [1967 Yearbook on Chinese Communism] (Taipei, 1968), p. 758; for available English references to the work of demobilization in China, see John Gittings, *The Role of the Chinese Army* (London and New York, 1967), pp. 25–29, 92–98, 176–178.

5. Yang Chan-hao, "Latest Upheavals in Sinkiang," *Fei-chin Yen-chiu*, Vol. 1, No. 2 (February 28, 1967), p. 26.

6. Chin Chien-li, *Odyssey in North China*, pp. 411–412.

7. Ibid., pp. 413–419, 436.

8. Hai Feng, *Kuang-chou Ti-ch'u Wen-ke Lieh-chen Shu-lueh* [An Account of the Cultural Revolution in the Canton Area] (Hong Kong, 1971), pp. 61–63.

9. Neale Hunter, *Shanghai Journal: An Eyewitness Account of the Cultural Revolution* (Boston, 1969), pp. 229–230.

10. *Yomiuri* (Tokyo), January 19, 1967, and *Mainichi* (Tokyo), January 25, 1967, as cited in Chao Tsung, "An Account of the 'Great Proletarian Cultural Revolution,' " (Part 30), *Tsukuo* [China Monthly], No. 76 (July 1, 1970); this was later corroborated by the official paper *Kuang-min Jih-pao*, January 31, 1967.

11. *Yi-chiu Liu-pa Chung-kung-nien-pao* [1968 Yearbook on Chinese Communism] (Taipei, 1969), p. 426 (hereafter cited by English title).

12. The report was published by "The Revolutionary Rebel Corps of Sinkiang Army Corps" in *Pin-tuan Nung-hsueh-yuan Ke-min-chao-fan-pin-tuan* (Sinkiang), January 28, 1967, as reprinted in Chao Tsung, "An Account of the 'Great Proletarian Cultural Revolution,' " (Part 31), *Tsukuo*, No. 77 (August 1, 1970), pp. 17–18.

13. Yang Chan-hao, "Latest Upheavals in Sinkiang," p. 28.

14. *Radio Sinkiang* reported on May 4, 1965, that there were "260,000 intellectual youths" with the Production and Construction Corps of Sinkiang; Shanghai youths accounted for 50,000. *Radio Shanghai* reported on May 3, 1966, that the number of Shanghai youths in Sinkiang was increased to 70,000; see Yang Chan-hao, "Latest Upheavals in Sinkiang," p. 29.

15. *CCP Documents of the Great Proletarian Cultural Revolution, 1966–1967* (Hong Kong, 1968), p. 258 (hereafter cited as *CCP Documents*).

16. Reuters news dated February 1, 1967, from Tokyo quoting Japanese correspondents' accounts, see Chao Tsung, "An Account of the 'Great Proletarian Cultural Revolution,' " (Part 31), *Tsukuo*, No. 77 (August 1, 1970), p. 18.

17. Ting Wang, ed., *Chung-kung Wen-hua Ta-ke-ming Tze-liao Hui-pien* [A Collection of Documents on the Great Proletarian Cultural Revolution] (Hong Kong, 1972), p. 332 (hereafter cited as *Collection of Documents*).

18. *Radio Nanchang*, 0315 GMT, January 20, 1967; also in Chao Tsung, "An Account of the 'Great Proletarian Cultural Revolution,' " (Part 31), *Tsukuo*, No. 77 (August 1, 1970), p. 14.

19. Hai Feng, *Account of the Cultural Revolution in Canton*, p. 62; Ting Wang, *Collection of Documents*, pp. 316–317.

20. Hai Feng, *Account of the Cultural Revolution in Canton*, pp. 61–63.

21. Gordon A. Bennett and Ronald N. Montaperto, *Red Guard: The Political Biography of Dai Hsiao-ai* (Garden City, N.Y., 1972), p. 187.

22. Hai Feng, *Account of the Cultural Revolution in Canton*, pp. 104–196.

23. *Chingkangshan*, March 8, 1967, in *Red Guard Publications*, Group X-2 (hereafter cited as RGP).

24. Hai Feng, *Account of the Cultural Revolution in Canton*, p. 190.

25. Ken Ling, *The Revenge of Heaven: Journal of a Young Chinese* (New York, 1972), p. 65.

26. Leaflet distributed by the "Revolutionary Rebels of Taishan *Hsien*, Kwangtung province," trans. in *Survey of China Mainland Press* (Hong Kong: U.S. Consulate General), No. 4038, pp. 12–15.

27. *Chingkangshan*, March 8, 1967, in RGP, Group X-2.

28. *Kan Pa-i*, October 15, 1967, in RGP, Group X-4.

29. *Chung-kung Wen-hua Ta-ke-ming Chung-yao Wen-chien Hui-pien* [Important CCP Documents of the Great Proletarian Cultural Revolution] (Taipei, 1973), p. 204.

30. *1968 Yearbook on Chinese Communism*, p. 108.

31. Ibid., p. 109.

PART THREE
CONFLICT
& ORDER

8

CONFLICT RESOLUTION

Γhe Cultural Revolution in China, which began as an authentic induced conflict by a section of the elite, had, by August 1967, become a runaway movement involving violent group conflict. Numerous groups voluntarily joined the movement to seek redress of real and imagined wrongs. The major cities, particularly in the South, reported a great increase in crime. The residents of Canton formed vigilante groups to patrol the neighborhood and they erected roadblocks.[1] Armed workers, together with the police in Shanghai, rounded up gangs of juvenile delinquents who "model[led] themselves after . . . hoodlums."[2] Looting was reported in Peking and a Red Guard group was armed and entrusted to patrol the streets.[3] The movement obviously no longer served a useful purpose for the leaders around Mao Tse-tung and the problem of bringing the conflict to a close proved to be difficult and protracted.

The effort to end the conflict in 1967 and 1968 was hampered by the lack of an impartial mediator. The new political culture in China explicitly denounced political neutralism and everyone was formally required to draw a line between the people and the enemy, and between the Left and the revisionists. Dai Hsiao-ai reports that "everyone naturally took the view that one's political standpoint was a matter of life and death."[4] That political and social context made it extremely difficult to find an impartial mediator. Another obstacle to the resolution of conflict during the Cultural Revolution was the lack of a clear goal—thus it was essentially a large-scale induced conflict. Mao Tse-tung may have had a goal, but it was difficult to identify given his duality of thought. Also, the competing goals of the combating groups were too numerous and often too particularistic to admit compromise. And, of course, Mao's reluctance to use force presented a third obstacle to conflict resolution. As reported earlier, the Army's use of coercion in March 1967 was censured by the leaders in Peking.

The serious situation in August and September 1967, however, did not permit the leaders to remain passive and, despite the difficulties mentioned above, they moved to control and terminate group conflict. Since there was no impartial and neutral mediator among the conflicting groups, the leaders in Peking had to find a substitute. They apparently decided to "de-radicalize" the image of leaders like Chiang Ch'ing and Mao Tse-tung and strengthen Chou En-lai's image of "moderation." To do so, a "line must be drawn" between Chiang Ch'ing and Mao Tse-tung on one side and the "ultra-leftists" on the other. The "ultra-leftists" also denigrated Chou En-lai's reputation (or so the government claimed). In September 1967, the leaders in Peking publicly condemned the "May 16th Corps," who were accused of "ultra-leftism." Several onetime "close comrades-in-arms" of Chiang Ch'ing were included in this group. The list of political sins committed by the corps was headed by its attack on Chou En-lai and its effort to create dissension between Chou and the Cultural Revolution Group.[5] Following the condemnation of the "May 16th Corps," more "ultra-leftists" were dragged out, including Wang Li, the hero of the Wuhan Incident of July 20. These actions brought the image of a central or moderate group to the forefront and Chou En-lai's position was strengthened. Chou was then apparently put in charge of mediating the conflict and bringing it to a close. Chou's actions indicated that he was a specialist in conflict resolution.

Pacification & Recognition

Chou first moved to improve public relations and beginning in August 1967, he personally received several delegations, mostly of students but also from other groups. Most of the warring factions were invited to send delegates to Peking and they were made to attend special classes and conduct talks with Chou's subordinates to work out mutual agreements concerning the cessation of armed struggle and future representation on the revolutionary committees. Depending on the progress made in mediation by his lieutenants, Chou selectively granted long audiences with the delegations. These talks never settled matters of substance or even discussed them in depth; rather, the talks were intended as symbolic gestures of recognition. Several scholars have noted that recognition is a first step in reducing violent conflict to the point where it becomes nonviolent and more manageable. Chou also used the subject orientation of the Chinese people to good effect in these talks. There was little back talk by the delegates, who seemed to be awed by Chou's presence. They, like repentant children, probably enjoyed his gentle scolding.[6]

Moderation of Language

Chou's sensitivity to cultural factors was reflected in his attempt to moderate the use of extreme language. He also tried to eliminate Shanghai as a focal point of radicalism. For example, during one of his long audiences, Chou objected to the use of the phrase "surround and attack" *(wei-ch'ao)* in describing the government's effort to combat factionalism.

> These two words "surround-attack" are not proper. Who has used them to talk about factionalism? ([Li] Fu-ch'un: The press.) The *Wen-hui Daily* [Shanghai] and the *Peking Daily* reprinted them. It is better to say the overcoming of bourgeois and petit-bourgeois factionalism and strengthening the Party spirit of the proletariat. "Surround-attack" can be easily mistaken as dealing with the contradictions between the enemy and us. The use of "surround-attack" is apt to confuse the nature of contradiction and widen conflict. It might even lead to masses attacking masses. I do not remember I ever used these words in my report. . . . *Comrade Chiang Ch'ing said that Shanghai does not always lead everything. Peking has its merits.* We must use scientific analysis [emphasis added].[7]

Significantly, Chou invoked the name of Chiang Ch'ing to neutralize the radical influence emanating from Shanghai. Probably unknown to Chou, extreme language was still being used in that city by Wang Hung-wen. As a security official with newly acquired power and status, Wang reported to his colleagues at the "No. 29 State Cotton Mill" in February that he had "surrounded" and "attacked" factionalism with a vengeance. Wang also mentioned the arrest and detention of "agents" and "traitors."[8] Yet Chou, in the talk quoted above, objected to the word "overthrow" in dealing with Yu Ch'iu-li (Yu was in charge of the petroleum industry) for fear of putting Yu "up against the wall."

After trying to moderate the language of the radicals, Chou attempted to build a new image for Mao and Chiang Ch'ing. Specifically, Chou tried to deny the radicals the use of Mao as their patron saint in their violent actions. Chou was joined in this effort by other leaders. For example, he told the delegates from the northeastern provinces on September 28, 1967, that Mao's statement in his "Report on an Investigation of the Peasant Movement in Hunan" about "striking the landlord down to the dust and keeping him there" was a "figure of speech" and that "Chairman Mao never advocated corporal punishment."[9] Chang Ch'ung-ch'iao, the Shanghai leader, similarly told a group in Honan that Mao's statement that "revolution is not playing host at dinner" applied only to "landlords, enemies and captives in the past," not to present cadres.[10] The Red Guards were thus denied in their attempt to transfer their "superego" function to Mao—an attempt which would have facilitated their aggressions against other groups.

Chou also tried to absolve Chiang Ch'ing of blame for the Red Guard attack on the military. He received the delegation from Canton on September 27, 1967, and declared: " 'To drag out a small group of leaders from the army' is an incorrect slogan. This error was first discovered by Chiang Ch'ing. Comrade Chiang Ch'ing should be given the credit for this."[11] Actually, the public on mainland China knew that Mao Tse-tung was the leader who first objected to the call of "dragging out a small group from the army," and Chou's attempt to credit Chiang Ch'ing was a transparent attempt to give her a moderate image.[12] The radical youths were thus deprived of another patron in their rebellion against the Party authorities.

Return to Centralized Segregation

Chou En-lai and other leaders also strongly emphasized the need for dissolving "cross-trade" organizations and the elimination of the "link-up" movement. Their policy was intended to facilitate a return to integration through segregation—the policy which obtained prior to the Cultural Revolution. Chou made this plain to delegates from the northeastern provinces on September 28, 1967:

> We demand that students do not go on "link-up" trips anymore. The "cross-trade" organizations must be separated. The workers and employees of the railway system must have their own organization. Those in defense industries must not join other organizations. We have now decided that the defense industry in Peking will organize its own alliance, not to link up with other industries or schools; otherwise no guarantee of production can be made.
>
> "Cross-trade" organizations must be separated step by step. Universities, high schools, workers, poor and lower middle peasants,

all of them must set up representative councils *within* themselves. On that basis we can unite and form provincial revolutionary committees [emphasis added].[13]

The breaking up of "cross-trade" organizations and the suspension of "link-up" movements proved to be the most difficult steps taken to resolve conflict. The government moved as early as February 1967 to break up some of the most militant "cross-trade" groups, e.g., the veterans, contract and temporary workers, and students returned from the countryside—they were the most disruptive. As soon as the old groups were dissolved, new ones were formed. The activists apparently resolved not to be subjected again to the tactic of "divide and rule." Nine months after Chou's talk with the northeasterners (on June 12, 1968), he received a delegation from Wuhan and despairingly stated that "so far as the 'cross-trade' organizations are concerned, the five provinces in the Central-South have not found a solution." General Huang Yung-shen, the military commander in charge of Central-South China, reaffirmed Chou's statement: "The problem of 'cross-trade organizations' has not been solved in Wuhan and not in Canton either."[14] New "cross-trade" organizations were actually formed in Canton as a backlash following the reimposition of control by the national leaders. The Kwangtung Provincial Revolutionary Committee was still calling mass rallies to denounce "cross-trade organizations" in August 1968.[15]

Stopping the "link-up" movement proved to be just as difficult. The government initiated a series of measures designed to put a stop to the link-up movement as early as November 12, 1966. Free travel on trains by students was banned on November 16, 1966.[16] Then specific groups were forbidden to participate in the "link-up" movement—schoolteachers (January 19, 1967),[17] personnel in the defense industry,[18] and students of military art and literary institutes.[19] The "link-up" movement as such was explicitly banned by the government on March 19, 1967.[20] These efforts had little effect and students from military institutes and other military personnel refused to respond. Military personnel were first ordered to report back to their units on February 8, 1967, yet the government was still appealing for their return on April 17.[21] Chou En-lai and Chiang Ch'ing delivered an ultimatum on September 17 to students in Peking who were the most vigorous in the "link-up" movement. The students were ordered to return to their schools in one month or be expelled. The seniors were to be denied work assignments.[22] The ultimatum was formalized by another state decree on September 23.[23] Yet small groups of radical students apparently continued to defy state orders. The "link-up" movement continued in Szechwan in December 1967, and violent group conflict persisted through the spring of 1968. The Szechwan students used "propaganda teams" and "exchange experiences in education revolution" as an excuse for travelling around the province.[24] As mentioned earlier, radical student leaders who desired to set up a "correspondence network" convened a conference in Peking in July 1968.

The government meanwhile directed the attention of students and workers who returned to their units to the formation of a grand alliance *(ta-lien-h'o)*. Following Chou En-lai's earlier instructions, each trade was to have a grand alliance but there were to be no cross-trade alliances. The alliance among railway workers received special emphasis, and the French reporter Jean Vincent noted:

> The grand alliance—the fusion of different revolutionary groups to which Chinese railworkers belong—could be the decisive factor in China's return to political and economic order.[25]

Chou maintained that the following method would be effective in dealing with the intransigent groups. First, he proposed to identify the leaders. Second, an attempt would be made to mobilize group members in a struggle against the "black heads" to separate leaders and followers and thus limit the struggle. Third, Chou planned to prevent "the real rightists and past power-holders" from demanding a reversal of verdict.* Finally, the educational value of the whole process was to be stressed to all the members.[26] The plan was, of course, to limit antagonistic struggle to avoid provoking stronger group cohesion and prolonged resistance. Chou claimed that his method effectively dealt with the activities of a group in the agricultural and forestry ministry and limited factional fights between student groups in Chekiang. Chou's method of fragmenting the opposition was not new; the Communist Party used it in the early 1950s to deal with the secret societies and other quasireligious sects within Chinese society. Vogel summarizes this tactic as "careful preparation by detailed investigation and swift elimination of leading opponents to intimidate the rest of the opposition."[27]

Despite Chou En-lai's statement that excessive demands for reversals of verdict were to be prevented, there is evidence, at least in Canton, to indicate that there was a move toward reversal in February 1968. Teacher and bureaucrat groups were rather quickly exonerated and those wrongly sent to the countryside to serve at hard labor in June–August 1966 were returned to their homes and jobs. They were publicly given back their good names and were permitted to reestablish urban residences. They were paid overdue wages and loans were made available.[28]

---

*Redressing the wrongs done during the Cultural Revolution.

Whether all the victims of the Red Guard movement were thus rehabilitated in Canton or elsewhere is a moot question.

Social Control Reestablished

The breakup of "cross-trade" organizations and the stoppage of the "link-up" movement were accompanied by an assertion of social control —in particular, power was restored to the Public Security Bureau. The reports of crime in major cities provided a rationale for the return of police power. Yet, the spirit of populism and antiprofessionalism generated by Mao also had an effect on the use of police. Police from the Public Security Bureau were required to work in cooperation with Red Guards, the workers' militia and representatives of city residents. For example, a *Radio Shanghai* broadcast on December 26, 1967, reported that

> the Shanghai public security organization, Red Guards, armed workers, and revolutionary masses of Shanghai, under the leadership of the Mao Tse-tung's thought PLA propaganda team, took massive revolutionary action on 25 and 26 December against hoodlums and delinquent gangs who have been frenziedly disrupting the great proletarian Cultural Revolution and sabotaging the interests of the revolution.

Mass trials of criminals were televised in Peking. One case involved a

> televised trial of eleven men before a crowd of 10,000 in Peking's biggest stadium . . . followed by the immediate execution of two of the convicted. . . . The eleven defendants were described by the tribunal chairman as counter-revolutionaries. But for three of the eleven, the indictments and final pleas suggested that they were in fact guilty of common-law crimes.[29]

By using and publicizing the renewed power of the Security Bureau to exert social control, the government was probably trying to kill two birds with one stone. Jean Vincent aptly commented on the Shanghai anticrime campaign:

> It would appear that for tactical reasons Chinese officials are combining the normal fight against crime in a city area of ten million persons with the struggle against activists who refuse to obey the local revolutionary committee.[30]

Neither the method of dividing intransigent groups nor the use of police power was new. During the "Suppression of Counterrevolutionaries" campaign in Canton from 1950 to 1951, the Communists killed known criminals as well as "genuinely popular local leaders who might have been potential leaders against Communist rule."[31]

The Chinese Communist system of social control is noteworthy in that Mao Tse-tung and some other leaders seemingly shared a genuine desire to depart from the Soviet model, i.e., a separate and professional agency like the GPU or the MVD. Mao always emphasized mass involvement, particularly in the use of coercion. Thus the following speech by the late Hsieh Fu-ch'ih (the head of the Public Security Ministry) is extremely interesting and significant. While lecturing his staff on August 7, 1967, Hsieh stated:

> As long as we can carry out a policy through the masses, then let's do it through the masses. Let's not be so secretive. Only a minority of matters can not be done through the masses. We adopted the mass line in the first and second suppression of counterrevolutionaries campaign under the leadership of Chairman Mao. The Chairman has concluded that to use the mass line is to commit fewer errors than to rely on a small group of persons to do it. Even if we made mistakes under that circumstance, they could be more easily corrected. The Soviet way, to let security and defense agencies specialize and acquire special status, is to use the public security agency to supervise the masses not the other way around. This influenced our security agency quite deeply. Our security agency was not under the supervision of the masses. Instead we began to specialize and supervise others. We have not been able to change this tradition. . . . To use the instrument of dictatorship to shield bad people and suppress the masses is a characteristic of Soviet revisionism. That fellow Shelepin, after he became the chairman of Committee for State Security, did not even want to be the director of the Secretariat of the Central Committee. So you see the power of this security committee was greater than the central secretariat. . . . In my opinion, we should from now on reduce the status of the public security agency to that of a common servant. Anyone can command it. Its power must be small like a sesame seed. On this question of the scale of power, I had an argument with Lo Jui-ch'ing [former director of the Public Security Ministry]. I stated that the power of the Public Security Ministry was too great. Lo Jui-ch'ing said that this power was given to us by the Center. So at that central meeting we started arguing with each other. That "Lo, the long fellow" has long arms. Even if you gave him all the power he would still want more. I am not so capable and I can not handle so many things. We should not have that much power. Common

folks can supervise us. Can't the Public Security Ministry undergo
some fundamental changes? Our power must be small but our work
must be heavy.[32]

Hai Feng, a former resident of Canton, testified that "workers' pickets"
were formed in the city after March 1968 to restore order. Yet the
pickets were mostly from the conservative "Headquarters Faction,"[33]
conforming in spirit to the policy described by Hsieh Fu-ch'ih. In reality, there is some doubt whether the action of the pickets constituted a
form of mass supervision over the security police; they may have merely
been used to impart a populistic image to the police force. Nothing
Hsieh said clarified this point. To quote Vogel, "The regime made every
effort to gain as much popular support for the suppression as possible"
by organizing mass rallies and holding public exhibitions during the
"Suppression of Counterrevolutionaries" campaign between 1950 and
1951.[34]

In 1968, the government still relied on professional and special forces
to deal with dissidents. A special army was created in June 1968—the
"Central Support-the-Left Force" *(Chung-yang Tse-tso Pu-tui).* This
special force was

> authorized to check and correct the behavior of local troops partic-
> ipating in armed conflict in various provinces. It has power to
> arrest leaders of the troops involved and to disband their forces,
> if necessary. It also has authority to apprehend Red Guard leaders
> on the spot if their conduct is judged improper. . . . The . . . force
> is also invested with certain political power to nip local distur-
> bances fomented by political dissidents in the bud. The security
> force may round these elements and put them into concentration
> camps if necessary.[35]

The special force was quickly dispatched to Fukien, Yunnan, Kwangsi,
Tibet and Sinkiang—the five provinces that were the last to establish
revolutionary committees.

"New" Ruling Structure Established

All the measures discussed so far culminated in the eventual establishment of a new ruling structure—the revolutionary committees. The
radicals lost ground, since they wanted communes but were given committees.

On February 5, 1967, Shanghai proclaimed the formation of a new
ruling body, the "Shanghai People's Commune." The name was quietly

changed to "revolutionary committee" a week later. Chairman Mao reportedly preferred "committee" to "commune" and his reason was innocuous—"if many people's communes are established throughout the country, the name of the Chinese People's Republic will have to be changed to the Chinese People's Commune."[36] Mao's stated rationale for the change was probably specious. Analyst Chao Tsung notes that "commune" by definition meant "Paris Commune" in the Chinese setting and was meant to involve an election of officials. But Chou En-lai informed the "Flag Faction" (radicals) of Canton on November 3, 1967, that Mao preferred consultation, not decision by ballots which Mao said "is a bourgeois matter." Another leader, Ch'i Peng-yu, clarified Mao's stand further by saying, "If we had relied on the ballot we the Communists could not have won. The revolutionaries were always a minority at the start."[37]

Mao ultimately gave his blessing not to the "Shanghai Commune" but to the revolutionary committee of Heilunkiang on January 31, 1967. But the radicals in Heilunkiang also lost ground. In their first proclamation, they stated their goal, "all working staff shall be elected in accordance with the election system of the Paris Commune under extensive democracy. Those who are supported by the revolutionary masses may be re-elected, those incompetent may be dismissed at any time."[38] This was apparently no longer true in 1968, since Kang Shen told the delegates from Kirin province on March 6, 1968:

> The agreement among the Heilunkiang groups contains a good statement and I have recommended this to all the provinces. It says, "The Heilunkiang Revolutionary Committee is a provisional ruling agency based on revolutionary three-way alliance and personally approved by Chairman Mao." That means that this organization is not an alliance or a federation of all factions. It is certainly not a liaison station of the factions. It is not an organization of the masses. It is just a provisional ruling agency. . . . Its members are not the representatives of various factions. Those who join the revolutionary committee do not represent the interest of small groups.[39]

Kang Shen, a specialist in security matters, considered the revolutionary committee to be actually an "instrument of the dictatorship of the proletariat." He clarified his stand on July 25, 1968, when he and Chou En-lai received a delegation from Kwangsi:

> If you comrades have anything to say, then say it. The Center (*chung-yang*) is for democracy. But let me tell you one thing. You are not here on a law suit. You can not present conditions. You

can not present conditions to the proletarian headquarters led by Chairman Mao and Vice Chairman Lin. You come here to learn from the thought of Mao Tse-tung and the revolutionary way of Chairman Mao. It is not permissible to present demands to the proletarian headquarters. This meeting has been called by the Center and if you want to present conditions, then does the Center obey you or you obey the Center?[40]

The Cultural Revolution thus turned full circle and China reverted to the centralized institutionalization of conflict. Between the Center and the people, according to Kang Shen, there could not be any give and take. The young radicals of *Shen-wu-lien* were correct after all:

Our state apparatus is to a considerable extent a survival of the past and has undergone hardly any serious change. It has only been slightly touched up on the surface, but in all other respects it is a most typical relic of our old state machine [see Chap. 5, n. 35].

In the final analysis the methods leaders like Chou En-lai, Kang Shen and others used to terminate group conflict in the Cultural Revolution reflected their keen insight into the sociology of conflict. According to Oberschall, the conditions for a consolidated protest movement are the availability of a charismatic leader, emergence of a distinct subculture and establishment of a centralized organizational structure.[41] Chou En-lai's emphasis on destroying the "cross-trade" organizations was intended to prevent the emergence of a centralized organizational structure and the emergence of a mass leader. Chou's public relations work and the symbol of the Center *(chung-yang)* invoked by Kang Shen were designed to strengthen the subject and centralist orientation of the rebels to reduce or arrest the tendency toward establishment of a "subculture." Factionalism among the rebels facilitated the work of Chou and Kang, and that is a primary cause for the disintegration of protest movements. Chou En-lai's attempt to "drag out the black head" and limit the struggle to leaders was designed to further divide the rebel groups.

Conflict Unresolved

Chou En-lai, Kang Shen and others restored order and social control in China during 1967 and 1968, but there is little indication that the old conflicts were resolved. On the contrary, deeply rooted conflicts were exposed and became the cause of bitter fighting between the various groups. The result was that

> grievances begun or exacerbated during the movement would presumably be brought up again the next time there was a struggle. ... The cadres, especially, would harbor grudges against their critics, and the thought of class vengeance would never be far from the surface.[42]

During late 1967 and throughout 1968 the disaffection of students was the most immediate problem the government faced. Student reactions ranged from passivity to last-ditch resistance and Chou En-lai summarized their attitudes on January 17, 1968, when he received representatives from the northeastern provinces:

> *Ha-chun-kung* (Harbin Military Engineering College) which gave a proud performance during the initial period of rebellion, formed an alliance recently and lost two-thirds of its members after their return home. Is this called revolution? I think that many of you present here came from *Ha-chun-kung*. Don't you feel sorry at hearing this? This is bourgeois oscillation. You have engaged in the revolution for more than a year, and you must have got tired and wanted to go home to lie down for a rest. Those who do so are not so bad. The bad ones turn to love-making, playing poker, leading a dissipated life, having the ideas of the United Action Committee, writing reactionary handbills, etc.[43]

Ha-chun-kung was one of the most vigorous participants in the "link-up" movement and it established liaison stations in all the major cities in China. The "young aristocrats" (i.e., children of high ranking Party, state and military officials in Peking) formed the "United Action Committee" to attack the leaders of the Cultural Revolution.

The alleged attitude of dissipation on the part of certain rebels was the subject of a telling report prepared by the library staff of a school in Canton. The staff submitted a letter on March 4, 1968, to the editor of a Red Guard publication which stated that romantic literature had inundated the campus. During a three-month period, from December 1967 to the end of February 1968, 26,269 books were borrowed by the students; 16,107 (61 percent) were romantic literature including classical Chinese novels like *The Dream of a Red Chamber*, *Water Margin* and *Romance of the Three Kingdoms* and works by Maupassant, Balzac, Shakespeare and Tolstoy. Works written by these European authors were cleaned out and grabbed by students, and some students broke into the library in search of "yellow literature." Apparently the students had no desire to study Mao's works.[44] Another group of students allegedly buried their heads in mathematics and theoretical science and claimed: "Those who do research and engage in mental work make the greatest contribution to the state."[45] Wall posters in Peking reported that "counterrevolutionary performances were presented in Tientsin, Shanghai, and Peking in clandestine theaters set up in caves on the initiative of lawless Red Guards."[46]

Ken Ling contributed a vivid account of the students' disillusionment and passivity. He was brutally informed by Chen Po-ta in January 1968 that the Amoy rebels would either cease their factional war or suffer the consequences and he then reported:

> All the representatives walked out of the People's Hall together. There were many emotional outbursts. Some simply swore. . . . Others in a melancholy mood sang the lyrics of "Liang Shan-po and Chu Ying-tai," a love story with a tragic ending. The No. 1 leader of Ke Tsao Hui, putting his hands in his pockets as though he felt cold, said deliberately but with a touch of resignation, "Aside from Mao Tse-tung, who else can be emperor."
>
> We were deprived of official responsibilities and were no longer representatives. What did it matter? Everything was over. So we actually joined with our former opponents during the few days left to go about Peking. We went to restaurants together and reminded one another never to speak of the past.
>
> Ho Wei-ming seemed to become conscious of his age [he was the "thirty-eight-year-old" veteran turned Red Guard leader of Ken Ling's group]. . . . Most of the leaders said that they wanted to become hermits in some temple of western Fukien and renounce the mundane world. These were only words; anyway, everyone knew that under the present rule no one would be permitted to lead a life in seclusion for long.[47]

Chou En-lai mentioned other students who made a fighting last stand. A group in Canton declared that the "revolutionary committee must have its own armed force and that force is the Flag Faction of revolutionary rebels."[48] From late 1967 to mid-1968 Red Guard publications reported numerous reactionary and counterrevolutionary groups such as the "Extraordinary Committee of the Chinese Communist Party" in Peking,[49] the "Worker-peasant Joint Defense State" in Honan, "Young Communist Association" in Peking, "Anti-monarchical Restoration Association" in Shanghai, and the "Chinese Masses Party" in Inner Mongolia.[50] Neale Hunter commented on the return of almost all the old cadres to the Foreign Languages Institute in Shanghai: "I sensed that the deep factional divisions were not really bridged. The bitterness that remained would keep surfacing."[51]

Every society has conflicts, which are, after all, a natural concomitant of human relations. The group conflicts in China are noteworthy, however, because the state's mode of conflict management had such destructive consequences. Specifically, the leaders single-mindedly cultivated conflict as a norm, yet genuine conflicts were not allowed by the monistic power structure. There was also a lack of consistency and consensus among the leaders themselves regarding the manipulation of conflict. Over a period of time pent-up grievances and genuine conflict accumulated and when they finally surfaced, the adherents made such extreme demands that it was difficult, if not impossible, to aggregate them. Dahrendorf observed,

> . . . in the Communist countries of the East they have adopted an ideology of intense conflict. The two go together well: on account of the monistic structure of conflict (and many other) relations in totalitarian countries, these relations have gained, and continue to gain, in intensity. Whatever conflicts do occur involve both rulers and ruled with their whole personalities; and if these conflicts become open and violent, the cost of defeat is too high for both parties to allow graceful retreat. "Totality" distinguishes the totalitarian state in more than one respect, including the extent of the changes desired by those who, for the time being, are its powerless subject.[52]

Group conflict in the Cultural Revolution conformed to Dahrendorf's observation. The desires of new groups, i.e., contract and temporary workers, worker-peasants and students returned from the countryside, were expressed for the first time between 1967 and 1968. But the demands of students, workers, peasants and veterans had all been expressed before 1967, particularly in the "Hundred Flowers" campaign of 1957. Apparently these groups' discontent could not be entirely articulated via the formal structures of government prior to the Cultural Revolution. There were minor alterations in the formal structure after 1968, but those changes were no more conducive to the decentralized institutionalization of conflict than the structure which preceded the changes.[53] In fact, the standard technique of Chinese Communist leaders, Maoists or not, involves making minor concessions now and then. The aftermath of the "Hundred Flowers" campaign of 1957 was a case in point. Moreover, this technique is commonly used in all Communist states. According to Dahrendorf,

> Suppression of opposition is coupled with a careful and continuous scrutiny of the embryonic manifest interests of the potential opposition, and changes are introduced from time to time which incorporate some of these interests. In the latter case, suppression is not complete, and violent conflicts may simmer under the surface for a long time before they erupt . . .[54]

Ezra Vogel also describes how the Chinese Communist leaders coped with criticism in the "Hundred Flowers" campaign of 1957: "It was a familiar pattern: minor concessions were made to the alienated while the main concern, the discrediting of the severe attacks on the party and government was pursued with full vigor."[55] The Chinese leaders repeated these tactics in the aftermath of the Cultural Revolution, as indicated by their dissolution (more accurately, their promise to dissolve) the special prep schools for the children of high ranking officials, their requirement that cadres engage in manual labor (e.g., the "May 7th School") and their acceptance of a symbolic representation from the "masses" in the revolutionary committees. Actually, no fundamental adjustment was made specifically to accommodate the desires of any particular group. The group conflicts of 1967 and 1968 probably were a precursor of things to come and they may have increased the probability of renewed group conflict in the years ahead.

Prospect for Renewed Conflict

The conditions for mass group conflict mentioned earlier include divisions among the elite, a loosening of social control, the presence of precipitating events, the availability of focal points, and communications.

The Chinese Communist Party elite may have been more seriously divided during the 1970s than anyone ever anticipated, considering the impact of the Lin Piao affair and the recent "anti-Confucius" campaigns. The attempt to denigrate Confucius has been interpreted as another battle between radicals and moderates and it has even implicated Chou En-lai.[56] The present division of the Party elite, however, is not accompanied by a loosening of social control. But there have been reports about unrest in parts of China from January to August 1974.[57] There is little doubt that the imposition of social control is accepted by the majority of people who suffered during the Cultural Revolution. Yet, the decision to exercise control is not made by the people—that is a function of the elite. Divisions among the elite and the loosening of social control are intricately related in Communist systems.

The most significant change made during the Cultural Revolution involved communications. Prior to 1966, Peking was *the* center of ideological communication, but today Shanghai is as important as Peking in this respect. Two publications in Shanghai have taken a leftist line in ideological matters—the journal *Study and Criticism* (published by Futan University) and the newspaper *Wen-hui Daily*. It will be recalled that Futan University was a focal point of radical student activity during the Cultural Revolution. The *Wen-hui Daily* is significant, according to one observer, because a special category must be made for the newspapers and radio broadcasts of Shanghai, which since 1967 have consistently served as vehicles for points of view more radical or militant than the national media. It may be that Mao-intimates Chang Ch'ung-ch'iao and Yao Wen-yuan, both long-time Shanghai propagandists and associates of Chiang Ch'ing, have been able to use the Shanghai media as their own voice. . . . There were indications in 1969, however, that these media were not always more "leftist" than the national media; perhaps the term "vanguard" would describe their function exactly.[58]

The publication of these leftist organs appears to meet Mao's long-standing desire to have an ideological superego that will keep the compromising bureaucratic ego in line.[59] (Note that only journals more leftist than the national media are allowed to be published.) Mao's policy is obviously not liberalization.[60] It is entirely possible that the two sources of political ideology—Peking and Shanghai—may again be affected by a divided elite (as they were in 1966). If that occurs, the conditions for a civil war may result. The ideological and geographical dichotomy is infinitely more conducive to intense and violent group conflict than either a unicentered or multicentered situation. The development of coequal centers of ideological dispensation (though Shanghai is not yet entirely equal to Peking) might also lead to political pluralism, instead of civil war, provided certain fundamental changes in the political culture and the basic structure of political power in China also occur. There is no evidence to indicate that those changes are in the offing.

Several things may occur that qualify as precipitating events. When Mao dies, submerged tensions among the Party elite may again surface. The radical minority might then appeal to discontented groups for support in a struggle for power. Alternatively, the conservative majority might act first by initiating reprisals against radicals for the wrongs done in the Cultural Revolution. A genuine Chinese revolution in conflict management, a change toward decentralization in which conflict is regulated by explicit rules, predictable behavior and continuity, is only a slim possibility, given the existing centralist political culture and the continuing accumulation of social and economic unrest.

Notes

1.   *Hung-se Pao-tung*, August 22, 1967, trans. in *Survey of China Mainland Press* (Hong Kong: U.S. Consulate General), No. 4026, p. 12 (hereafter cited as SCMP).

2.   *Radio Shanghai*, 1300 GMT, December 26, 1967.

3. *AFP* (English broadcast), 1402 GMT, August 22, 1967.

4. Gordon A. Bennett and Ronald N. Montaperto, *Red Guard: The Political Biography of Dai Hsiao-ai* (Garden City, N.Y., 1972), p. 181.

5. *Jen-min Jih-pao* [People's Daily], September 3, 1967.

6. For examples of these talks, see Ting Wang, ed., *Chung-kung Wen-hua Ta-ke-ming Tze-liao Hui-pien* [A Collection of Documents on the Great Proletarian Cultural Revolution] (Hong Kong, 1972) (hereafter cited as *Collection of Documents*).

7. *Kuang-ya-pa-san-i*, May 1968, in *Red Guard Publications*, Group XI-1 (hereafter cited as RGP).

8. *Wen-ke Tung-hsun*, March 1968, in RGP, Group XI-2.

9. RGP, Group X-1.

10. *Cheng-fa Hung-chi*, No. 3–4 (October 17, 1967). Available translation in SCMP, No. 4070, pp. 1–12.

11. Hai Feng, *Kuang-chou Ti-ch'u Wen-ke Lieh-chen Shu-lueh* [An Account of the Cultural Revolution in the Canton Area] (Hong Kong, 1971), p. 255 (hereafter cited by English title).

12. *AFP* (English broadcast), 1718 GMT, November 26, 1967.

13. RGP, Group X-1.

14. Ting Wang, *Collection of Documents*, pp. 60, 63–64.

15. Ibid., p. 313.

16. *Chung-kung Wen-hua Ta-ke-ming Chung-yao Wen-chien Hui-pien* [Important CCP Documents of the Great Proletarian Cultural Revolution] (Taipei, 1973), pp. 130–132 (hereafter cited by English title).

17. Ibid., p. 115.

18. Ibid., p. 93.

19. Ibid., p. 69.

20. Ibid., p. 140.

21. Ibid., pp. 68, 76.

22. *Chu-ying Tungfanghung*, October 1, 1967, as reprinted in Chao Tsung, "An Account of the 'Great Proletarian Cultural Revolution,'" (Part 56), *Tsukuo* [China Monthly], No. 102 (September 1, 1972), p. 30.

23. *Important CCP Documents of the Great Proletarian Cultural Revolution*, p. 140.

24. Ibid., p. 142.

25. *AFP* (English broadcast), 2005 GMT, January 21, 1968.

26. *Tze-liao Chuan-ch'i*, February 28, 1968, in RGP, Group X-3.

27. Ezra F. Vogel, *Canton under Communism: Programs and Politics in a Provincial Capital, 1949–1968* (New York, 1971), p. 65.

28. *Tsui-hui Tze-fang-hsien*, February 1968, in RGP, Group X-3; *Chieh-fang-pao*, March 1968, in RGP, Group X-3.

29. *AFP* (English broadcast), 1549 GMT, January 28, 1968.

30. Ibid., 1552 GMT, December 28, 1967.

31. Vogel, *Canton under Communism*, p. 64.

32. *Important CCP Documents of the Great Proletarian Cultural Revolution*, p. 330.

33. Hai Feng, *Account of the Cultural Revolution in Canton*, pp. 360–364.

34. Vogel, *Canton under Communism*, pp. 63–64.

35. *AFP* (English broadcast), 1010 GMT, August 10, 1968. *AFP*'s report is based on Chinese Nationalist sources. Finally, the Nationalist government published the source, a document from the Yunnan Military District; see the text in *Important CCP Documents of the Great Proletarian Cultural Revolution*, pp. 79–81.

36. Tokyo General Overseas Service (English), 1300 GMT, March 4, 1967; Chao Tsung, "An Account of the 'Great Proletarian Cultural Revolution,' " (Part 26), *Tsukuo*, No. 72 (March 1, 1970).

37. Ting Wang, *Collection of Documents*, p. 40.

38. *Radio Harbin* (Mandarin), 1400 GMT, February 8, 1967.

39. *Li-hsin-kung*, March 6, 1968, in RGP, Group XI-1.

40. Ting Wang, *Collection of Documents*, pp. 71–72.

41. Anthony Oberschall, *Social Conflict and Social Movements* (Englewood Cliffs, N.J., 1973), pp. 143–145.

42. Neale Hunter, *Shanghai Journal: An Eyewitness Account of the Cultural Revolution* (Boston, 1969), p. 270. Hunter was commenting on the situation at a particular factory in Shanghai but his comments also generally describe the sentiments of major social groups involved in the Cultural Revolution.

43. *Hsiao-ping* (Canton), No. 22 (February 17, 1968), trans. in SCMP, No. 4134, pp. 1–2.

44. *Chung-ta Hung-chi*, March 15, 1968, in RGP, Group X-3.

45. *T'iao-ch'an*, March 1968, in RGP, Group XI-1.

46. *AFP* (French broadcast), 2120 GMT, March 20, 1968.

47. Ken Ling, *The Revenge of Heaven: Journal of a Young Chinese* (New York, 1972), pp. 384–385.

48. *Fang-yu-t'e-k'an*, May 26, 1968, in RGP, Group XI-1.

49. SCMP, No. 4115, p. 20.

50. All these groups, except the one in Honan, are described in "Excerpts from 'Brief Reports' in Red Guard Tabloids," *Tsukuo*, No. 53 (August 1, 1968), p. 42.

51. Hunter, *Shanghai Journal*, p. 286.

52. Ralf Dahrendorf, *Class and Class Conflict in Industrial Society* (Stanford, Calif., 1959), p. 317.

53. For a highly idealistic treatment of changes in Chinese political institutions, see Richard M. Pfeffer, "Serving the People and Continuing the Revolution," *The China Quarterly*, October–December 1972, pp. 620–653. Pfeffer apparently neglected to consider the new conflicts generated by the Cultural Revolution.

54. Dahrendorf, *Class and Class Conflict*, pp. 224–225.

55. Vogel, *Canton under Communism*, p. 211.

56. See, for example, Parris Chang, "The Anti-Lin Piao and Confucius Campaign: Its Meaning and Purposes," *Asian Survey*, Vol. 14, No. 10 (October 1974).

57. *The New York Times*, June 24, 1974; July 3, 1974; July 19, 1974. I have dealt with this and the other aspects of the new campaigns in the introduction to the paperback edition of my *Communication and National Integration in Communist China* (Berkeley, Calif., 1975).

58. The Editor, "1969 Through Peking's Eyes: A Survey of Chinese Media," *Current Scene*, Vol. 8, No. 3 (February 1, 1970), p. 8.

59. Mao Tse-tung, *Mao Tse-tung Ssu-hsiang Wan-sui* [Long Live the Thought of Mao Tse-tung], Vol. 1 (n. p., 1969), pp. 86, 95.

60. This should be viewed in the same context as Mao's promotion of the "Hundred Flowers" campaign. According to Stuart Schram, this "was never a policy of 'liberalization,' in the sense that it was intended to encourage diversity as desirable in itself":

    Mao's idea was rather that, Marxism being the only true form of thought, it would eventually triumph over all others if, within certain limits, a debate was encouraged among the partisans of various contending viewpoints. In the long run, this process would serve to educate non-Communist intellectuals, writers, and cadres, and transform them into socialist intellectuals. In the immediate future, the criticisms of the non-Marxists, even if they were partly false, would have the advantage of obliging the Marxists to re-think their own position.

    Stuart R. Schram, *Mao Tse-tung* (Baltimore, Md., 1967), p. 289.

GLOSSARY

Alliance of Poor Peasants in the Suburbs. A conservative peasant organization in the suburbs of Canton city that was formed in February 1967 and claimed a membership of 300,000.

Anting Incident. On November 10, 1966, the Shanghai workers' group called "Shanghai Workers' Rebellion Headquarters" commandeered a train to travel to Peking, which was stopped at the town of Anting and protracted negotiations followed between the workers and Shanghai Party officials.

April 22 Faction. A Red Guard group in Kwangsi that was involved in the violent struggles in that province.

August 1 Combat Detachment. A large veterans' group in Kwangtung during the Cultural Revolution.

August 5 Commune. A radical Red Guard group in Canton in late 1967 that was opposed to the establishment of the revolutionary committee.

Black elements. The five "outcast" groups in China: former landlords, rich peasants, counterrevolutionaries, bad persons and rightists.

Combat Army of Poor and Lower-Middle Peasants. A conservative peasant group in Chengtu, Szechwan province, that was involved in the bloody group conflict in May 1967 in that city.

Cross-trade organizations. Associational type of mass organizations that were formed during the Cultural Revolution, e.g., alliance between the veterans, workers and students.

Central Cultural Revolution Group. The ad hoc group formed in the Central Committee to direct the Cultural Revolution and the main figure being Chiang Ch'ing, wife of Mao Tse-tung.

Destroy the Four Olds campaign. Mass movement started by Mao Tse-tung in August 1966; the Red Guards were called upon to destroy all signs of old customs, habits, culture and thought.

District Headquarters. A large and conservative workers' group in Canton during the Cultural Revolution.

Doctrine Red Guards. A Red Guard group in Canton during the Cultural Revolution whose members were mostly sons and daughters of high-rank civil and military leaders of Kwangtung province.

Five kinds of red. Children of the family background of poor peasants, workers, soldiers, old cadres and revolutionary martyrs. Initially, in the Cultural Revolution, only those youths from these backgrounds could join the Red Guards.

Flag Faction. A large alliance of radical students and workers' groups in Canton in the Cultural Revolution.

Friends of Red Peasants. A youthful peasant group in the suburbs of Canton.

Grand alliance. In late 1967 and early 1968, an attempt by Chinese Communist leaders to break up factional strife promoted grand alliance in each social group such as students, workers and bureaucrats.

Headquarters Faction. A large alliance of conservative students and workers' groups in Canton during the Cultural Revolution.

January revolution. On January 3, 1967, a radical Red Guard group took over the Shanghai newspaper *Wen-hui Pao* and on January 7, the top leaders of Shanghai Municipal Party Committee were subject to a mass denunciation; these events were referred to by the participants in the Cultural Revolution as the "January revolution" of 1967.

Link-up movement. After the formation of the Red Guards in China in August 1966, the students were allowed to travel freely to Peking and various places on mainland China to exchange their "revolutionary experiences," which became known as the link-up movement.

May 7th School. According to Mao Tse-tung's instruction on May 7, 1966, all Party cadres must spend some time every year in manual labor in the countryside. The institutions set up to organize the cadres to do such labor are known as the "May 7th Schools" in China.

Power seizure movement. In January 1967, the Red Guard groups in China occupied the offices of local Party establishments and subjected the former Party officials to public denunciations. The Red

Guards then announced their "seizure of power" from former Party authorities.

Production and Construction Corps. Large veterans' groups organized by the government to settle in China's frontier regions, the most famous one being the Sinkiang Production and Construction Corps.

Revolutionary committees. The new governing organ in China's provinces and cities after the Cultural Revolution; the committee is supposedly based on an alliance of revolutionary cadres, soldiers and masses.

Scarlet Guards. A large and conservative workers' organization in Shanghai during the Cultural Revolution.

Shen-wu-lien. A radical student group in Hunan province ("The Great Union of Hunan Proletarian Revolutionaries") that sought to restructure China politically and socially.

United Action Committee. A Red Guard group in Peking that was composed exclusively of the sons and daughters of high-rank Party and state officials in Peking.

Weapons seizure movement. A wave of violent group conflicts with the use of modern weapons swept through China from May to the end of 1967; groups of Red Guards and workers seized weapons from the army and local militia to conduct violent struggles.

Work teams. In June 1966, the Party leaders in Peking dispatched numerous teams of Party cadres to various schools to direct students' movement against "bourgeois teachers."

Wuhan Incident. On July 20, 1967, a large workers' group in Wuhan city seized two emissaries from the Central Cultural Revolution Group and defied the order from Peking to release them. Because of the insubordination of the garrison command in Wuhan, Peking had to send outside troops to Wuhan to subdue the rebels.

BIBLIOGRAPHY

Theoretical Works on Group Conflict

Almond, Gabriel A., and G. Bingham Powell, Jr. *Comparative Politics: A Developmental Approach.* Boston: Little, Brown & Co., 1966.

Berkowitz, Leonard. *Aggression: A Social Psychological Analysis.* New York: McGraw-Hill Book Co., 1962.

———. "Words and Symbols as Stimuli to Aggressive Responses." In John F. Knutson, ed., *The Control of Aggression.* Chicago: Aldine Publishing Co., 1973.

Coser, Lewis. *The Functions of Social Conflict.* New York: Free Press, 1956.

———. *Continuities in the Study of Social Conflict.* New York: Free Press, 1967.

Dahrendorf, Ralf. *Class and Class Conflict in Industrial Society.* Stanford, Calif.: Stanford Univ. Press, 1959.

Di Palma, Giuseppe. *The Study of Conflict in Western Society: A Critique of the End of Ideology.* Morristown, N.J.: General Learning Press, 1973.

Erikson, Erik H. *Young Man Luther. A Study in Psychoanalysis and History.* New York: W. W. Norton & Co., 1962.

————. *Childhood & Society.* New York: W. W. Norton & Co., 1963.

Janis, Irving L., and Daniel Katz. "The Reduction of Intergroup Hostility: Research Problems and Hypotheses." *Journal of Conflict Resolution,* Vol. 3, No. 1 (March 1959).

Kecskemeti, Paul. *The Unexpected Revolution. Social Forces in the Hungarian Uprising.* Stanford, Calif.: Stanford Univ. Press, 1961.

Kerr, Clark. "Industrial Conflict and Its Mediation." *American Journal of Sociology,* Vol. 60 (1954).

Kornhauser, William. *The Politics of Mass Society.* Glencoe, Ill.: Free Press, 1959.

Lasswell, Harold D., and Abraham Kaplan. *Power and Society.* New Haven: Yale Univ. Press, 1963.

Lipset, Seymour Martin. *Political Man. The Social Basis of Politics.* Garden City, N.Y.: Doubleday & Co., 1963.

Mack, Raymond W., and Richard C. Snyder. "The Analysis of Social Conflict—Toward an Overview and Synthesis." *Journal of Conflict Resolution,* Vol. 1, No. 2 (June 1957).

Oberschall, Anthony. "Group Violence: Some Hypotheses and Empirical Uniformities." *Law & Society Review,* Vol. 5, No. 1 (August 1970).

————. *Social Conflict and Social Movements.* Englewood Cliffs, N.J.: Prentice-Hall, 1973.

Olson, Mancur, Jr. "Rapid Economic Growth as a Destabilizing Force." *Journal of Economic History,* Vol. 23, pp. 539–552.

Pye, Lucian W. *Politics, Personality, and Nation Building: Burma's Search for Identity.* New Haven: Yale Univ. Press, 1962.

————, ed. *Communication and Political Development.* Princeton, N.J.: Princeton Univ. Press, 1969.

Pye, Lucian W., and Sidney Verba, eds. *Political Culture and Political Development.* Princeton, N.J.: Princeton Univ. Press, 1969.

Pye, Lucian W. "Culture and Political Science: Problems in the Evaluation of the Concept of Political Culture." *Social Science Quarterly,* Vol. 53, No. 2 (September 1972).

Smelser, Neil J. *Theory of Collective Behavior.* New York and Glencoe: Free Press, 1963.

Waldman, Sidney R. *Foundations of Political Action. An Exchange Theory of Politics.* Boston: Little, Brown & Co., 1972.

Books on China

Bennett, Gordon A., and Ronald N. Montaperto. *Red Guard: The Political Biography of Dai Hsiao-ai.* Garden City, N.Y.: Doubleday & Co., 1972.

Brandt, Conrad, Benjamin I. Schwartz and John K. Fairbank. *A Docu-*

mentary History of Chinese Communism. New York: Atheneum, 1966.

CCP Documents of the Great Proletarian Cultural Revolution, 1966–1967. Hong Kong: Union Research Institute, 1968.

Chen Kuang-sheng. *Lei Feng, Chairman Mao's Good Fighter*. Peking: Foreign Languages Press, 1968.

Chin Chien-li. *Pei-kuo Chien-wen-lu* [Odyssey in North China]. Hong Kong: Union Research Institute, 1973.

Chuang, H. C. *The Great Proletarian Cultural Revolution: A Terminological Study*. Monograph. Berkeley, Calif.: Center for Chinese Studies, August 1967.

Chung-kung Wen-hua Ta-ke-ming Chung-yao Wen-chien Hui-pien [Important CCP Documents of the Great Proletarian Cultural Revolution]. Taipei: Institute for the Study of Chinese Communist Problems, 1973.

The Diary of Wang Chieh. Peking: Foreign Languages Press, 1967.

Eckstein, Alexander. *Communist China's Economic Growth and Foreign Trade. Implications for U.S. Policy*. New York: McGraw-Hill Book Co., 1966.

An Economic Profile of Mainland China. Studies Prepared for the Joint Economic Committee, U.S. Congress, Vol. 2 (February 1967).

Granquist, Hans. *The Red Guard: A Report on Mao's Revolution*. Translated by Erik J. Friis. New York: Frederick A. Praeger, 1967.

Hai Feng. *Haifeng Wen-hua Ke-ming Kai-shu* [A General Account of the Cultural Revolution in Haifeng County]. Hong Kong: Chung-pao Chou-k'an, 1969.

————. *Kuang-chou Ti-ch'u Wen-ke Lieh-chen Shu-lueh* [An Account of the Cultural Revolution in the Canton Area]. Hong Kong: Union Research Institute, 1971.

Hunter, Neale. *Shanghai Journal: An Eyewitness Account of the Cultural Revolution*. Boston: Beacon Press, 1969.

Ken Ling. *The Revenge of Heaven: Journal of a Young Chinese*. New York: G. P. Putnam's Sons, 1972.

Li Chi. *General Trends of Chinese Linguistic Changes under Communist Rule*. Monograph. Berkeley, Calif.: Center for Chinese Studies, July 1956.

Lifton, Robert J. *Thought Reform and the Psychology of Totalism. A Study of "Brainwashing" in China*. New York: W. W. Norton & Co., 1969.

Liu Shao-ch'i Wen-ti Tze-liao Ch'uan-ch'i [A Special Collection of Materials on Liu Shao-ch'i]. Taipei: Institute for the Study of Chinese Communist Problems, 1970.

MacFarquhar, Roderick. *The Hundred Flowers Campaign and the Chinese Intellectuals*. New York: Frederick A. Praeger, 1960.

Mao Tse-tung. *Mao Tse-tung Ssu-hsiang Wan-sui* [Long Live the Thought of Mao Tse-tung]. Vol. 1. N.p., 1969.

————. *Miscellany of Mao Tse-tung Thought (1949–1968)*. Part II. Joint Publications Research Service (February 20, 1974).

Nee, Victor, and Don Layman. *The Cultural Revolution at Peking University*. New York: Monthly Review Press, 1969.

People's Republic of China: An Economic Assessment. A Compendium of Papers Submitted to the Joint Economic Committee, U.S. Congress (May 18, 1972).

Ridley, Charles Price, Paul H. B. Godwin and Dennis J. Doolin. *The Making of a Model Citizen in Communist China*. Stanford, Calif.: Hoover Institution on War, Revolution, and Peace, 1971.

Shabad, Theodore. *China's Changing Map. National and Regional Development, 1949–71*. New York: Frederick A. Praeger, 1972.

Schram, Stuart R. *Mao Tse-tung*. Baltimore, Md.: Penguin Books, 1967.

Schurmann, Franz. *Ideology and Organization in Communist China*. Berkeley: Univ. of California Press, 1968.

Snow, Edgar. *The Long Revolution*. New York: Random House, 1972.

Ting Wang, ed. *Chung-kung Wen-hua Ta-ke-ming Tze-liao Hui-pien* [A Collection of Documents on the Great Proletarian Cultural Revolution]. Hong Kong: Ming Pao Monthly, 1972.

Tung Chi-ping and Humphrey Evans. *The Thought Revolution*. New York: Coward-McCann, 1966.

Vogel, Ezra F. *Canton under Communism: Programs and Politics in a Provincial Capital, 1949–1968*. New York: Harper & Row, 1971.

Wu, Yuan-li, H. C. Ling and Grace Hsiao Wu. *The Spatial Economy of Communist China. A Study on Industrial Location and Transportation*. New York: Frederick A. Praeger, 1967.

Yi-chiu Liu-ch'i Chung-kung-nien-pao [1967 Yearbook on Chinese Communism]. Taipei: Institute for the Study of Chinese Communist Problems, 1968.

Yi-chiu Liu-pa Chung-kung-nien-pao [1968 Yearbook on Chinese Communism]. Taipei: Institute for the Study of Chinese Communist Problems, 1969.

Journal Articles on China

Chao Chung (Tsung). "An Account of the 'Great Proletarian Cultural Revolution'" (Part 13). *Tsukuo* [China Monthly], No. 58 (January 1, 1969).

————. "An Account of the 'Great Proletarian Cultural Revolution'" (Part 22). *Tsukuo*, No. 68 (November 1, 1969).

———. "An Account of the 'Great Proletarian Cultural Revolution' " (Part 31). *Tsukuo*, No. 77 (August 1, 1970).

———. "An Account of the 'Great Proletarian Cultural Revolution' " (Part 42). *Tsukuo*, No. 88 (July 1, 1971).

———. "An Account of the 'Great Proletarian Cultural Revolution' " (Part 50). *Tsukuo*, No. 96 (March 1, 1972).

———. "An Account of the 'Great Proletarian Cultural Revolution' " (Part 55). *Tsukuo*, No. 101 (August 1, 1972).

———. "An Account of the 'Great Proletarian Cultural Revolution' " (Part 57). *Tsukuo*, No. 103 (October 1, 1972).

———. "An Account of the 'Great Proletarian Cultural Revolution' " (Part 58). *Tsukuo*, No. 104 (November 1, 1972).

———. "An Account of the 'Great Proletarian Cultural Revolution' " (Part 74). *Chung-hua Yüeh-pao*, No. 709 (October 1, 1974).

Chen Pi-chao. "The Political Economics of Population Growth: The Case of China." *World Politics*, Vol. 23, No. 2 (January 1971).

———. "Overurbanization, Rustication of Urban-Educated Youths, and Politics of Rural Transformation." *Comparative Politics*, April 1972.

Chien Ta-chin. "Leading Personnel of New CCP Shanghai Municipal Committee." *Tsukuo*, No. 84 (March 1, 1971).

Dittmer, Lowell. "The Structural Evolution of 'Criticism and Self-Criticism'." *The China Quarterly*, October–December 1973.

Goldman, Rene. "Peking University Today." *The China Quarterly*, July–September 1961.

———. "The Rectification Campaign at Peking University: May–June, 1957." *The China Quarterly*, October–December 1967.

Hickrod, Lucy Jen Huang, and G. Alan Hickrod. "The Communist Chinese and the American Adolescent Sub-culture." *The China Quarterly*, April–June 1965.

I Fan. "Industry, Communication and Transport of Communist China in 1967." *Tsukuo*, No. 48 (March 1, 1968).

———. "Cotton Production in Communist China." *Tsukuo*, No. 81 (December 1, 1970).

Marcuse, Jacques. "The Myth Who Speaks for Mao." *New York Times Magazine*, November 1, 1964.

Ma Sitson. "Cruelty and Insanity Made Me a Fugitive." *Life*, June 2, 1967.

"Recent Speeches of CCP Leaders." *Tsukuo*, No. 46 (January 1, 1968).

"Selected Statements of Chang Ch'ung-ch'iao." *Tsukuo*, No. 56 (November 1, 1968).

Shu Huei. "New Crisis and New Trend of the CCP's 'Send-down' Movement of Young Intellectuals." *Chung-kung Yen-chiu* [Study on Chinese Communism], Vol. 4, No. 11 (November 10, 1970).

————. "Send-down Work of Chinese Youth." *Chung-kung Yen-chiu*, Vol. 6, No. 3 (March 10, 1972).

The Editor. "Source of Labor Discontent in China: The Worker-Peasant System." *Current Scene*, Vol. 6, No. 5 (March 15, 1968).

————. "1969 Through Peking's Eyes: A Survey of Chinese Media." *Current Scene*, Vol. 8, No. 3 (February 1, 1970).

Tao Yuan-chang. "The New Members of the Politburo of the Chinese Communist Party." *Chung-hua Yüeh-pao*, No. 697 (October 1973).

Vogel, Ezra. "From Friendship to Comradeship: The Change in Personal Relations in Communist China." *The China Quarterly*, January–March 1965.

INDEX